MICROCOMPUTERS

No. 1406
$17.95

MICROCOMPUTERS

What they are *and* how to put them to productive use!

BY A. J. DIRKSEN

TAB BOOKS Inc.

BLUE RIDGE SUMMIT, PA. 17214

FIRST EDITION

FIRST PRINTING

Originally printed in the Dutch language
by Kluwer Technische Boeken BV - Deventer © 1978

English language edition © 1982 W. Foulsham & Co. Ltd
Published in the English language in 1982 by TAB BOOKS Inc.

This edition not for sale outside the United States of America, its possessions, and the Phillippines.

Printed in the United States of America

Library of Congress Cataloging in Publication

Dirksen, A.J.
    Microcomputers.

    Includes index.
    1. Microcomputers. I. Title.
QA76.5.D5623   001.64′04   81-18266
ISBN 0-8306-0063-9   AACR2
ISBN 0-8306-1406-0 (pbk.)

Contents

Introduction

This book was translated from the original Dutch text. During this process, the 8080 chip went out of production. There are, however, still many 8080 systems around.

Even though the illustrations and examples draw heavily on the 8080 chip, this book is by no means obsolete. The techniques explained here are applicable to any microcomputer system and, in most cases, directly translatable to the Z80, which remains the most widely used chip today.

Chapter 1
What Is a Computer?

As the name implies the word *computer* comes from the term to compute, meaning to calculate. Early computers were referred to as calculators. In this book we shall confine ourselves to the term "computer."

In addition to doing calculations a computer can perform processes which, at first, appear to have little to do with calculating. This can be translating texts, adding words to texts (or deleting them), transferring data, bookkeeping, and process control.

In this book a computer will be considered as a device with which data can be processed, using a program. We can represent this data as a series of binary digits. This series of digits (ones and zeros) is translated into electronic signals. We shall, therefore, be speaking about an electronic device, the *digital computer*.

Fig. 1-1.

The definition of *microcomputer* refers to computers in which the greater part of the electronic circuitry is contained in one integrated circuit (IC). They differ from 'normal' computers only in their size and price. Such an IC has a surface area of 6.75 cm² (fig. 1-1). The circuitry is contained in an area of only 1 cm². Together, the electronic circuits perform a *series* of processes on the data fed to them. Because the electronic circuits are assembled on a very small area, the IC is called a *microprocessor*. The price of microprocessors is so low that by combining a microprocessor with a memory and an input/output device one can make an inexpensive microcomputer.

The purpose of this book is to provide the knowledge for understanding microcomputers. This knowledge will relate to the *hardware*, i.e., the choice of equipment, and the *software*, i.e., programming as a whole.

In this chapter we will discuss a block diagram of a computer and the basic principles of computer programming.

THE COMPUTER IS AN ELECTRONIC DEVICE

The block diagram in fig. 1-2a is applicable to any electronic system. The input signal converter changes the given information into an electronic signal which is processed by the signal processing unit. The processed signal is then converted by the output signal converter into a non-electrical signal.

In fig. 1-2b an audio-amplifier system is shown using the same diagram as in fig. 1-2a. The signal processing unit is called the amplifier. The microphone is the input signal converter which changes the given information (sound) into an electrical signal (alternating current). The

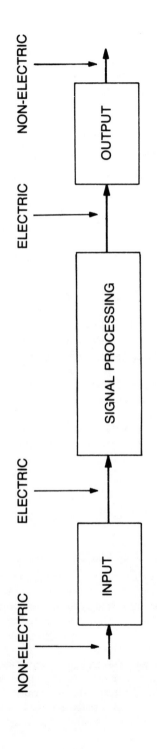

NON-ELECTRIC   ELECTRIC   ELECTRIC   NON-ELECTRIC

INPUT   SIGNAL PROCESSING   OUTPUT

Fig. 1-2A.

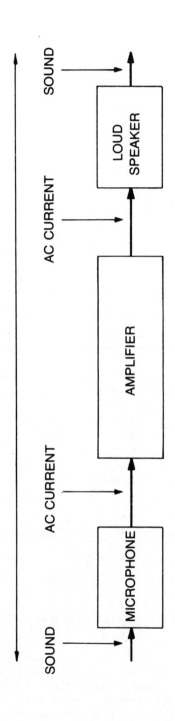

SOUND   AC CURRENT   AC CURRENT   SOUND

MICROPHONE   AMPLIFIER   LOUD SPEAKER

Fig. 1-2B.

loudspeaker does the opposite. For computers the terms given in fig. 1-3 are used.

The *Input* device converts data; for example, a *paper tape reader* converts a code consisting of holes on a punched tape into electrical impulses. This data is processed in the *Central Processing Unit*, the CPU. The *Output* device, for example a line printer, translates these electrical impulses into text. These Input and Output devices collectively are called I/O devices.

HOW IS INFORMATION PROCESSED?

A computer processes information exactly as we do. We will first see an example of how a *person* does this, in order to understand better how a computer works. This example can be seen in fig. 1-4.

If we want to process information we have to use our memory. The following is a simple example. You are given the following information: the next 3 numbers are the data—2, 5, and 3. Multiply the first number by the third and store the answer. Give the result.

To complete this task you have had to continually use your memory. While feeding in the data, you had to store the numbers, 2, 5, and 3 in your memory. You also had to store the result of the multiplication in your memory. The *data* (2, 5, 3) and the *program* (multiplying the first and third numbers together) were fed in (input) through your sense of sight. In order to feed-in this information, light was changed into electrical impulses which reached your brain through the nervous system and then stored in your memory. Your brain then processed this information under the direction of the program. The result which is now present in your memory is fed back through your mouth - the output device. This output device says, 'six.'

The program which has been described here is so simple that you could execute it immediately. In other cases you might not have sufficient knowledge of the facts to complete the task given. You might then refer to a card file and take data from there. You would read this data into your memory in order to be able to return to the processing of the program.

BLOCK DIAGRAM OF A COMPUTER

Refer to fig. 1-5 throughout this section.

Information

When we refer to information or data in this context we are talking about a task which is given to a computer. It can be in the form of letters, punctuation marks, num-

bers, or impulses related to a given action. This information is stored in the *main memory*.

Program

A program comprises a number of instructions. All the instructions that a computer can execute are contained in the *instruction set*. (See Appendix A.) The data which is to be processed *and* the program to be executed are stored in the main memory.

Input

Data and the program are changed into electric signals using the Input device. These electronic signals activate certain sections of the main memory so that their condition reflects the data and the program which has been stored. Input devices will be studied later in this chapter. A more detailed description will be given in chapter 20.

Control Unit

The control unit directs *every activity* which takes place between the various components of the computer. The control unit may make use of a number of *registers* for temporary storage. One of these registers is the instruction register, in which the instruction to be executed, after being taken from main memory, is stored. The instruction which, at a given moment, is in the instruction register tells the control unit:

●The location in which the data is stored. It could be in main memory or a register.

●Where this data must be transferred. Again, to main memory or a register.

●What operation must be executed?

Under the direction of the program the control unit regulates the flow of information in the computer. When an instruction has been completed, the *program counter* in the control unit sends a signal. This signal "fetches" the next instruction from the main memory and stores it in the instruction register.

Arithmetic and Logic Unit

The Arithmetic and Logic Unit, generally called the ALU, should be viewed as an assistant to the control unit. The ALU can perform *arithmetic* operations such as adding and subtracting and *logical* operations. It can manipulate numbers, using the AND, OR, or EXOR functions. The ALU also has a register at its disposal usually called the *accumulator*.

When the instruction that is in the instruction register of the control unit demands that a fixed arithmetic or

3

4

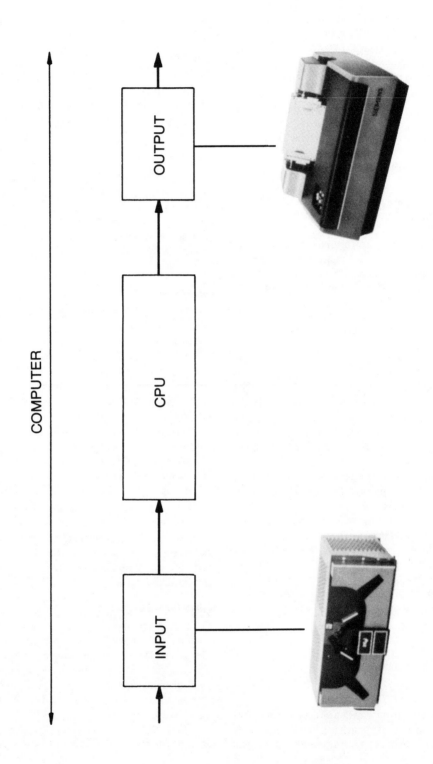

COMPUTER

INPUT → CPU → OUTPUT

Fig. 1-3.

logic operation is to be performed on certain data, this data is taken out of the main memory or register and presented to the ALU. The ALU then processes the data as instructed by the control unit. After the operation has been performed, the result - new data - is stored in the accumulator.

Central Processing Unit

In large computers, used for administrative and scientific applications, the central processing unit is considered to be a combination of the control, arithmetic and memory sections.

With microcomputers, the central processing unit may be seen as a combination of the control unit and arithmetic and logic unit, together with the associated registers that serve as memory space. This terminology has been developed because in microcomputers the control unit and arithmetic and logic unit are contained on one chip and are physically separate from the main memory.

Because this course concerns itself with the working of microcomputers, we will confine ourselves to the terminology in current use. In other words, the term CPU includes the control unit, the arithmetic and logic unit and its associated registers.

Output

The Output devices present the result of operations in legible form. On the instruction of the computer, or the computer operator, the signals representing the results of the operations are either printed or displayed.

MEMORY

To be able to process data according to a given program, a computer must have a memory at its disposal in which the instructions and the data to be processed are stored. The memory in a computer system can be divided as follows:

The Main Memory

The following are stored in the main memory:

●The instructions, which together form the program.

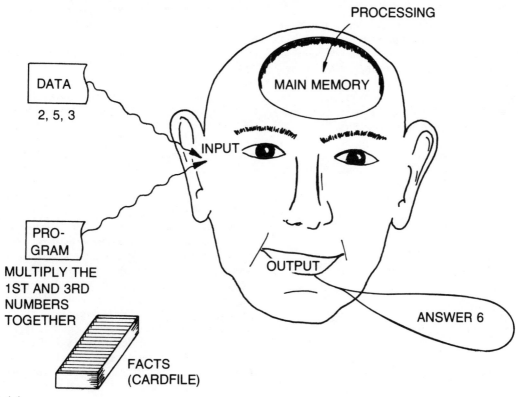

Fig. 1-4.

5

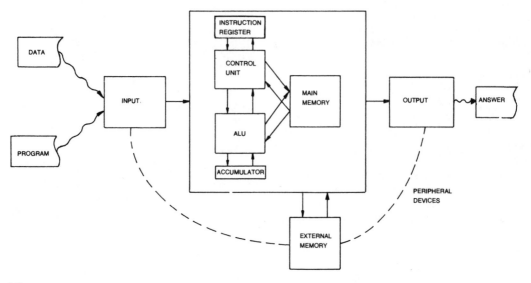

Fig. 1-5.

●The data which is to be processed in a given situation.

The part of the main memory in which the instructions are stored is called the *program memory*. When a computer is to be used only for a special purpose, the program can be permanently stored in the main memory. Such a computer is called a special-purpose or *dedicated computer*. This is often the case with microcomputers. According to the requirements of the user, the manufacturer provides a preprogrammed memory.

If the computer is general purpose, the program must be exchangeable. This, for example, is true when a computer is used for salary administration and stock control for different firms. In order to execute a certain program, that program has to be *read in* to the main memory.

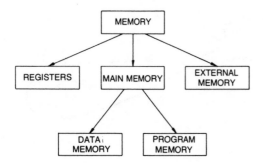

Fig. 1-6.

Note

Preprogrammed memories can also be used with general-purpose computers as long as the number of programs is limited and they don't occupy too much memory space. The various main programs can then be stored in the remaining memory and executed as required.

The section of the memory where data is temporarily stored is called the *scratch-pad* memory. This part of the memory can be seen as fulfilling the same function as a scratch-pad. It only retains the results of an operation until they can be transferred to the output device. Even a dedicated computer must have some scratch-pad memory.

External Memory

Whenever data or programs must be stored for future processing or reference, *external memory* is used. In most cases this is in the form of a magnetic tape or disc. Figure 1-7 shows an example of a magnetic tape unit. In microcomputers, this magnetic tape usually comes in the form of a cassette. This cassette is similar to the cassette found in modern audio cassette recorders.

The magnetic disc is called a floppy disc. It is made from flexible magnetic material and is stored in a sort of envelope. A disc closely resembles a flexible stereo record, except for the fact that it can be erased and used again just like a magnetic tape. The unit that "plays" the disc is shown in fig. 1-8.

Fig. 1-7.

Fig. 1-8.

Registers

Registers to store data temporarily are spread throughout the entire CPU. In addition to the control unit and the ALU, sometimes the Input/Output devices also contain such registers.

Note: The word computer is sometimes *not* meant to represent the installation as a whole, but rather that part which is *exclusive* of the peripheral devices. The system as a whole, including the peripheral devices, is called a computer system or computer installation. In this book, in order to avoid confusion, we shall be referring to the system as a whole when we say computer.

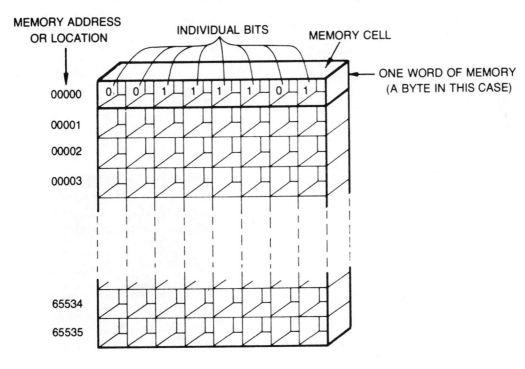

Fig. 1-9.

ORGANIZATION OF THE MAIN MEMORY

The instructions and data stored in the main memory must be easily retrievable. The memory is thus divided into blocks of equal size (fig. 1-9). These blocks are called *memory locations, memory addresses,* or *byte.* A memory location is divided into *memory cells.*

In most microcomputers, the memory location contains eight memory cells. In such a case we speak of an 8-bit computer. Each cell can contain a single binary number (1 or 0). Each memory location can thus contain 8 bits (*b*inary dig *its*). Because 8 bits = 1 byte, we say that the word length of a microcomputer is 1 byte.

The zeros and ones in the 8 memory cells together form the *contents of the memory location.* Each memory location has an *address.* Most microcomputers can address a maximum of $2^{16} = 65.536$ addresses, so there is no point in having a larger main memory, since extra memory locations couldn't be addressed and therefore couldn't be used.

INPUT/OUTPUT DEVICES

You will see these abbreviated as I/O Devices.

Paper Tape Reader and Paper Tape Punch

Punched tape is often used to feed data to microcomputers. This punched tape is a continuous thin strip of paper on which data is recorded by means of round or square holes. A character on the punched tape consists of a number of holes in line across the breadth of the tape. Depending upon the code used, this could be 5, 6, 7 or 8 holes. Figure 1-10 is an example of a tape with a maximum of 7 holes. Using these 7 holes we can code a total of $2^7 = 128$ different characters.

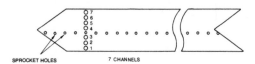

SPROCKET HOLES   7 CHANNELS

Fig. 1-10.

For transport the tape has a row of smaller holes (sprocket holes) along the middle. Fig. 1-11 shows a combination paper tape reader/punch. Used as a reader, it converts data on the tape into electrical signals for the computer. Used as a punch, it converts electrical signals from the computer into holes on the tape.

Fig. 1-11.

Line Printer

The line printer (fig. 1-12) is the output medium most frequently used. Line printer paper is usually folded in the form of an accordion. This is sometimes called continuous form, or form fold paper.

Fig. 1-12.

Display

A display is, strictly speaking, merely a video screen which displays data in the form of words, numbers or graphics. In most cases the display is combined with a keyboard which acts as an input device, and such a combination is also referred to as a display (fig. 1-13). Using the

Fig. 1-13.

keyboard, information can be requested from the computer and be displayed on the screen.

Teletype

A teletype (fig. 1-14) is suited for the input as well as the output of data. A teletype is a typewriter which serves the programmer (input) as well as the computer (output). In addition, it may have a paper tape reader and punch.

Fig. 1-14.

THE FLOWCHART

When properly instructed, a computer can perform calculations very quickly. The use of a computer is therefore most profitable when the same procedure must be carried out repeatedly using variable data. The computer only needs instructing once. The procedure which the computer must carry out is caled the *program*.

The separate steps used to carry out this program are called the *instructions*.

To program a computer for a specific problem we must schematically define the consecutive operations that lead to the solution. This schematic definition is called a *flowchart* or *flow diagram*. When making a flowchart one has to take into consideration the properties of the computer in question. The form of a flowchart depends on the person who made it. Making a flowchart demands not only knowledge and experience, but also creativity. Computer programming is as much an art as it is a science. People's characters differ both in creativity and in depth. By means of an example we will try to help you to become familiar with flowcharts. This topic will be discussed in more detail in Chapter 14.

Problem

Find the sum of a column of consecutive, positive, whole numbers, beginning with P and ending with N. P and N can be chosen at random. We will choose P = 2 and N = 5.

Note: We must bear in mind that:

● A computer can only add 2 numbers at a time.

● That the amount of data to be read in should be kept to a minimum.

The amount of data to be read in can be kept to a minimum by reading in only the initial value P and the final value N. Starting from the initial value the computer can then fill in the values between. The initial P is supplied to a memory location to which we shall designate the *symbolic address* NUMBER (fig. 1-15a).

NUMBER	P
FINAL-VALUE	N
SUM	O

Fig. 1-15A.

Note

In subsequent program-writing lessons we shall see that this is something that we do repeatedly. Symbolic addresses are given in the form of a name. The computer then calculates the appropriate address numbers. We don't have to concern ourselves with this. Calculating the address is done by an assembly program. This will be discussed fully in Chapter 18 and to a certain extent in

Chapter 3. When the number P has been processed, the address NUMBER is filled with the succeeding number. We indicate this as:

$$\text{NUMBER} \leftarrow (\text{NUMBER}) + 1$$

This notation must be read as follows:
The memory location with the address NUMBER is filled with the sum of the present contents of the memory address plus the value 1.
When we wish to indicate the content of a word in memory, we put the address of the word in parentheses.

When the content of the memory location with the address NUMBER is equal to N the computer must stop the program. We must therefore continually compare the content of the address NUMBER with the content of the memory location in which we have put the value N. N has been put in the memory location with the symbolic address FINAL-VALUE. The check to see if the content of the address NUMBER is equal to N is shown in fig. 1-15b. If the content of the address NUMBER is the same as N, the program continues in the direction 'yes.' If the contents are not equal to N, the program continues in the direction 'no.'

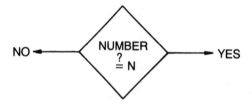

Fig. 1-15B.

Because a computer can only add 2 numbers at a time, we assign the memory location in which the running total is stored the symbolic address SUM. This memory word is filled with the value 0. We then add to the content of SUM step-by-step.

We first add P to the content of location SUM. The content of the address SUM then becomes

$$\text{SUM} \leftarrow (\text{SUM}) + P$$

We then add the second number to the new content of SUM. The content now becomes P + (P + 1). The third number is added to this new content. Since P is stored in the memory location symbolically addressed by NUMBER, we define this process as:

$$\text{SUM} \leftarrow (\text{SUM}) + (\text{NUMBER})$$

This must be read as follows:
The memory location with the address SUM is loaded with the sum of its former content and the content of the word in memory which has the address NUMBER.

It should be clear that after each addition the content of the memory word with the address NUMBER must be incremented by 1.

Solution

The method for solving the problem may be summed up in a flowchart (fig. 1-16). The command START indicates that the program must begin. The values required to continue are then read in. In this case the memory locations NUMBER, FINAL-VALUE, and SUM are filled

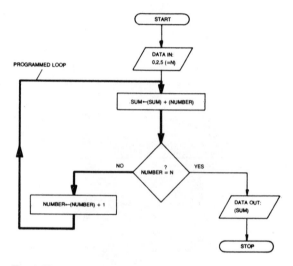

Fig. 1-16.

with 2, 5 and 0, respectively (fig. 1-17a). We now proceed to the processing stage.

$$\text{SUM} \leftarrow (\text{SUM}) + (\text{NUMBER})$$

The content of the address SUM becomes 0 + 2 = 2 (fig. 1-17b). We must then check to see if the content of the address NUMBER is equal to 5. The content of the address NUMBER is 2. The result of the comparison is thus 'no.'

We now find ourselves in what is called a *programmed loop*. (This loop is executed continually until the content of the address NUMBER is equal to 5). Subsequently, the calculation NUMBER←(NUMBER)+1 is performed. Because of this calculation the content of the address NUMBER becomes 2 + 1 = 3. The contents of the memory locations are shown in fig. 1-17b.

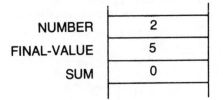

NUMBER	2
FINAL-VALUE	5
SUM	0

Fig. 1-17A.

Afterwards, the calculation SUM ← (SUM) + (NUMBER) is repeated. The content of the address SUM thus becomes $2 + 3 = 5$. The content of the address NUMBER is then compared to 5. The result is 'no'.

NUMBER	3
FINAL-VALUE	5
SUM	2

Fig. 1-17B.

Therefore the calculation NUMBER ← (NUMBER) + 1 must be repeated. The content of the address NUMBER thus becomes $3 + 1 = 4$. The contents of the memory locations are shown in fig. 1-17c.

NUMBER	4
FINAL-VALUE	5
SUM	5

Fig. 1-17C.

The calculation SUM ← (SUM) + (NUMBER) is performed again. The content of the address SUM becomes 5 + 4 = 9. A comparison is then made. Because the content of the address NUMBER is still less than 5. The calculation NUMBER ← (NUMBER) + 1 is performed. The content of the address NUMBER becomes $4 + 1 = 5$. The present contents of the memory words are shown in fig. 1-17d.
The calculation SUM ← (SUM) + (NUMBER) is repeated again. The content of the address SUM becomes 9 + 5 = 14 and the comparison is made again. Because the content of the address NUMBER is equal to

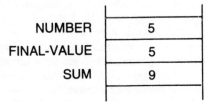

NUMBER	5
FINAL-VALUE	5
SUM	9

Fig. 1-17D.

N, the content of sum, which is 14, is output. The execution of the program is therefore stopped fig. 1-17e.

PROGRAMMING LANGUAGES

The procedure that a computer must follow in order to complete a given task is called the *program*. The separate steps in the program are called the instructions. When writing a program, one can use a *machine oriented* langauge or a *problem oriented* langauge.

NUMBER	5
FINAL-VALUE	5
SUM	14

Fig. 1-17E.

Instead of the term problem oriented language, the expression high-level programming language is often used.

PROGRAMMING LANGUAGES

Problem oriented languages	Machine oriented languages
BASIC	Assembly
Fortran	
PL/M	
Cobol	

In a machine oriented language the instructions are a direct reflection of the potential of the computer concerned. The disadvantage of writing in a machine oriented language is that one must be completely familiar with the characteristics of the computer concerned. The advantages of writing in a machine oriented language are that the programs are shorter and require less memory space.

Programming microcomputers in a machine oriented language is certainly advantageous from an economic point of view. The machine oriented language used with microcomputers is called *assembly language.* Because of the differences between the microcomputers produced by various manufacturers, there are differences in the assembly languages. However, these are small.

When writing a program in a problem oriented language, one must have a good command of that particular language. A program is then written based on the problem itself. The problem oriented languages used with microcomputers are BASIC and PL/M. The latter is an abbreviation for Programming Language for Microcomputers. Cobol is used in writing programs for administrative applications. Fortran is used for writing programs for scientific applications. There are, however, versions of both of these languages for microcomputers.

ASSEMBLY LANGUAGE

A computer is constructed in such a way that when a particular instruction is fetched from the main memory and presented to the control unit, a number of functions controlled by electronic signals are automatically executed. The instruction set states which operations the computer can execute. An example of a typical instruction for a microcomputer can be seen below:

Instruction	Instruction Code
ADD D	1 0 0 0 0 0 1 0

This instruction signifies that the content of register D in the ALU will be added to the content of the accumulator. The sum will be placed in the accumulator.

The instruction code tells us how we can activate the memory cells of the memory at, for instance, address A. This could be done, for example, as indicated in fig. 1-18. The instruction is fed in through the use of switches, one

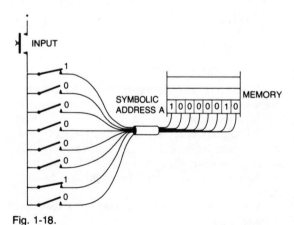

Fig. 1-18.

switch for each digit. Depressing the Input button causes the memory cells connected to the closed switches to be set to the '1' state.

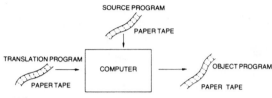

Fig. 1-19.

Consecutive instructions can be fed to consecutive memory addresses in this manner. Instructions expressed in ones and zeroes are in machine language. If consecutive instructions make a program, the program is said to be written in object code and is called an *object program.*

When we have a given problem, for instance, the automatic control of traffic lights, we will ultimately have to run an object program as this is the only form of program upon which the computer can act. This does not mean that the programmer will have to write his program in the form of an object program. Writing a program in object code could have 2 disadvantages:

●Because of the nature of the instructions, mistakes are easily made.

● One cannot easily understand which operation is to be performed from reading the object code.

This is the reason a programmer writes a program in mneumonics, which are an abbreviation of the operation to be performed.

The instruction 'addition' could, for example, be represented by the word 'ADD'; the instruction 'subtraction' by 'SUB'; the instruction 'bring to' by 'MOVE', etc. A program which has been written using this sort of abbreviation is called an *assembly program.* Any program in readable form is also called a *source program.*

TRANSLATING PROGRAMS

After a program has been written in assembler, BASIC or PL/M, it must be converted into an object program. This is done using a translation program. If our microcomputer uses paper tape for external storage, we would follow this procedure.

The translation program is put onto punched tape. This is loaded into the computer. The instructions in the source program are typed in on a teletype which produces a punched tape. The information on the punched tape is fed to the computer. Using the translation program, the computer converts the source program into an object program. The object program can be stored on punched tape or magnetic tape for use as needed.

The translation program for a program written in assembly language is called the *assembler*. The translation program for a program written in a higher language is called a *compiler*. Translation programs will be discussed in detail in Chapter 18.

HEXADECIMAL NOTATION

The addresses and contents of memory areas are in binary code in the computer. It is very easy to make mistakes in addresses and contents with binary notation. Therefore, we make use of a notation called hexadecimal. In hexadecimal notation a group of 4 bits is represented by a digit or letter taken from the hexadecimal digits as shown in the adjoining table. The hexadecimal system contains 16 digits, from 0 to 9 and from A to F.

Binary Notation	Hexadecimal Notation
0000	0
0001	1
0010	2
0011	3
0100	4
0101	5
0110	6
0111	7
1000	8
1001	9
1010	A
1011	B
1100	C
1101	D
1110	E
1111	F

SUMMARY

1. A computer is a device which processes data under the direction of a program.

2. A computer works in a similar way to other electronic systems. As can be seen in the block diagram, it has an Input signal converter, a signal processing unit (the CPU) and an Output signal converter.

3. A microcomputer is a computer in which the electronic circuitry, which executes tasks, is contained on one IC. This IC is called the microprocessor.

4. Information or data can be considered as words, numbers, and so forth, which are given to a computer to be processed.

5. A program is a series of instructions which are executed consecutively in order to achieve a given result.

6. The instructions which a computer can execute are stated in the instruction set of the computer.

7. The control unit of the computer directs every activity in and between the various parts of the computer. The control unit has several registers at its disposal, including the instruction register.

8. Arithmetic and logical operations take place in the ALU. The ALU has a register at its disposal. This register is called the accumulator.

9. When considering microcomputers, the CPU is thought of as a combination of the control unit, and the ALU with its associated registers. In large computers the main memory is also considered as part of the CPU.

10. The program, which describes in detail the instructions to be executed, is stored in the main memory, so that it can be referred to at will.

11. The data to be processed must be stored in the main memory so that it can be processed at will.

12. The memory functions of a computer are divided among the main memory, the external memory, and the registers.

13. We may think of the main memory as being split into the data memory, where the data to be processed is stored, and the program memory, where the instructions are stored.

14. A dedicated computer is designed for *one* purpose only. A general purpose computer is designed for general use.

15. External memories are used for storing data or programs which must be later processed or referred to. Magnetic tapes, magnetic discs, cassettes, floppy discs, and paper tape are all types of external memories.

16. The memory of a computer must be strictly organized. For this reason, the memory is divided into memory locations of equal length. The word length in microcomputers is usually 8 bits = 1 byte.

17. Each word in memory has an address and contents. A word and its address are inseparable. The contents can be changed.

18. With the help of the Input device, non-electronic signals are converted into electronic signals which the computer can process. The output device converts signals from the computer into visual form.

19. The I/O devices most used with microcomputers are the keyboard and video screen.

20. The most useful programming language for microcomputers is assembly language. With the help of an assembler a program written in assembler language is converted into machine code.

21. Whenever one writes a program based on a given problem without taking into consideration the characteristics of the particular computer, the program is being written in one of the high-level programming languages.

22. The consecutive instructions of an object program are expressed as zeroes and ones.

23. Representation in a form other than the object program is called the source program.

24. The translation program for assembly language is called the assembler.

25. The translation program for high-level programming languages is called a compiler.

26. We use hexadecimal code whenever discussing conditions within the computer.

REVIEW EXERCISES

1. Name a few operations that a computer can perform.

2. Draw a simple block diagram of a computer system.

3. Draw a more complete block diagram of a computer system.

4. What is the meaning of the word data?

5. What is the meaning of the word program?

6. What is stored in the main memory?

7. In what two functional parts can the main memory be divided?

8. What is a preprogrammed memory?

9. a. What is the function of an external memory?

b. What is the most usual form of external memory?

c. Name two forms of external memory used with microcomputers.

10. a. What is a memory location?

b. Which two things typify a memory location?

11. What is a byte?

12. Which 2 parts makes up the CPU of a microcomputer?

13. What does the control unit do?

14. What does one call the storage space available to the control unit?

15. What can an instruction which is in instruction register inform the control unit of?

16. What sort of operations can the Arithmetic and Logic Unit perform?

17. What does one call the storage space available to the ALU?

18. Which medium is most used with microcomputers in order to store data in a non-electronic form?

19. How is data recorded on a punched tape?

20. What is the purpose of sprocket holes in a punched tape?

21. What is the most used output medium?

22. In what form does the line printer present the paper?

23. What is a terminal?

24. What is the commonest I/O device?

25. What do we call the schematic description which represents the procedure to be carried out by the computer?

26. What is a program loop?

27. What can be understood from the instruction set of a computer?

28. What is the sum total of the instructions which are represented by zeros and ones called?

29. What is an object program?

30. What are the disadvantages of writing a program in object code?

31. What is the advantage of hexadecimal representation as compared to representation in binary form?

32. What do we call a program which is written in readable code?

33. What do we call the translation program which changes a program written in assembly language into an object program?

34. What is the advantage of a machine oriented language as compared to a problem oriented language?

35. What do we call the translation program used with the high-level programming languages?

36. Name a high-level programming language used with microcomputers.

ANSWERS

1. Calculating, translating texts, transporting data, controlling a process.

2. See fig. 1-3.

3. See fig. 1-5.

4. That information which is given to a computer in the form of letters, numbers or punctuation marks.

5. A number of instructions which are executed in a predetermined order.

6. a. The instructions which, when taken together, form the program.

   b. The data to be processed.

7. The program memory and the data memory.

8. A memory which, according to the needs of the user, is delivered by the manufacturer in a preprogrammed form and cannot be erased.

9. a. It is used for storing data to be used later.

   b. In the form of a magnetic tape or disc.

   c. Cassette tape and floppy disc.

10. a. A fixed location in the memory.

    b. The address and the contents.

11. A word with a length of 8 bits.

12. A control unit and the Arithmetic and Logic Unit (ALU).

13. It directs every activity which takes place in and between the various parts of the computer.

14. The instruction register.

15. a. In which memory position or register the data to be processed is stored.

    b. Where the data must go to.

    c. Which operation must be performed on the data.

16. Arithmetical and logical.

17. The accumulator.

18. The cassette, which is magnetic tape.

19. By the use of a vertical row of round or square holes.

20. They are used to transport the tape.

21. The video screen.

22. In the form of an accordion.

23. A combination of a video screen on which the data can be displayed and a keyboard which can be used to feed data to the computer.

24. The terminal.

25. The flowchart.

26. A part of the program which repeats itself until a certain result has been reached.

27. a. Which operations a computer can execute.

    b. How these operations are coded.

28. The machine language.

29. A program stored in machine language.

30. a. It is easy to make a mistake because of the long binary instructions.

    b. One cannot understand from the object code which operation is to be performed.

31. Fewer mistakes are made because a byte in hex is only 2 digits long, and more dicernable.

32. Source program.

33. The assembler.

34. Less memory space is needed, and you have more control of the computer.

35. The compiler.

36. PL/M or BASIC.

Chapter 2

What Is a Microcomputer?

In the previous chapter it was stated that a microcomputer is a computer with the CPU on one or two ICs. The CPU is then called a microprocessor. In this chapter we shall consider the construction of the microcomputer in block schematic terms. First, something about the history of the electronic computer and the origin of the microcomputer.

In 1943 Eckert, Mauchly, and Goldstine began building the first vacuum tube digital computer at the University of Pennsylvania. This ENIAC (Electronic Numeric Integrator And Calculator) comprised 55,000 tubes and its power consumption was 150 kW. The ENIAC was specially developed for ballistic calculations for the American artillery and worked about 1000 times faster than the few relay computers that were invented in about 1935.

In 1946 John von Neumann, the noted mathematician, proposed the following idea in a paper written for a development group:

"If instructions are dealt with in the same way as data, a program can modify itself during its execution. Through the use of jump or branch instructions, the execution or not of certain parts of the program will depend upon the result of certain operations".

Eckert, Mauchly and von Neumann developed the first 'stored program' computer, the UNIVAC-1, based on this idea. In this computer, the information and the program were stored in the memory and were switched in as needed.

In 1958 the transistor made its entrance into computer construction and the size of the computer was considerably reduced.

In 1965 the integrated circuit replaced discrete (transistor) components. Computers became smaller yet. The speed of processing also increased.

In 1969 the designers of Datapoint, USA made a great step forward. They designed a very simple control and arithmetic unit and commissioned both Texas Instruments and Intel to realize this on one chip. Intel succeeded, but it transpired that the first microprocessor worked at about one-tenth of the speed that Datapoint had expected. The deal was therefore cancelled. Intel held onto a prototype (of which the development costs were already paid). They could have shelved the prototype, but instead they decided to risk production. In this way the well-known Intel 4004 became the first microprocessor on the market.

An example of a microcomputer is given in fig. 2-1. This diagram will be used in this and following chapters.

ORGANIZATION OF A MICROCOMPUTER

The block diagram in fig. 2-2 represents a microcomputer. As can be seen from fig. 2-2, the usual peripheral equipment such as the floppy disc, teletype, and punched tape reader can be used to supply data to the computer. Data originating from a process can also be supplied *directly*. If this data is in analog form, for example temperature control in an industrial installation, it must first be converted to digital form since a computer can only work with zeros and ones. This conversion is done by the use of an Analog to Digital converter (A/D). Similarly, the output of the computer, data for process control, can be converted into analog form by a Digital to Analog (D/A) converter. Addresses, data and control signals are transferred via the bus lines.

Data presented to the *input device* passed to the *data bus* in the form of either an 8-bit parallel signal, or a series pulse train via an input port. Address selection chooses which input port or memory mapped address will feed data to the data bus at any given moment.

The main memory consists of ROMs and RAMs. The contents of a memory word in a ROM (Read-Only Memory) cannot be erased. For this reason, the ROM is used as a program memory which the manufacturer has pre-programmed as required by the user. Thus, a different ROM or part thereof must be used for each program.

A ROM can be compared to a book from which one can only read things. The various forms of ROM will be discussed in more detail in the next chapter.

The data memory in microcomputers is a RAM (Random-Access Memory). A RAM can be compared to a book in which things can be written as well as read. The data present in the RAM is erased when the power supply is interrupted. This can be prevented by using buffer batteries which are connected in parallel to the power supply.

When the terms RAM and ROM are used we must remember:

RAM = data memory
ROM = program memory

The data fed into RAM is processed in the CPU under the direction of the program stored in ROM. The results of the processing in the CPU is stored in the accumulator or in the RAM. They are Output, on command, via one of the *Output Ports* to the *Output device* connected to that port. The desired Output port is chosen via the *address selection* circuit.

THE BUS STRUCTURE OF A MICROCOMPUTER

A block diagram of a microcomputer is given in fig. 2-2. The *bus structure* is used to connect the various parts of the computer. A bus is a multicore cable. A microcomputer has 3 different buses.

Address Bus

The number of lines in the address bus is determined by the number of bits in a memory address. Most microcomputers have 16-bit addresses, which we will assume to be the case from now on.

Data Bus

The number of data lines is equal to the word length of the microcomputer. This is almost always 8 bits. A data bus thus has 8 lines.

Control Bus

This bus contains the control lines. The number depends on the type of microcomputer. The commands that tell the various parts to perform are transmitted via the control bus.

BUS STRUCTURE CONTINUED

Whenever we mention buses in a microcomputer, we are talking about *internal* buses. The microcomputer has an extensive internal bus structure, represented in fig. 2-2 by broken lines. Arrows indicate whether a certain part receives and/or transmits signals. If signals are both received and transmitted, the related connection is bidirectional.

Note 1

The bus structure makes it possible to connect new parts directly. This is of great advantage, as we can add 4 extra RAMs and one ROM to the system shown in fig. 2-1.

Note 2

The data bus itself is bidirectional. Naturally, this doesn't apply to the connection between the data bus and the ROM.

COUPLING THE PARTS
OF THE COMPUTER TO THE BUSES

Information may be placed on a given bus by only one part of the microcomputer at any given moment. For example, information can only be placed on the data bus by one of the following parts: CPU, ROM, RAM, or the input ports. A three state buffer (fig. 2-3) is used on each bus Output line of every port in order to accomplish this. The three state buffer is like a switch which is opened or closed by a control signal.

The name 'three state' comes from the fact that, viewed from a given port, an external line can assume any of three different states. When, under influence of a control signal, a three state buffer operates as an open circuit, there is no connection between the internal and external lines. The resistance between the internal lines of the part concerned and the external lines is now high. This condition is, therefore, called a high impedance state. It can also be called *floating*.

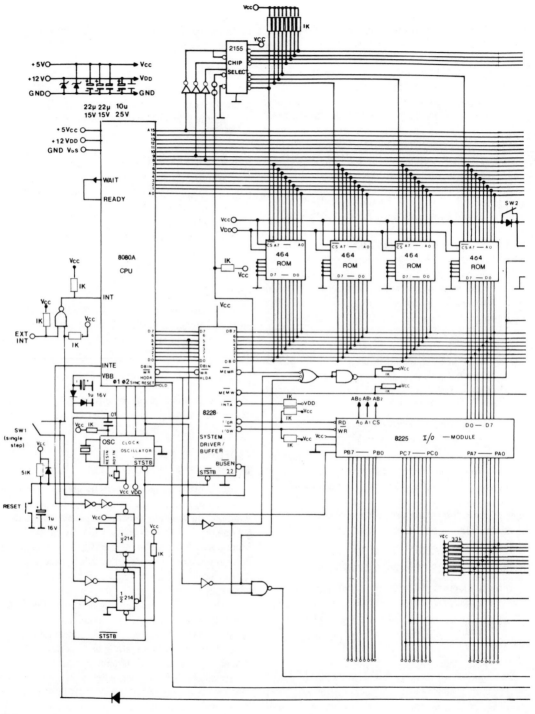

Fig. 2-1.

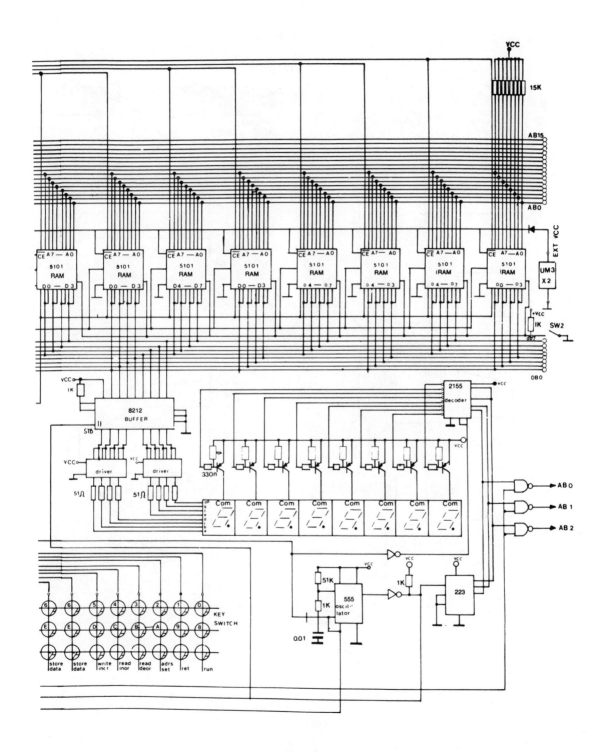

19

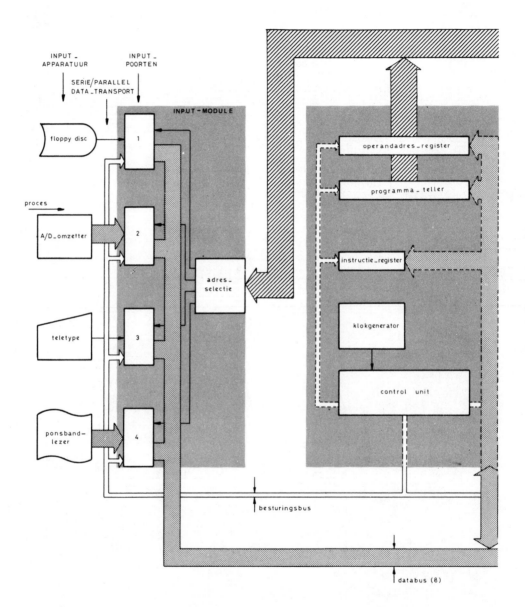

Fig. 2-2.

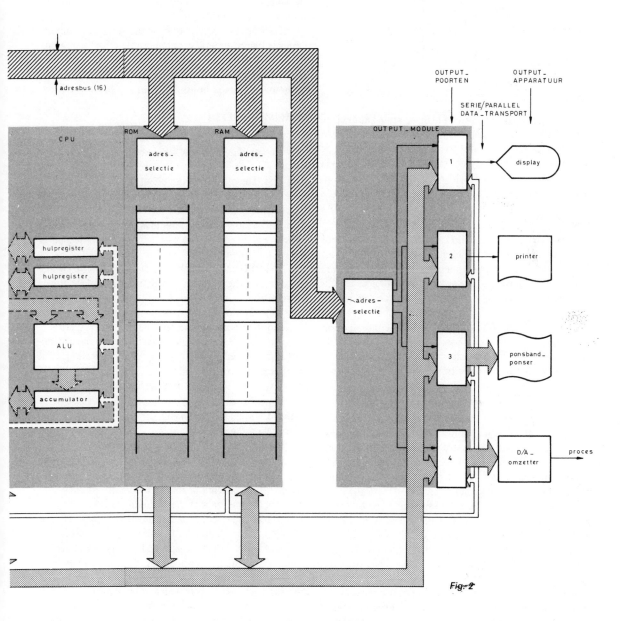

adresbus (16)

OUTPUT_
POORTEN

OUTPUT_
APPARATUUR

SERIE/PARALLEL
DATA_TRANSPORT

CPU

ROM

RAM

OUTPUT_MODULE

adres_
selectie

adres_
selectie

1

display

hulpregister

hulpregister

2

printer

ALU

adres-
selectie

accumulator

3

ponsband_
ponser

4

D/A_
omzetter

proces

Fig. 2

21

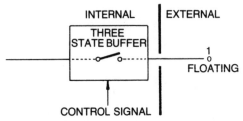

INTERNAL | EXTERNAL

THREE STATE BUFFER

FLOATING

CONTROL SIGNAL

Fig. 2-3.

The signals which switch the three state buffers into the desired condition come from the control unit. When switched on, the buffer will pass the logic high and logic low signals on the data lines. In this manner we can, via the control unit, select which device can place signals on the bus at any given moment.

CONTROL UNIT

The activities of the CPU are cyclic. The processor performs the same sort of operations continually. In other words, the CPU continually fetches an instruction from the memory, performs the process indicated in the instruction, and fetches the next instruction. This sequence of events requires *timing*.

A clock generator (or clock) is built into the microcomputer for this purpose. The clock generator is coupled with the control unit which provides the necessary signals for all the activities of the microcomputer.

PROGRAM COUNTER

The instructions which, as a set, form a program are stored sequentially in the program memory. The CPU fetches these instructions from the program memory to determine which activities it must undertake. This implies, however, that the CPU must know where the instruction can be found.

The CPU retains the address in the program memory where the next instruction to be executed can be found in a register. This register is called the program counter (PC). The CPU increments the program counter each time it has executed an instruction. Thus the program counter always contains the address of the next instruction to be executed. The programmer must make sure that he has stored the instructions in program memory in the proper order. The instructions are then processed in ascending address sequence; 00, 01, 02, etc.

The programmer can interrupt this sequence by using a jump instruction to any other place in memory instead of the following one. A jump instruction contains the address of the next instruction to be executed. In this manner the next instruction can be stored in a random memory location as long as its address is given in the previous instruction. *Programmed jumps make the programmer's job much easier.*

One of the greatest advantages of programmed jumps is that programs with loops are not as long as they would be if they were written out in full. One can jump back and repeat a piece of the program. Therefore, using programmed jumps limits the memory space required.

INSTRUCTION FETCH

An instruction is fetched from the program memory in two steps (fig. 2-4). The CPU sends the address given by the program counter to the program memory in the first step. The memory word belonging to this address is selected. In the second step the program memory gives the *contents* of the addressed memory word to the CPU. The CPU stores these contents which represent an instruction in the *instruction register*. The program counter is now incremented.

The CPU uses the contents of the instruction register to control the activities which must take place during instruction execution. The circuit in which the processor translates the instruction code for these specific actions is called the *instruction decoder*.

One part of the instruction now stored in the instruction register serves to indicate which operation must take place (for example: addition). This part is called the *operation code*. The other parts of the instruction serves to indicate the place where the data is to be processed can be found (called the *operand*), and where to put the answer (called the *destination*).

In Chapter 1 we saw the instruction

ADD D or 10000010

which means that the contents of register D must be added to the contents of the accumulator. 10000 = the adding of the contents of the accumulator and 010 = the place where the operand can be found = register D. The destination, the accumulator, is implied. 10000 is the operation code; 010 is the operand address. (Register D is one of the general-purpose registers in the CPU).

This is an example of a 1 byte instruction. It is, therefore, an instruction which takes up one memory word in an 8-bit microcomputer. An instruction can sometimes be 2 or 3 bytes long. Thus, in an 8-bit computer, 2 or 3 memory words are needed to store such an instruction in the program memory. This is the case, for example, when the instruction contains the address in the data memory where data is located.

If we have a microcomputer with a CPU which can

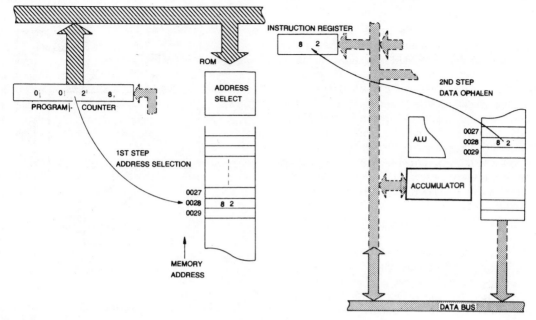

Fig. 2-4.

address 65, 536 memory locations, the addresses of the memory words are then 16 bits = 2 bytes long. In this case the total instruction will take up 3 bytes (fig. 2-5). The byte forms the operation code. This indicates which operation must be executed. When fetched the operation code enters the instruction register. The following 2 bytes, which indicate the *operand address* in the information memory, are stored in the *operand address register* during the execution of an operation. This is usually called the *address register*.

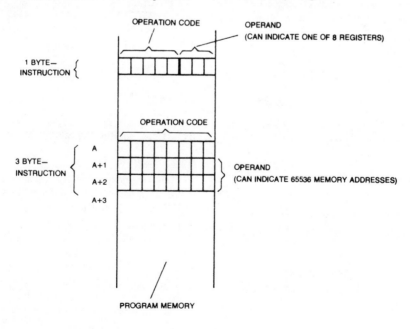

Fig. 2-5.

Note

During the execution of a 3 byte instruction, the program counter has to be incremented 3 times. If the program counter points to address A, the contents of address A goes to the instruction register. The program counter is then incremented by 1. It now becomes A + 1. The content of this address is brought to the address register. The program counter is then incremented by 1. It now becomes A + 2. The content of this address is also brought to the address register. During the execution of the instruction, the counter becomes A + 3, indicating the next instruction to be fetched. For other instructions and other machines different rules may apply. We will deal with this later.

ALU

The arithmetic and logical operation a microcomputer must perform take place in the ALU. Two operands are required for a great number of these arithmetic operations; for example, add A to B. The operands are presented to the ALU from 2 general-purpose registers and then processed. The result is stored in the accumulator.

In this sort of operation the computer must give the address of both operands; thus we speak of a *two address machine* (fig. 2-6a). In many microcomputers though the content of the accumulator is fed back into one of the inputs of the ALU. In this case, one of the operands is *always* in the accumulator, so that we only have to give the address of the other operand. This is a *one-address machine* (fig. 2-6b).

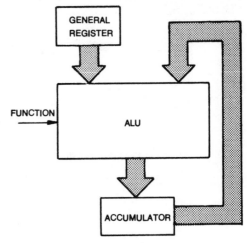

Fig. 2-6B.

Note

The ALU is sometimes represented as shown in fig. 2-6c, in which two pieces of data are presented with 1 result.

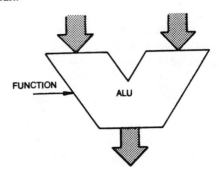

Fig. 2-6C.

DATA FLOW WITHIN THE MICROCOMPUTER

From the CPU to Memory

The memory-write operation (writing in to the memory) is performed in order to write data from the CPU into a selected memory location. The following steps are executed:

1. The address of the memory word where a word has to be written goes from the CPU to memory.

2. The address is decoded by the address selection.

3. The CPU puts a word on the data bus, and at the same time sends a *write* command.

4. The word is stored in the selected address.

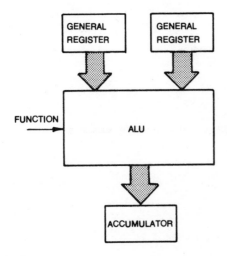

Fig. 2-6A.

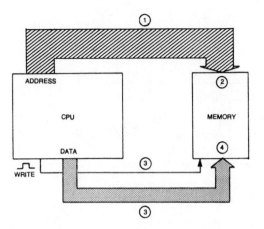

Fig. 2-7.

From Memory to the CPU

A memory-read operation (reading out of memory) is performed in order to transport data present in a given memory location to the CPU. The following steps are executed:

1. The address of the memory address, the contents of which must be brought to the CPU, goes from the CPU to memory.

2. The address is decoded by the address selection.

3. The CPU sends a read command to memory.

4. The contents of the selected memory address are brought to the CPU.

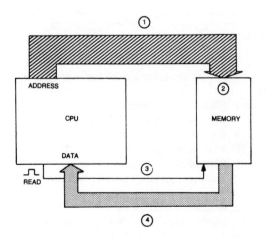

Fig. 2-8.

Note

An instruction which causes data to be brought to or taken from memory is called a *memory reference* instruction.

From Input to the CPU

An Input operation is executed in order to bring data from an Input device to the CPU where it can be processed further. The transfer of data from the Input to the CPU takes place in the following manner (fig. 2-9):

1. The CPU sends an I/O selection address to the I/O module via the address bus. This indicates from which input port the data must be taken. Note: This method of selecting an I/O port is called memory mapped I/O. Some CPUs have separate IN and OUT signals for I/O. This is called Port Addressed I/O.

2. To indicate that this involves an input operation, the CPU sends the command READ to the I/O module via the control bus.

3. The data presented to the selected Input port put on the data bus where the CPU reads it.

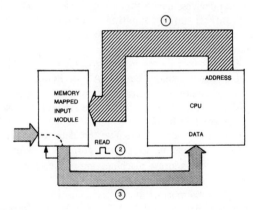

Fig. 2-9.

From the CPU to Output

An Output operation is executed in order to transport data from the CPU to a selected Output port, as follows:

1. The I/O selection address, which determines the Output port through which data must be brought to the Output device, goes from the address bus to the I/O module.

2. The CPU puts the data to be transported on the data bus. It then executes a WRITE command.

3. The data processed by the CPU goes out the selected Output module.

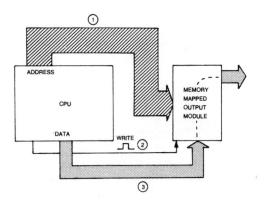

Fig. 2-10.

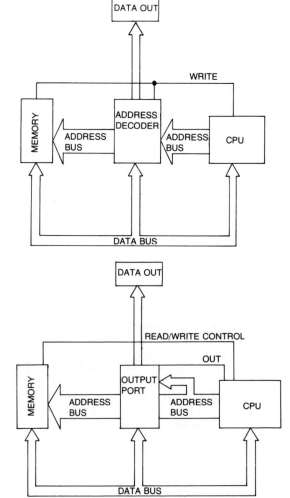

SUMMARY

1. The various parts of a microcomputer are connected to one another by a bus system.

2. The bus consists of a number of data lines, address lines and control lines.

3. In addition to inputting data with the usual peripheral devices, data from a process can also be fed direct into a microcomputer. Because a computer can only work with zeros and ones, the data has to be converted to digital form first.

4. The data memory in a microcomputer is RAM and the program memory can be RAM or ROM.

5. Arithmetic and logical operations take place in the ALU. The results are stored in the accumulator unless directed elsewhere.

6. In a two-address machine the data to be processed can be found in two general purpose registers.

7. In a one-address machine, one of the operands can be found in the accumulator.

8. The memory-write operation is executed in order to take data from the CPU and write a selected memory location or address.

9. The memory-read operation is executed in order to bring data from memory to the CPU.

10. An Input operation is executed in order to bring data from a selected Input Port in the CPU.

11. An output operation is executed in order to take data from the CPU to a selected Output Port.

REVIEW QUESTIONS

1. What is a microcomputer?
2. What is a bus system?
3. What do we call the 3 sets of bus lines?
4. Why is a clock generator built into a microcomputer?

Fig. 2-11.

5. What is stored in the program counter?
6. In what sequence are the instructions stored in memory?
7. What is a jump instruction?
8. What is the fetch cycle?
9. What is stored in the instruction register?
10. What is the operand?
11. What parts make up an instruction?
12. What is stored in the operand address register?
13. What does ALU mean?
14. What is the difference between a one-address machine and a two-address machine?
15. What does the D/A converter do?

26

16. A memory-write operation is executed using what steps?

17. An Output operation is executed using what steps?

18. Draw a block diagram of a microcomputer, showing the bus system in detail.

ANSWERS

1. If the CPU is contained on one or two chips (called a microprocessor), the computer is a microcomputer.

2. An external extension of the address, data, and control lines to which parallel components can be connected.

3. Data lines, address lines and control lines.

4. To regulate the timing of all actions in the microcomputer.

5. The address of the next instruction to be fetched.

6. In ascending consecutive order.

7. A jump instruction contains the address of the following instruction to be executed. It is possible in this way to store the next instruction in a random memory location.

8. An instruction is brought from memory to the CPU during the fetch cycle.

9. The instruction.

10. The part of the instruction that tells what to do.

11. An operation code and the location of the operand.

12. The address of the operand.

13. Arithmetic and Logic Unit.

14. In a one-address machine the accumulator is used to store one of the two operands as well as the result of the operation. In a two address machine only the result of the operation is stored in the accumulator. Two general-purpose registers are available for the two operands, both of which can be addressed by the CPU.

15. A D/A converter converts digital data from the computer into analog form for an external process.

16. The address is put on the address bus, data on the data bus, and a WRITE signal is then sent to memory.

17. For memory mapped I/O, the address on the address line is decoded. If it is correct, the Output Port is enabled. Data is put on the data bus, and the WRITE signal strobes it to the external lines.

For Port I/O, a part of the address bus selects a Port. Data is placed on the data lines and an OUT signal on the control lines strobes the data out to external lines.

Chapter 3

The Microcomputer in General

The first two chapters served as an introduction to the microprocessor. One could say that the fourth revolution in the history of electronics has begun with the arrival of the microprocessor. First the vacuum tube, then the transistor, after that the integrated circuit, and now the microprocessor. A new phase of technological development is introduced. That it is indeed a new phase can be clearly understood when you realize that we're no longer working with semiconductor devices, but with a *system*.

By using a microprocessor a microcomputer system is created. It isn't just a matter of soldering the components together. By mounting the components on a printed circuit board and connecting them together, you have constructed the system *hardware*.

To make the system function according to your requirements, you have to *program* it; in other words, provide it with a program. Writing such a program replaces the calculations which are needed to design conventional circuitry. As an example, two circuits which can perform addition are shown in fig. 3-1. Figure 3-1a shows a circuit with an operational amplifier and resistors. Figure 3-1b shows a circuit with a computer. The computer program contains an instruction to add the values fed in.

To attain an error-free smooth-running program you must set up and adapt the circuit. You don't do this, as you would in conventional electronics, by using a multimeter and an oscilloscope (fig. 3-1a), but rather by using *sub-programs* (fig. 3-1b). These sub-programs, which have the collective name *system software*, are provided by the microcomputer manufacturer.

The advantages of a computer system can be clearly seen in the examples just given. If one wanted to multiply (or divide), U_1, U_2 and U_3 by each other, one would have to feed in a new work program. The circuitry itself (the hardware) wouldn't have to be changed.

Once written, programs can be changed much more quickly and easily than circuitry. From this it can be seen that a microcomputer is indeed more economic when many different or very complex functions are required.

In this chapter we will address the subject of how to use system software. We will cover this in more detail in Chapter 18. Also in this chapter we will consider some general points concerning the microcomputer, such as types of memory, application possibilities, and considerations when selecting a microprocessor.

FROM THE IDEA TO THE OBJECT PROGRAM
Phase 1

When a designer has an idea or gets an assignment to automate a process, he usually begins by defining the problem. He then finds a method of solving the problem and draws a flowchart. The functions which the computer must perform are given in this flowchart step-by-step, in the proper sequence. From the flowchart the programmer writes a program, either in one of the lower-level programming languages (assembly language, for example) or in a high-level programming language (PL/M for instance). This hand-written program is called the *source program*.

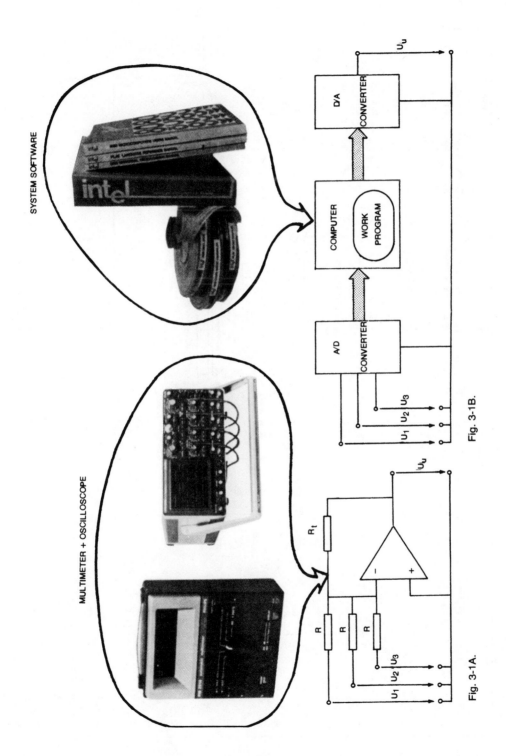

SYSTEM SOFTWARE

MULTIMETER + OSCILLOSCOPE

Fig. 3-1B.

Fig. 3-1A.

29

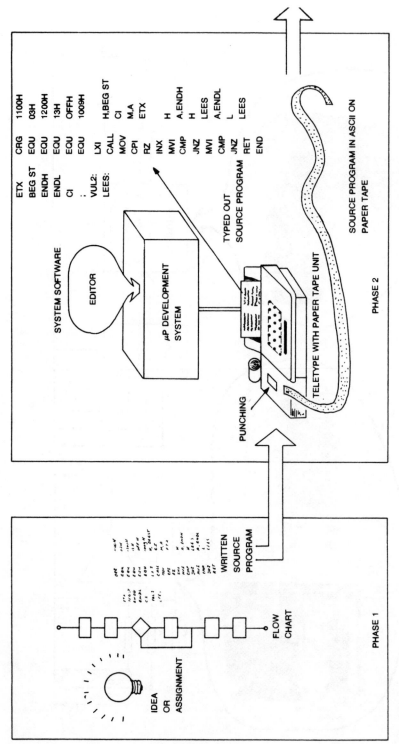

Fig. 3-2A.

30

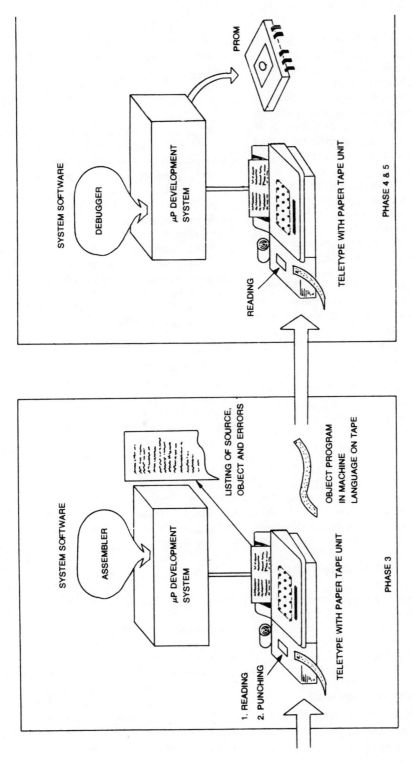

Fig. 3-2B.

Phase 2

The computer cannot read the source program. It must first be translated into machine instructions—the *object program*. A *microprocessor (µP) development system* is used to make the translation. A development system is a complete microcomputer, and its software, used specifically for the development of other software. The development system has a large amount of memory at its disposal for storing its own sub-programs, the source ASCII code, the translated object code, and control programs for the necessary peripheral devices.

To translate a source program into an object program, the source program must first be fed into the memory of the development system. To do this we type out the source program on an input device; a teletype in this case. Each letter, number, and character in the source becomes a character coded in ASCII, which is stored in the main memory of the development system. (For a furthr description of ASCII, see Chapter 4.) Inputting the characters into the development system and storing them in the main memory is controlled by one of the development programs called the *editor*. Typing errors can also be corrected by the editor, if necessary.

When the entire program has been stored, letter-by-letter and character-by-character, in the data memory of the development system, it is saved in external memory; punched on paper tape in this case. This paper tape is called the *source tape* (because it contains the source program).

Phase 3

A second development program now makes its appearance, because the microcomputer cannot read the information on the source tape, as these are not machine instructions. Using a translation program (for instance, an *assembler* in assembly language or, a *compiler* in higher programming languages) the source program is converted into machine instructions suitable for the microcomputer.

When the development system has been loaded with the translation program, the source tape produced in Phase 2 is fed in. The information present on the source tape is also stored in the memory of the development system. The translation can begin.

FROM OBJECT PROGRAM TO WORK PROGRAM

We shall now examine the result of Phase 3. We see in fig. 3-2b that the development system produces the following output via the teletype:

● A list containing the ASCII coded source program as well as the binary coded object program.

● A list containing all the mistakes which have been found . . .

● . . . or a paper tape containing the object program, *if* the source program is error free.

When you see the outcome of Phase 3 for the first time, don't be discouraged. In most cases the list of errors will be extremely long and you won't get a paper tape of the object program. You must return to Phase 2, where the errors can be corrected with the editor. This means that the contents of certain memory words in which ASCII characters are stored will be re-written. After this a new source tape is made. This is then fed into the development system for a second time. You repeat this process so long as errors appear. At last, to your relief, the message "assembly complete—no errors" will appear. This message implies only that the translating program has found no errors. It doesn't necessarily mean that the program works.

Phase 4

Now that you have a paper tape containing the object program at your disposal, this program must be read into the memory of the development system to see if the program runs properly. In most cases the program doesn't run the first time it's tried. You must get to work to track down your mistakes. These are usually fundamental, i.e. a mistake in the flowchart or using the wrong instruction. Had you built a conventional system that didn't work, you'd get busy with soldering iron and oscilloscope. In a development system we can make use of a software tool—the *debug program*, sometimes shortened to *debugger*.

The debugger (which literally helps you "get the bugs out" of your program) enables you to put your finger on the weak points in your program, using a teletype instead of an oscilloscope. Therefore you feed the debugger into the program memory of the development system, where the object program is already stored. You now give the commands, such as "Run through my program from point to point, then stop and tell me what is stored in the memory". The teletype will give you the typed answer. In this manner you can run through the program step-by-step and check the contents of all the registers and memory locations. Each section of the program can be independently examined and corrected until it is error free. In the end you arrive at an error-free object program, the *work program*.

Phase 5

In the last phase the program is stored in a PROM which can be connected into the microcomputer for which the program finally has been designed.

TYPES OF MEMORY

Before moving on to a simple example of a computer system, let us examine the various forms of memory more closely.

The main memory of a computer system can be divided into program memory and data memory (fig. 3-3). The instructions are stored in the program memory and the data to be processed is stored in the data memory. Roms can only be used *as* program memory, RAMs are a must *for* data memory. Both types of memory come under the heading of semiconductor memories.

Information is permanently stored in a ROM. It can only be read out and cannot be changed or updated. Three types are available:

● ROMs preprogrammed by the manufacturer. During production the manufacturer puts a series of bit patterns into memory according to the needs of the user. Later updating is impossible. This type of ROM is suitable when large numbers of identical ROMs are needed.

● Programmable ROMs, sometimes called PROMs. The user can program a PROM with a PROM programming device which burns out certain diodes. Once this has been done, further changes are impossible. This method is practical whenever small numbers of different ROMs are needed.

● EPROMs (Erasable PROM). With these devices a program can be erased using ultraviolet light. Reprogramming takes place with an EPROM programming device. The advantage is that mistakes can be corrected and that program changes can be affected without having to discard ROMs or PROMs.

A RAM is a memory which the processor can read from or write to. This memory is particularly suitable for storing intermediate results of calculations and various types of variable data. Its function is, in fact, that of a scratch-pad.

Note

RAM is an abbreviation of Random Access Memory. The name RAM is used to describe READ/WRITE memory even though a ROM can also be randomly addressed. As the name implies, information can only be read out of a ROM, so it is not randomly accessible, only randomly readable.

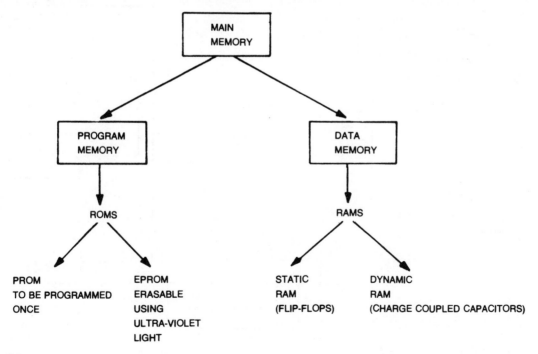

Fig. 3-3.

With RAMs, a distinction is made between static and dynamic circuits. Static RAMs consist of flip-flops, in which the information is stored until the related flip-flop is addressed and rewritten with new information. Usually, static RAMs are used when speed is not important, and only a small amount of memory is needed. Dynamic RAMs do not use flip-flops, but rather integral capacitances. Because leakage current is not negligible, the leakage loss has to be compensated every few milliseconds. This process is called *refresh* and extra hardware is needed for it. Dynamic RAMs would be used if a large amount of data is to be processed and if integrated refresh-circuitry is available. Some microprocessors supply a refresh cycle.

EXAMPLE OF AN APPLICATION

In order to give a practical example of the working of a microcomputer we will use the control of a washing machine by a microcomputer (fig. 3-4) as an example.

The data fed in—such as the temperature and level of the water—must be converted into signals which the CPU can recognize using A/D converters. The signals sent out by the CPU control the heating coils, water-supply valve, drainage pump and the motor for washing and spin-drying. This is done via solid-state relays, triacs, and SCRs. The various washing programs are stored in the ROMs. It is easy for the manufacturer to expand the number of washing programs or to change a program simply by replacing one or more ROM ICs.

To show the control process, a part of the fine-wash program is shown in fig. 3-5. This program is permanently stored in the fine-wash ROM. The underlined parts of fig. 3-5 indicate what is permanently stored in ROM. These include water temperature, water-level and the time necessary for washing and spin-drying the wash. A decision must be made every time the water level, the temperature, or the time is measured. The decision is arrived at by comparing the measured value with the value stored in the ROM.

With the fine wash the temperature of the water must not be more than 40°C. If the measured value is equal to or higher than 40°C, the heating element is turned off and the drive motor turned on. Now go through the flowchart carefully for yourself.

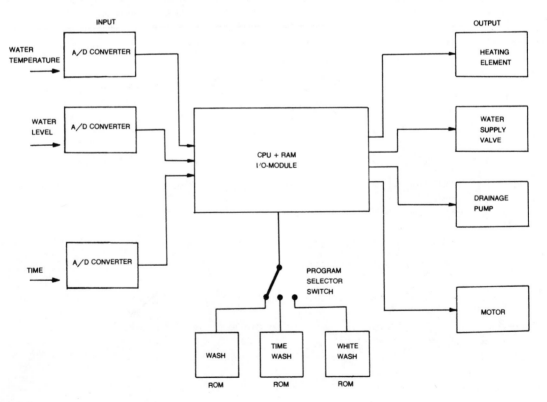

Fig. 3-4.

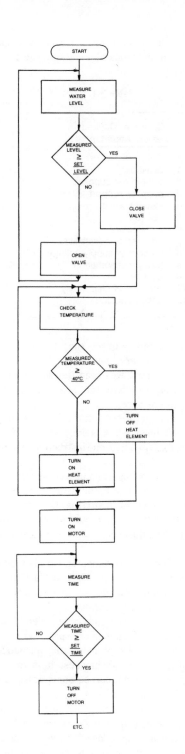

Fig. 3-5.

APPLICATIONS FOR MICROCOMPUTERS

Known application areas for microcomputers are:

Consumer	Automatic petrol stations Cash registers Automatic change machines Toys Pin-ball machines Cable television Automobiles Microwave ovens Sewing machines Radio Television
Medicine/biology	Diagnostic devices Laboratory tests Patient monitoring Physiological test systems Patient administration
Communication	Transfer equipment Channel control Bandwidth reduction
Physical devices	Reactor control accelerators Mass spectrometers Alarm systems for monitoring air pollution
Measuring instruments	Oscillographs Spectrum analysis Component test equipment Logic for sorting Scales Radar devices Fail-safe measuring equipment Dosing systems
Decentralized on-board computers for:	Aircraft Ships Trucks Military systems Rocket systems (space travel)

Industrial control	Process control
	Regulating traffic
	Controlling lifts
	Decentralized control systems (subsystems)
	Robot systems
	Machine control
	Production control
	Press control (Printing presses)
	Central unit for closed-loop control
	Test system for ICs and printed circuits
Computer peripherals	Displays
	Punched-card readers
	Floppy discs
	Control of tapes/ cassettes
	Printers
Data processing	"Intelligent terminals"
	Invoicing devices
	Memories
	Multiprocessing (a system composed of various microprocessors)
	Emulation of micro-computers
	Pocket calculators
	Banking installations (the control of checks, etc.)
	General office use (organization of a card system)
	Automatic typewriters
	Photocopying machines

EVALUATING THE MICROCOMPUTER

After deciding to solve a problem with a microcomputer, we have to decide which computer system is best suited for the purpose. The answer is not simple, since there are so many systems on the market and so many criteria which play a role in our decision.

The criteria for evaluating a computer can be divided into technical and nontechnical. A public-opinion survey among customers of one of the leading computer manufacturers in America showed that non-technical factors play the major role in the choice of a microcomputer (table 3-1). We will now look at some of these points a little more closely.

Table 3-1.

```
              Customer Ranked
              Feature Importance

          1.  availability
          2.  trust in the supplier
          3.  supplier support
          4.  instruction set
          5.  speed
          6.  architecture
          7.  addressing possibilities
          8.  number of supply voltages
          9.  power consumption
         10.  service
         11.  diversity of chip family
         12.  documentation
```

Having a second source, that is alternative suppliers, for an IC is very important.

By supplier support we mean the supply of subprograms, and assistance with the development of the work program, where necessary

The microcomputer's instruction set plays an important role here. We must ask ourselves whether a given operation can be executed with one instruction, or if more are needed.

Speed is often very important in process control. As strange as it may seem, a microprocessor can sometimes work too slowly. When a calculation may need as many as 100 to 200 instructions, each requiring up to about 2 μseconds, 0.2 to 0.4 milliseconds are needed to complete it.

When ordering a microcomputer we also have to take its architecture into account. The construction of the buses, memory organization, etc., are important if we are to allow for expansion at a later date.

We will discuss how operands can be identified and located in Chapter 13. Much memory space can often be saved by the proper choice of addressing technique or combination of addressing techniques. It is therefore often advantageous if the microprocessor can make use of a variety of addressing techniques.

When purchasing a microprocessor one should examine the rest of the chip family very closely. Where, for example, a certain brand doesn't have I/O modules available, we are forced to obtain modules of a different type, which usually causes problems.

Table 3-1 shows that such aspects as availability, confidence in the supplier and supplier support weigh more heavily than the technical aspects. This is really not surprising. You will usually find that more than one microcomputer system matches a given application, and make a decision based on nontechnical features.

While systems are often equivalent in performance and differ little in price, they are not interchangeable. One must choose with care, and take a considerable risk with regard to continuity of supply. One is advised to choose a supplier from among the leading firms, one of long standing, and one which gives sound technical support. Finally, choose a genuine (one who manufactures, not one who buys in) second source to protect your supply line.

SUMMARY

1. Software development takes place in the development system.

2. When developing software, use is made of several auxiliary programs and system software supplied by the manufacturer.

3. The editor is used to enter and correct the source program.

4. A translation program translates the source program into the object program.

5. A translation program used with a program which has been written in assembly language is called the assembler. A translation program used with a program which has been written in one of the higher programming languages is called a compiler.

6. The object program which results from Phase 3 is read into the memory of the microcomputer with the help of the loader.

7. The debugger is used to track down and correct the mistakes in the object program.

8. The final result is the work program which is stored in a PROM.

9. ROM can only be used as program memory. RAM is mostly used as information memory.

10. PROM is a type of memory which the user programs once. EPROM is a memory device in which the stored information can be erased using ultraviolet light.

11. RAM can be divided into two types; static and dynamic.

REVIEW EXERCISES

1. What is system software?

2. Into what phases can we divide the development of the work program?

3. What is the function of the editor, the assembler, and the debugger?

4. What is source tape?

5. What output does the teletype give at the end of Phase 3?

6. Which types of memory do we use for the data and program memories?

7. Name two types of programmable ROMs.

8. What types of RAMs are there, and what is the difference between them?

ANSWERS TO REVIEW EXERCISES

1. Sub-programs delivered by the manufacturer and used in the development of the work program.

2. Writing, editing, assembly, debugging, and PROM programming.

3. The editor inputs and corrects the source program.
The assembler translates the source program into the object program.
The debugger helps find errors in the object program.

4. A tape with an ASCII-coded source program stored on it.

5. A listing of the source program that has been fed in, and the object code.
A listing of all the mistakes found.
If there are no mistakes, a papertape which contains the object program.

6. RAM is used for the data memory.
ROM is used for the program memory.

7. PROM = Programmable Read Only Memory
EPROM = Erasable PROM

8. Static RAMs, consisting of flip-flops, and dynamic RAMs, where the memory is based on internal capacitances.

Chapter 4
How Does a
Computer Compute?

Digital electronic circuitry, which includes computers, can assume only 2 states. This can be visualized as switches that may be open (*nonconducting*) or closed (*conducting*). The non-conducting state is indicated by a '0'. The conducting state is indicated by a '1'.

A group of such 2-state circuits forms a combination of states, i.e. *a combination of zeros and ones*. If we have an agreed code, such a combination of zeros and ones can represent a number, a letter, or a character.

Various codes exist to represent letters and characters. Here we will discuss the two codes used with microcomputers: *ASCII* and *EBCDIC*.

The code used to represent a number using zeros and ones is called binary or base-2 notation ($bi = 2$). A binary digit is called a *bit*. This is an abbreviation of *bi*nary dig*it*. We will deal with calculations in binary digits first. Because we have grown up with decimal (or base 10) notation, we need time to get used to the binary system. In fact, calculating in binary is much easier than in decimal notation. There are only 2 digits (0 and 1), whereas there are 10 digits (0 to 9) in decimal notation. To express negative numbers in a computer, where we are limited to ones and zeros, we use the *2's complement*.

This chapter will also deal with *hexadecimal representation*, i.e., an abbreviated method of representing a combination of ones and zeros using the hexadecimal system.

DECIMAL NOTATION

To understand the binary system better, we can first examine the familiar decimal system. 10 Symbols are used in base-10 notation, namely:

0, 1, 2, 3, 4, 5, 6, 7, 8 and 9.

One uses these symbols whenever one wants to indicate a number or an amount. For a number greater than 9, we use a *combination of digits*. This combination is accidental, but accords with definite rules.

When we represent an amount by a number we do it in such a way that the place of the digit has a meaning. In the number 247, the number 2 is the most important. We say that in the number 247 the digit 2 has the greatest *weight*.

The weight is the factor by which a digit must be multiplied in order to find the real value of the digit in the number.

In base-10 notation, the right-hand digit has a weight of 1, the digit to its left the weight 10, that next 100, etc. We can write a number as the sum of the powers of ten. The number 247 is equal to $2 \times 100 + 4 \times 10 + 7 \times 1 = 200 + 40 + 7 = 2 \times 10^2 + 4 \times 4 \times 10^1 + 7 \times 10^0$. Depending on the weight (or significance) of the position, we speak of units, tens, hundreds, thousands . . . .

Note

Units are recorded as 10^0 because, by definition, the zero power of any number is 1.

BINARY NOTATION

In the decimal system we work as follows:
When we add 1, the number in the first (right-hand) column moves to the next, higher value. When we add 1 to 38 it becomes 39. The first column is now full (nine is the highest whole number). Figure 4-A. If we again add 1, the first column jumps back to 0, and 1 is added to the next column to the left (a CARRY). This second column now becomes 4. We add again ones to the first column until it reaches its maximum (9). After this, another carry is

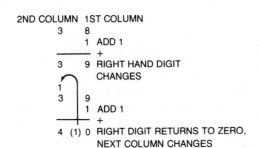

```
2ND COLUMN  1ST COLUMN
     3         8
               1    ADD 1
   ─────────        +
     3         9    RIGHT HAND DIGIT
                    CHANGES
     1
     3         9
               1    ADD 1
   ─────────        +
     4  (1)    0    RIGHT DIGIT RETURNS TO ZERO,
                    NEXT COLUMN CHANGES
```

Fig. 4-A.

produced. The digit in the 2nd column thus indicates how many times the maximum in the first column has been completely filled.

In the base-2 system, only 2 symbols are available, i.e. 0 and 1. Thus, when adding in this system the columns fill very quickly (see Table 4-1). The first column becomes full the first time that 1 is added. With the second increment of 1, the first column returns to zero and the carry is brought from the first to the second column. With the third increment of 1, the first column jumps back to 1 (from 0). Both columns are now full.

With the fourth increment of 1 to the amount 4, the first column jumps first to 0. We must now carry 1 over to the second column. This column is already full and thus jumps back to 0. The carry must now be brought over to the third column. We continue adding in this manner. *You are strongly advised to practice this method of addition until you understand it completely.*

That the binary and decimal systems are basically the same can now be clearly seen. In the binary system too, a digit in a given column indicates how many times the column to its right has been filled.

Converting from Binary to decimal

Because a full column consists of 2 digits, a binary number can be written as the sum of a power of 2. The binary number 101101 is equal to:

$$1 \times 2^5 + 0 \times 2^4 + 1 \times 2^3 + 1 \times 2^2 + 0 \times 2^1 + 1 \times 2^1 + 1 \times 2^0 =$$
$$32 + 0 + 8 + 4 + 0 + 1 = 45.$$

By writing a binary number as a sum of a power of 2, it can be rewritten as a decimal number.

Note

The combination of digits 100 has two different meanings:
- In decimal notation this combination of digits represents the amount *one hundred.*
- In binary notation this combination of digits represents the amount *four.*

If it isn't sufficiently clear which notation is used, we put the type of notation in parentheses in the lower right-hand side of the number for example $100_{(2)}$. To avoid confusion, we do not name binary numbers. Instead, we say the digits. In binary notation, $1001_{(2)}$ is spoken of as one, zero, zero, one.

DECIMAL TO BINARY

A decimal number is converted into a binary number in the following manner: To change $31_{(10)}$ (31 in decimal notation) into a binary number, you must write 31 as a sum of the powers of 2. First look for the highest power of 2, that can be subtracted. For 31 that is $16 = 2^4$. From the remainder (15), the next highest power of 2 is subtracted, i.e. $8 = 2^3$, then $4 (2^2)$, then $2 (2^1)$, then $1 (2^0)$. Therefore:
$$31_{(10)} = 1 \times 2^4 + 1 \times 2^3 + 1 \times 2^2 + 1 \times 2^1 + 1 \times 2^0 = 11111_{(2)}$$

Placing the coefficients we have found in sequence, gives us the binary number.

Note

The left-hand bit in a binary number is often called the MSB—the *M*ost *S*ignificant *B*it (the bit with the highest weight). The right-hand bit is often called the LSB-*L*east *S*ignificant *B*it (the bit with the lowest weight).

ADDING BINARY NUMBERS

Binary numbers are added in exactly the same way as decimal numbers. Because a column is filled more

Table 4-1.

decimal	binary
0	0
1	1
2	10
3	11
4	100
5	101
6	110
7	111
8	1000
9	1001
10	1010
11	1011
12	1100
13	1101
14	1110
15	1111
16	10000

Table 4-2.

decimal	binary
0 + 0 = 0	0 + 0 = 0
0 + 1 = 1	0 + 1 = 1
1 + 1 = 2	1 + 1 = 10
1 + 1 + 1 = 3	1 + 1 + 1 = 11

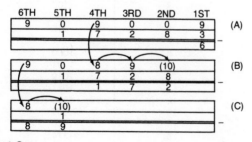

Fig. 4-B.

quickly (see table 4-1), we have to carry to the next column more frequently when adding in binary.

By adding A and B in the above picture we will illustrate that the same rules apply when adding in binary and in decimal. In the first column 0 and 0 are added, giving 0. In the second column 1 and 0 are added, 1. In the third column 0 and 1 are added, also resulting in 1. In the fourth column 1 and 1 are added. The result of adding 1 and 1 is 10. The 1 is now 'left over' and is placed above the fifth column as a carry. Thus, adding the 1, 0 and 0 which are above each other produces the sum 1. In the sixth column we again have 1 and 1. The sum is 10. The 1 is again brought over, to column 7, as a carry; we thus get three 1s above each other. The sum of this is 11. The carry is placed above the eighth column where we have no further numbers—the sum of column 8 is thus 1.

SUBTRACTING BINARY NUMBERS

Again we'll look first at subtracting in decimal in order to see what steps we actually take.

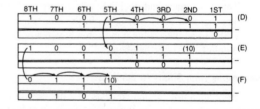

Fig. 4-C.

The number 17283 (subtrahend) must be subtracted from the number 909009 (minuend). We mark this by putting a minus sign to the right of the double line under the problem. When subtracting, we always begin with the right-hand column. To subtract 3 from 9 is easy. The result is 6 (see a). Going one column to the left, we see that we must subtract 8 from 0. That's impossible, since 8 is larger than 0. In other words, we can't decrement 0 by 8. To proceed with our calculation we must now find a number that is not 0. In this case it's 9. We borrow 1 from 9 and the 9 thus becomes 8 (see b). We can add the 1 to the zero in column 2 and thus get 10 in this column. *The zeros which lie between are changed to 9.*

We can now take 8 away from 10 in the second column, and find that the answer is 2. In the third column we must subtract 2 from 9. The answer is 7. In the fourth column we subtract 7 from 8, giving 1. In the fifth column we again meet an impossible situation, because we must subtract 1 from 0. Again we borrow, going to the left until we find a number that is not equal to 0. The 9 there then becomes an 8. The 0 becomes a 10 and any zeros in between (in this case none) become 9. Now we can proceed with our subtraction (see c). Perhaps you had never realized that when subtracting you were actually performing all these calculations.

After this refresher course, subtracting in binary should be easier to explain. We shall do this using the numbers below.

Fig. 4-D.

Subtracting the right-hand column is straightforward. $1 - 1 = 0$. In the second column we have to subtract 1 from 0. Which doesn't go. *Therefore, we move as many places to the left as are needed to arrive at a 1.* We put this 1 with the 0 in the second column, which changes it into 10 (one-zero). *We change the zeros which lie between into 1 (see e).* Now we continue with our subtraction. $10 - 1$ is, of course, equal to 1. We can further subtract in both the third and fourth column. In the fifth column we must again subtract 1 from 0. We must again borrow 1. We move to the left until we find a 1. We place this 1 with the 0 in the fifth column, making this 10 (one-zero). The zeros which lie between have been changed into ones and we can again continue with our subtraction (see f).

In the above example the minuend was larger than the subtrahend. We therefore obtain a normal positive result. Where, however, the subtrahend is larger than the minuend, the answer is negative. How we deal with a subtraction where the result will be negative is shown below:

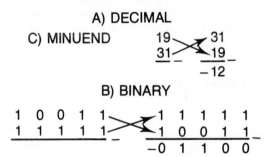

A) DECIMAL

C) MINUEND

B) BINARY

Fig. 4-E.

Where the minuend is smaller than the subtrahend, we first reverse the minuend and the subtrahend; subtract, and put a minus sign before the result.

THE 2'S COMPLEMENT METHOD

Because a computer only works with zeros and ones without plus or minus signs, it has certain limitations when doing arithmetic. To work with both positive and negative numbers, we must first agree how negative numbers are to be processed. In order to acquaint you with the most usual method, we will begin with an example of an 8-bit number, since most microcomputers work with words of this length. The general representation of an 8-bit number is:

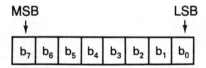

Fig. 4-F.

$b_0 - b_7$ are 0 or 1. Here the decimal value is always positive. We can operate with both positive and negative numbers if we represent the decimal value as follows:

$$b_7 \times - 2^7 + b_6 \times 2^6 + \ldots \ldots + b_0 \times 2^0$$

This is called the 2's complement representation. Thus we do not assign the weight 2^7 to the MSB of this figure (in this case b_7), but rather $- 2^7 = - 128$.

If the MSB is 1, it represents the decimal value $- 128$. Such a number must be negative since $b_6 - b_0$ combined can, at most, have a decimal value of 127. We can thus see that in the 2's complement value the number 10110001 is equal to:

$$1 \times - 128 + 0 \times 64 + 1 \times 32 + 1 \times 16 + 0 \times 8 + 0 \times 4 + 0 \times 2 + 1 \times 1 = - 79.$$

If the MSB is 0, the MSB represents the decimal value 0 and the number is positive because $b_6 - b_0$ represents positive decimal values. Therefore:
$$00100100 = 0 \times - 128 + 0 \times 64 + 1 \times 32 + 0 \times 16 + 0 \times 8 + 1 \times 4 + 0 \times 2 + 0 \times 1 = 36.$$

Writing a *positive* number in binary using the above method is straightforward. We write it as a sum of powers of 2. We must, however, select a word-length in which the MSB is equal to 0. If we want to write a *negative* number using the above method, we can do this easily using the 2's complement method.

The 2's complement of 77, for example, is formed by first writing 77 in binary and inverting all the digits (1's complement), and then adding 1.

$$
\begin{array}{ll}
77 = 01001101 & \\
\underline{10110010} + & \text{1's complement} \\
-77 = 10110011 & \text{2's complement}
\end{array}
$$

With 8-bit numbers, the values that can be represented range from $10000000 = - 128$, to $01111111 = + 127$ (see table 4-3).

Table. 4-3.

binary	decimal
10000000	−128
10000001	−127
10000010	−126
10000011	−125
.	.
.	.
.	.
11111110	−2
11111111	−1
00000000	0
00000001	1
00000010	2
00000011	3
.	.
.	.
.	.
01111101	+125
01111110	+126
01111111	+127

If this range is too small for our calculations, we must use 16-bit numbers. This is done by joining two 8-bit words together, forming a 16-bit word. When using this system, we must assign the value $b15 \times -2^{15}$ to the MSB of the word and the most negative number is:

$$1000\ 0000\ 0000\ 0000 = -2^{15} + 0 \times 2^{14} \ldots \ldots 0 \times 2^0 = -32768.$$

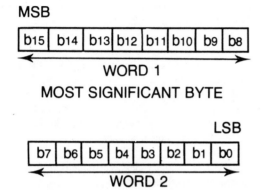

MSB

| b15 | b14 | b13 | b12 | b11 | b10 | b9 | b8 |

WORD 1

MOST SIGNIFICANT BYTE

LSB

| b7 | b6 | b5 | b4 | b3 | b2 | b1 | b0 |

WORD 2

LEAST SIGNIFICANT BYTE

Fig. 4-G.

The most positive number is now:

$$0111\ 1111\ 1111\ 1111 = 0 \times (2^{15}) + 1 \times 2^{14} + \ldots \ldots + 1 \times 2^0 =$$

The 2's complement method makes it much easier to subtract one binary number from another. It is clear that subtraction and addition are exactly the same. For example, $17 - 22 = 17 + (-22)$. Thus, to solve $00010001_{(2)} - 00010110_{(2)}$, we add $00010110_{(2)}$ to the inverse of $00010110_{(2)}$. The inverse of $00010110_{(2)}$ is the 2's complement.

The 2's complement of $00010110_{(2)}$ is found by first inverting all the bits and then adding 1.

INVERTED

```
00010110  ──────▶   11101001      1'S COMPLEMENT
                           1  +          (+1)
                    ─────────
                    11101010        2'S COMPLEMENT
```

Fig. 4-H.

Therefore, $00010001_{(2)} - 00010110_{(2)}$ can also be written as:

```
0 0 0 1 0 0 0 1
1 1 1 0 1 0 1 0
─────────────── +    Fig. 4-I.
1 1 1 1 1 0 1 1
```

The 2's complement notation is often an inherent part of microcomputers. When we use the SUB instruction (subtraction) to command the microcomputer to subtract one number from another, it will use the 2's complement method. In computers where the 2's complement method is not inherent, the programmer can first instruct the computer to find the 2's complement of the subtrahend and add that to the minuend using the ADD instruction.

MULTIPLYING BINARY NUMBERS

$0 \times 0 = 0$ The multiplication tables
$0 \times 1 = 0$ in binary notation are very
$1 \times 0 = 0$ simple. All possible
$1 \times 1 = 1$ combinations are given on the left.

```
  1 0 0 1
    1 1 ×
  ───────
  1 0 0 1
  1 1 0 1 +
  ───────
1 1 0 1 1
```

We multiply binary numbers by each other just as we do decimal numbers. This is shown on the right. If we multiply binary numbers containing more than two 1s, the addition must be performed in steps. For example:

```
      1 1 0 1
      1 0 1 1 ×
      ───────
      1 1 0 1
    1 1 0 1     +          Fig. 4-J.
    ─────────
  1 0 0 1 1 1
  1 1 0 1       +
  ───────────
1 0 0 0 1 1 1 1
```

Multiplying by 0 always results in zeros; so we don't have to note them. It is sufficient to shift one place to the left. Multiplying by 1 results in the same number (just as in decimal notation).

TERMS

One drawback of the binary system is that the numbers are longer than they are in decimal notation. To be able to work with these longer numbers, a number of general terms were developed. The expression bit, which comes from the term binary digit, means exactly what it says; a binary digit. The *binary number* as a whole is called a *word*. An important specification of a computer is its *word length*. Word length defines the number of bits that a word contains. A group of 4 bits is called a *tetrad* or *nybble*. A group of 8 bits is called an *octane* or *byte*.

HEXADECIMAL NOTATION

Hexadecimal or base-16 notation is also applied in digital technology, not to perform calculations but to abbreviate binary numbers. In other words, hexadecimal notation is used as a means of coding binary numbers. There are 16 symbols in hexadecimal notation; 0, 1, 2, 3, 4, 5, 6, 7, 8, 9, A, B, C, D, E, F. Addition is exactly the same as in binary and decimal (see table 4-4).

Table 4-4.

decimal	binary	hexadecimal
0	0000	0
1	0001	1
2	0010	2
3	0011	3
4	0100	4
5	0101	5
6	0110	6
7	0111	7
8	1000	8
9	1001	9
10	1010	A
11	1011	B
12	1100	C
13	1101	D
14	1110	E
15	1111	F

To represent a given number, fewer digits are needed than in binary representation. It's very easy to convert from a binary into a hexadecimal number and vice-versa. To write a binary number in hexadecimal notation, one must first divide the binary number into groups of 4 bits, or nybbles. Each nybble can be represented by a single hexadecimal character. The word 101100101001_2 can be divided into 1011 0010 1001. The hexadecimal representation of this number is now $B29_{(16)}$. It is just as easy to convert a hexadecimal number into a binary number. $3FA_{(16)} = 0011\ 1111\ 1010_{(2)}$ (see table 4-4).

Because binary numbers can be so easily converted into hexadecimal and back, hexadecimal notation is used as an abbreviated method of writing binary numbers.

BCD CODE

The BCD code is used to convert the decimal digits 0 through 9 into zeros and ones in a computer (table 4-5). BCD is an abbreviation of *Binary Coded Decimal*.

Table 4-5.

Decimal	BCD
0	0000
1	0001
2	0010
3	0011
4	0100
5	0101
6	0110
7	0111
8	1000
9	1001

In each decimal digit, the BCD code is represented by 4 binary bits. Although 4 bits could represent the decimal digits 0 to 15, the code to represent 10 - 15 is not used in BCD. For example, to code the number 13 using the BCD code, the digits 1 and 3 are coded separately. 13 thus becomes 0001 0011.

Many microprocessors have instructions for converting binary to BCD. This is called *decimal adjust*.

CODE SYSTEMS

A computer only works with zeros and ones. In our day-to-day life, however, we exchange information by using letters, symbols, and numbers. By arranging the 26 letters of the alphabet in a meaningful order, we compose sentences. We punctuate with other symbols. Examples are . , ? ; %. Ten digit symbols are used (0 to 9), and with these we form numbers. To make this information acceptable to the computer or a digital system, we must devise a sort of code, consisting of a combination of zeros and ones. Two of these codes, often used with microcomputers, are ASCII (pronounced ASS-KEY) and EBCDIC (pronounced EBB-SEE-DICK). ASCII is the American Standard Code for Information Interchange and EBCDIC is the Extended Binary Coded Decimal Interchange.

Table 4-6 shows how a combination of 8 bits can encode letters, symbols, and digits using the ASCII and EBCDIC codes. The combination of ones and zeros which goes with each symbol is represented in hexadecimal. Because ASCII is, in fact, a 7-bit code, we usually omit the left-most bit. Some microcomputers have special characters that use the 8th bit, and even though these are not a part of the standard ASCII, they are still *called* ASCII codes.

SUMMARY

1. A number consists of digits, each of which has its own weight based on position.

2. The weight of a digit in a number is that factor by which the digit must be multiplied in order to find the actual value.

Table 4-6.

Hexadecimal notation	ASCII (7 bits)	EBCDIC (8 bits)	Hexadecimal notation	ASCII (7 bits)	EBCDIC (8 bits)
0			40		blank
1			41	A	
2			42	B	
3			43	C	
4			44	D	
5			45	E	
6			46	F	
7			47	G	
8			48	H	
9			49	I	
A			4A	J	
B			4B	K	
C			4C	L	<
D			4D	M	(
E			4E	N	+
F			4F	O	!
10			50	P	&
11			51	Q	
12			52	R	
13			53	S	
14			54	T	
15			55	U	
16			56	V	
17			57	W	
18			58	X	
19			59	Y	
1A			5A	Z	
1B			5B		
1C			5C		$
1D			5D		*
1E			5E		)
1F			5F		
20	blank		60		
21	!		61	a	
22	"		62	b	
23	#		63	c	
24	$		64	d	
25	%		65	e	
26	&		66	f	
27	'		67	g	
28	(		68	h	
29	)		69	i	
2A	*		6A	j	
2B	+		6B	k	
2C	,		6C	l	%
2D	-		6D	m	
2E	.		6E	n	>
2F	/		6F	o	?
30	0		70	p	
31	1		71	q	
32	2		72	r	
33	3		73	s	
34	4		74	t	
35	5		75	u	
36	6		76	v	
37	7		77	w	
38	8		78	x	
39	9		79	y	
3A	:		7A	z	
3B	;		7B		‡
3C	<		7C		
3D	=		7D		
3E	>		7E		=
3F	?		7F		"

Hexadecimal notation	ASCII (7 bits)	EBCDIC (8 bits)	Hexadecimal notation	ASCII (7 bits)	EBCDIC (8 bits)
80			C0		
81		a	C1		A
82		b	C2		B
83		c	C3		C
84		d	C4		D
85		e	C5		E
86		f	C6		F
87		g	C7		G
88		h	C8		H
89		i	C9		I
8A			CA		
8B			CB		
8C			CC		
8D			CD		
8E			CE		
8F			CF		
90			D0		
91		j	D1		J
92		k	D2		K
93		l	D3		L
94		m	D4		M
95		n	D5		N
96		o	D6		O
97		p	D7		P
98		q	D8		Q
99		r	D9		R
9A			DA		
9B			DB		
9C			DC		
9D			DD		
9E			DE		
9F			DF		
A0			E0		
A1			E1		
A2		s	E2		S
A3		t	E3		T
A4		u	E4		U
A5		v	E5		V
A6		w	E6		W
A7		x	E7		X
A8		y	E8		Y
A9		z	E9		Z
AA			EA		
AB			EB		
AC			EC		
AD			ED		
AE			EE		
AF			EF		
B0			F0		0
B1			F1		1
B2			F2		2
B3			F3		3
B4			F4		4
B5			F5		5
B6			F6		6
B7			F7		7
B8			F8		8
B9			F9		9
BA			FA		
BB			FB		
BC			FC		
BD			FD		
BE			FE		
BF			FF		

3. The base-2 system or binary notation (bi = 2) uses the digits 0 and 1.

4. A bit is an abbreviation of binary digit.

5. The zero power of a number is by definition 1; $10^0 = 1$.

6. A binary number can be converted into a decimal number by adding up the powers of 2.

7. A decimal number can be converted into a binary number by continually subtracting powers of 2 beginning with the highest possible and then putting the coefficients in sequence so that the coefficient with the highest power of 2 has the greatest weight.

8. The method of notation which is to be used is placed in parentheses as a subscript.

9. A carry is a transfer to the next column.

10. If you must borrow when subtracting, the next 1 becomes a 0, the column for which we have borrowed becomes 10, and the zeros that lie between become 1.

11. Where the subtrahend is larger than the minuend, we subtract the minuend from the subtrahend, and place a minus sign before the difference.

12. 1 byte = 2 nybbles = 8 bits.

13. Binary numbers can be represented in abbreviated form by hexadecimal numbers.

14. The decimal digits 0 to 9 can be coded into binary using the BCD code.

REVIEW EXERCISES

1. How many digits in binary notation, and what are they?

How many digits in hexadecimal notation, and what are they?

How many digits in decimal notation, and what are they?

2. What are the advantages of working with the binary system when arithmetic processes must be performed using electronic circuits?

3. Indicate how a binary number can be converted into a decimal number.

4. Indicate how a hexadecimal number can be converted into a binary number.

5. Indicate how a binary number can be converted into a hexadecimal number.

6. Indicate how a decimal number can be converted into a binary number.

7. What is a bit?

8. What is a word?

9. What is a carry?

10. What is the main reason that hexadecimal notation is used in digital technology?

11. What is a nybble?

12. What is a byte?

13. Write the following decimal numbers in binary notation; 15, 29, 38, and 53.

14. Write the following binary numbers in decimal notation; 1010, 1101, and 11101.

15. Using a vertical column count to 18 in binary.

16. Add $101101_{(2)}$ and $110100_{(2)}$.

17. Subtract $101001_{(2)}$ from $110000_{(2)}$.

18. Write the following binary numbers in hexadecimal notation; 10110101, 11000111, and 1001 1101 1100 0100.

19. Multiply $1011_{(2)}$ by $1001_{(2)}$.

20. How are negative numbers represented in a computer?

21. How do we find the 2's complement of a number?

22. Name 2 codes with which we can encode letters, digits, and punctuation marks using zeros and ones.

ANSWERS TO REVIEW EXERCISES

1. Binary notation comprises two digits; 0 and 1. Hexadecimal notation comprises 16 symbols; 0, 1, 2, 3, 4, 5, 6, 7, 8, 9, A, B, C, D, E and F.

Decimal notation comprises ten digits; 0, 1, 2, 3, 4, 5, 6, 7, 8, 9.

2. The advantage is that we can work with 2-state circuits such as relays, switches and electronic circuits which operate as switches. One position is equal to 0, the other position to 1.

3. The binary number is converted to decimal by writing it as a sum of powers of 2. For example, $1011_{(2)} = 1\times2^3 + 0\times2^2 + 1\times2^1 + 1\times2^0 = 8 + 0 + 2 + 1 = 11_{(10)}$.

4. A hexadecimal number can be converted into a binary number by replacing its digits with their binary equivalents (table 4-4). $3F1_{(16)} = 001111110001_{(2)}$

5. A binary number is converted into a hexadecimal number by dividing the binary number into groups of 4 bits and by replacing each group of 4 bits by a hexadecimal digit. $0101\ 1010\ 0001_{(2)} = 5A1_{(16)}$.

6. A decimal number can be converted into a binary number by writing the decimal number as a sum of the powers of 2. One must look for the highest possible power of 2, subtract this, and again look for the highest possible power of 2 in the remainder, etc.

7. Bit is an abbreviation of binary digit. A bit is a simple digit in a binary number.

8. A word is the total number of bits in the largest binary number that a given computer can treat as a single entity.

9. A carry is the transference of an amount to the adjacent column.

10. Hexadecimal notation is used mainly because it is a shorter way of writing binary numbers.

11. A nybble is a group of 4 bits.

12. A byte is a group of 8 bits.

13. 1111, 11101, 100110, and 110101.

14. 10, 13, and 29.

15. See table 4-1.

16. $1100001_{(2)}$.

17. $111_{(2)}$.

18. B5, C7, and 9DC4.

19. $1100011_{(2)}$.

20. As the 2's complement of the corresponding positive number.

21. All the bits are first inverted, and then as 1 is added.

22. ASCII and EBCDIC code.

Chapter 5
Circuitry in a Computer

This chapter mainly covers digital circuitry and is likely to be a revision for you if you have a hardware background, less so if your specialty is programming.

The CPU is only one of the many integrated circuits in a microcomputer. The purpose of this chapter is first to familiarize you with the functions of the other circuits, and secondly to introduce you to some of the circuits found *in* the CPU so that you may better understand the instructions related to these circuits. The first category includes circuits such as *NAND, NOR, NOT* gates and *flip-flops*. The second category deals with *AND, OR* and *EXOR* functions, *registers* and *counters*.

For your guidance, a diagram of the microcomputer (fig. 2-1 from the chapter "What is a Microcomputer?") is shown in fig. 5-24 at the end of the chapter. Here you see the circuits present in a microcomputer and how they are connected to the lines of the data bus and address bus.

The *microprocessor* (type 8080A) and the *clock generator* (type 8224) are discussed in the chapter "CPU Architecture 1 and 2".

The *main memory* consists of ROMs (4x type 464) and RAMs (6x type 5101), as covered in the chapter "Main Memory".

In the chapter "Architecture of a Microcomputer" the *I/O module* will be included. This is 8255 in fig. 5-24.

The *displays* and *hexadecimal keyboard* can be seen in the lower right-hand side of fig. 5-24. There will be more about these in the chapter "Simple Programming".

All circuits covered in this chapter are *digital* circuits. They work on 2 voltage levels only, i.e. *no voltage* (0V) or *voltage* (for instance 5V). The presence or the absence of voltage is represented by 1 and 0, respectively. The circuits will be treated in a logical sequence.

AND GATE

The schematic symbol for an AND gate in fig. 5-1a conforms with the American MIL specification, that in fig. 5-1b conforms with the European standard. These symbols show an AND gate with 3 Inputs—A, B and C. The Output is indicated by the letter F.

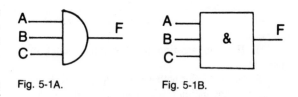

Fig. 5-1A.   Fig. 5-1B.

The voltages applied to A, B, and C are referenced to ground. If we work with 2 voltage levels, 0 and 5V, then A, B and C will be connected to one or the other of these levels. Using these voltages on A, B and C we obtain 8 combinations as shown in the table.

If we let 0 and 1 represent 0 and 5V, we can make a table such as the one below. Such a table is called a *truth table*. The Output voltage depends on the voltages present at the inputs. The following is true for an AND gate:

The output of an AND gate is 1 only if all the inputs are 1.

Table 5-1.

UA (V)	UB (V)	UC (V)
0	0	0
0	0	5
0	5	0
0	5	5
5	0	0
5	0	5
5	5	0
5	5	5

Thus F can only equal 1 if A=1, B=1, and C=1. If one or more of the inputs are 0, the output is 0. The fact that F is only 1 if A AND B AND C are 1 is written as:

$$F = A \cdot B \cdot C \cdot$$

AND is written as a dot. This notation is taken from *Boolean algebra*. Boolean algebra is the arithmetic of system using logical circuitry. In Table 5-2 all possible combinations of zeros and ones are now applied to the inputs of the AND gate. A 0 means that 0V is applied to the input concerned. A 1 means that 5V is applied to the input concerned.

Table 5-2.

A	B	C	F
0	0	0	0
0	0	1	0
0	1	0	0
0	1	1	0
1	0	0	0
1	0	1	0
1	1	0	0
1	1	1	1

The ALU of the microcomputer (fig. 5-1c) has 8 AND gates, each with 2 inputs. With these gates the microcomputer can process two 8-bit words, A and B, as

an AND function. When the ALU processes the words 10110110 and 01001111 with an AND function, the result is 00000110 since only the second and third bits of both words are 1.

OR GATE

Figure 5-2a shows the MIL specification symbol for an OR gate. Fig. 5-2b shows the current European standard for the same function. This is an OR gate with three inputs.

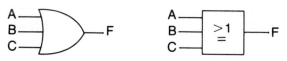

Fig. 5-2A.   Fig. 5-2B.

The output of an OR gate is 1 if one or more inputs are 1. Thus F=1 if A=1 and/or B=1 and/or C=1. This is written as follows:

$$F = A + B + C$$

The plus sign (+) indicates and/or. This indication again originates from Boolean algebra and does *not* have the same meaning as in normal algebra.

Table 5-3.

A	B	C	F
0	0	0	0
0	0	1	1
0	1	0	1
0	1	1	1
1	0	0	1
1	0	1	1
1	1	0	1
1	1	1	1

In the ALU of a microcomputer there are 8 OR gates, each with 2 inputs, which can process 2 words of 8 bits using the OR function (fig. 5-2c). If a computer, for example, processes the words 10010110 and 11100001

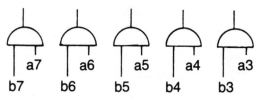
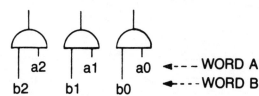

a7 a6 a5 a4 a3   a2 a1 a0 ◄--- WORD A

b7 b6 b5 b4 b3   b2 b1 b0 ◄--- WORD B

Fig. 5-1C.

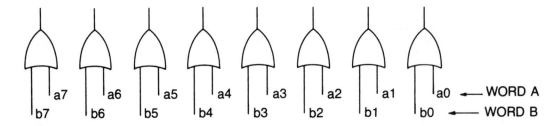

Fig. 5-2C.

using the OR function, the result is 11110111. Only the fourth bit is 0, because in both words the fourth bit is 0.

INVERTER

The inverter has one input and, like all gate circuits, one output. The output of an inverter is the opposite of the input. We can thus say that the output of an inverter is not equal to the input. If the input is 0, the output is 1. If the input is 1, the output is 0.

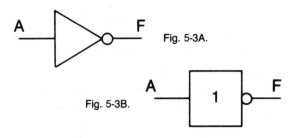

Fig. 5-3A.

Fig. 5-3B.

Figure 5-3a shows an inverter following MIL specification. The circle indicates the NOT function. The European standard schematic symbol for an inverter is shown in fig. 5-3b. Because with an inverter the output is

the opposite of the input, the inverter is also called a *NOT GATE*, or I gate (from *Invert*), and sometimes a *negator*. F is the opposite of A and is written as:

$$F=\overline{A}$$

The line above the A is read as 'not'. $F=\overline{A}$ is read 'F is not A'.

In fig. 5-4 the gates which we have discussed so far are combined to form a gate circuit. Gate 1 is an AND gate, its output is 0. Because 3 is an inverter, B is 1. 2 is an OR gate, its output is 1. Because 4 is an inverter, D becomes 0, and because the input to gate 5 from B is 1, the output from this OR gate (E) is 1.

The microcomputer makes considerable use of inverters (see fig. 5-24). In the ALU, for example, all bits of a word may be inverted to obtain the complement.

NAND GATE

In the truth table next to fig. 5-5, D can only have the value 1 if all the inputs are 1. So only the last square of column D has a 1. As a result of inversion, F is the opposite of D. Thus only the last square of column F is 0, and F is only 0 if all inputs are 1.

If we combine the AND gate and the NOT gate we get the NAND gate. NAND gates are often used because

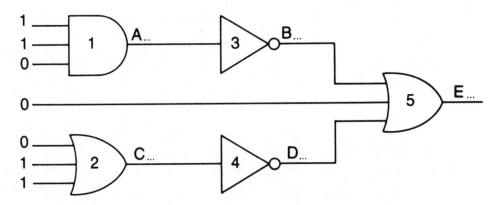

Fig. 5-4.

Table 5-4.

A	B	C	D	F
0	0	0	0	1
0	0	1	0	1
0	1	0	0	1
0	1	1	0	1
1	0	0	0	1
1	0	1	0	1
1	1	0	0	1
1	1	1	1	0

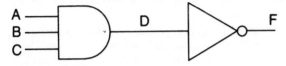

Fig. 5-5.

all possible logical circuits can be made by combining only NAND gates. Only one type of circuit is really needed. Remember, a NAND gate produces a 0 only if all the inputs are 1.

The symbol for a NAND gate is that of an AND gate with a small circle placed at the output (fig. 5-6). In Boolean algebra, the NAND function is written as follows:

$$F=\overline{A \cdot B \cdot C}$$

$$\boxed{F = \overline{A.B.C}} \quad (4)$$

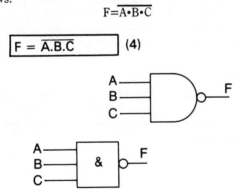

Fig. 5-6.

A, B and C are thus first combined in an AND function and the result is inverted.

As opposed to AND, OR and NOT gates, there are no NAND gates in the ALU. Even so, the microcomputer can process two words using the NAND function. The words are first processed using the AND function and then all bits in the result are inverted. In fig.

5-24 it can be seen that various NAND gates are used separately.

NOR GATE

In the truth table next to fig. 5-7 we see a 0 only in the first square in column D. Because of the inversion function of a NOT gate, a 1 appears in the first block of column F only.

Table 5-5.

A	B	C	D	F
0	0	0	0	1
0	0	1	1	0
0	1	0	1	0
0	1	1	1	0
1	0	0	1	0
1	0	1	1	0
1	1	0	1	0
1	1	1	1	0

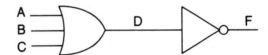

Fig. 5-7.

If we combine an OR gate and a NOT gate in one symbol, we get a *NOR gate*. NOR is a combination of 'not' and 'or'. Be careful! In the circuitry the 'not' comes *after* the 'or'.

In a NOR gate the output is 1 only if all inputs are 0. In Boolean algebra the NOR function is written as follows:

$$F=\overline{A+B+C}$$

A, B and C are first combined in the OR function and the result is inverted. The symbol of a NOR gate is that of an OR gate, with a small circle placed at the output (fig. 5-8).

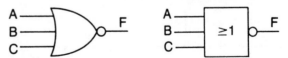

Fig. 5-8.

Just as with NAND gates, one can form all possible logical circuits using only NOR gates. Again, there are no NOR gates in the ALU. To process two words in the microprocessor with a NOR function, they must first be processed with the OR function and then all bits in the result must be inverted.

EXCLUSIVE OR GATE

In an EXCLUSIVE OR, often also called *EXOR*, the output is 1 if only *one* of the inputs is 1. With the EXOR function, 2 words of 8 bits can be processed in the ALU. For this purpose the ALU has 8 EXOR gates, each with 2 inputs. If, for instance, the words 01001111 and 10001111 are processed following the EXOR function, the result is 11000000.

A	B	F
0	0	0
0	1	1
1	0	1
1	1	0

Table 5-6

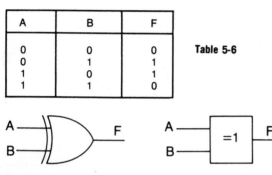

Fig. 5-9.

THE FLIP-FLOP

A flip-flop is a digital circuit with 2 outputs. The signals at the outputs are opposite. If one output is 1, the other is 0 and vice versa. This is expressed by indicating the outputs as Q and $\overline{Q}$. $\overline{Q}$ is the opposite of Q. ($\overline{Q}$ is expressed verbally as 'not Q').

A flip-flop also has inputs. There is always at least one *set input*, indicated by S, and a *reset* input, indicated by R. A pulse at the set input brings the flip-flop to the state Q = 1. This is known as setting the flip-flop. The input where a signal must be applied to yield the value Q = 1 is therefore called the set input. Depending upon the internal construction, either 1 or 0 at the set input will set the flip-flop.

The reset input is used to bring the flip-flop to the state Q = 0. This is called resetting the flip-flop. The set input is sometimes called the *preset input*. The reset input is sometimes called the *clear input*.

The symbol for a basic flip-flop is shown in fig. 5-10a. As the circle already indicates the NOT function, the notations Q and $\overline{Q}$ could be omitted. Instead of Q and $\overline{Q}$, the symbols Q_1 and Q_2 are often used. The most important application of the flip-flop is as a *memory element* (also called *latch*). Each memory cell in a static semiconductor memory is a flip-flop. An 8 bit memory word thus comprises 8 flip-flops.

Another application is as a *divide-by-two circuit*. The two most important types of flip-flops used in microcomputers are:

● The D flip-flop (only as a memory element).
● The J-K master-slave flip-flop (can be used as a memory element or as a divide-by-two circuit).

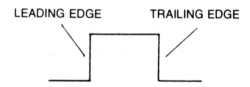

Fig. 5-10B.

Both flip-flops have a clock input, the clock pulses being delivered by a clock generator. When the information is transferred to the output depends on the type of flip-flop. The D flip-flop reacts to the leading edge of the clock pulse and the J-K master-slave to the trailing edge (fig. 5-10b).

D Flip-Flop

The symbol for a D flip-flop is given in fig. 5-11. A D flip-flop *always* has two inputs, C(lock) and D(ata); and two outputs, Q and $\overline{Q}$. Usually S(et) and R(eset) inputs are also available.

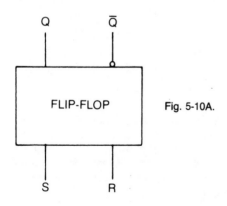

Fig. 5-10A.

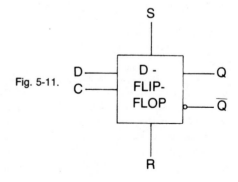

Fig. 5-11.

Fig. 5-12 shows the operation of a D flip-flop. The signal present at the D input is transferred to the Q output when the clock signal (C) goes from 0 to 1. The signal at Q is retained even if D changes later, which is how the flip-flop functions a memory. At $t = t_2$, when the clock pulse again goes positive, the data present at D is transferred to Q and stored.

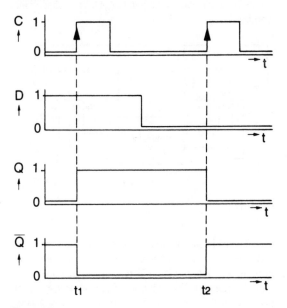

Fig. 5-12.

Note

The flip-flop mentioned in this chapter is the edge-triggered flip-flop. There are other types of flip-flops. The clocked flip-flop gives the input information to the output during the entire length of the clock pulse. After the clock pulse, this flip-flop continues to retain the last information present at the input. The D master-slave flip-flop copies the information that was present during the trailing edge of the clock pulse to the output.

J-K Master-Slave Flip-Flop

Figure 5-13 shows the symbol for a J-K master-slave flip-flop. There could be any number of J and K inputs, tied to logic gates. J and K inputs are the inputs for the steering signals. The set and reset inputs are used only for setting or resetting. In the quiescent condition S = R = 1 and the flip-flop is free to operate. If R becomes 0, then Q = 0; $\overline{Q}$ = 1. If S becomes 0, then Q = 1 and $\overline{Q}$ = 0. If S = 0 and R = 0, the flip-flop oscillates between the two states.

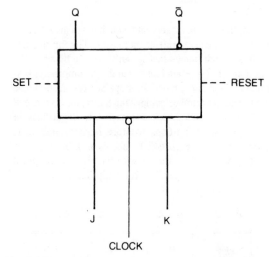

Fig. 5-13.

The functions J and K are executed within the flip-flop. The time just before the clock pulse goes positive is called t_n. The time just after the clock pulse returns to zero is called t_{n+1} (fig. 5-14). A number of very important conclusions can be drawn from this table:

●If J = 0 and K = 0, the output combination is the same after the clock pulse as it was before (first line).

●J = 0; K = 1 is transferred at the trailing edge of the clock pulse to the outputs as Q = 0; $\overline{Q}$ = 1 (second line).

●J = 1; K = 0 is transferred at the trailing edge of the clock pulse to the Outputs as Q = 1; $\overline{Q}$ = 0 (third line).

●The J-K master-slave flip-flop behaves as a *memory circuit* for the combinations J = 0; K = 1 and J = 1; K = 0.

●If J = 1 and K = 1, the outputs are switched after the clock pulse (fourth line). This means that $Q_{n+1} = \overline{Q}_n$. In other words, at t_{n+1}, Q is the opposite of what it was at t_n, that is to say Q has been switched.

●From (e), the J-K master-slave flip-flop can function as a *divide-by-two* circuit, provided all J and K inputs are at 1. You will find an example of the application of the J-K master-slave flip-flop in the chapter "Automatic Traffic-Light Control".

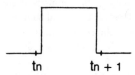

Fig. 5-14.

Registers

In the previous sections you have learned about flip-flops that can operate as memories. The flip-flop has 2 states, which means that it can store the binary numbers 0 and 1. To retain binary numbers comprising several zeros and ones, more flip-flops are required. To be able to retain a number comprising 8 bits, for instance, 8 flip-flops are needed, one for each bit. Regardless of length, a row of flip-flops to store binary numbers is called a *register*. Figure 5-15 shows a 4 bit register. Flip-flop 4 is used for the bit with the highest weight. If we want to store the number 1000, flip-flop 4 retains the 1.

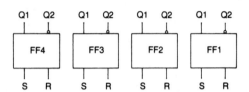

Fig. 5-15.

A 4 bit register can hold words of up to 4 bits. The numbers 0 to 15 can be represented by 4 bits. By examining the condition of the flip-flops in a register, one can see which binary number is stored. Only the Q_1 outpus are used.

As we can see from fig. 5-16, Q_1 in flip-flop 4 is 0; in flip-flop 3, $Q = 0$; in flip-flop 2, $Q = 1$, and in flip-flop 1, $Q = 0$. The register thus contains the binary number 0010. The zeros to the left of the 1 can be neglected, so the number stored in the register is 2.

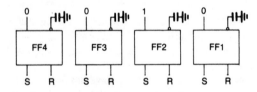

Fig. 5-16.

Entering data into a register is called reading-in. When reading-in the flip-flops are set to 0 or 1. We can do this by feeding a pulse to the flip-flops at the set input or the reset input. To store a decimal number, for example 12, the Q_1 inputs of the register must be brought to the state 1100, by resetting flip-flops 1 and 2 and setting flip-flops 3 and 4.

A microprocessor is largely made up of registers, such as the accumulator, general-purpose, and instruc-

tion registers. In an 8 bit microcomputer, these registers are made of 8 flip-flops, so that 8 bit words can be stored.

COMPARATOR

With microcomputers, one often needs to *compare* the contents of 2 registers or the contents of a register and a counter (fig. 5-17). An example is in process control, where one counts the number of bottles that go into one box.

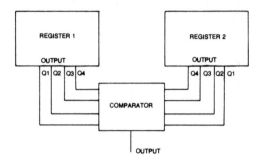

Fig. 5-17.

The requisite number is entered into the register, and a counter is used to count the number of bottles put into the box. When the box is full, the filling mechanism must be stopped. The contents of the counter are compared with the contents of the register using a comparator When they are equal, we must have a signal to stop the filling machine. Such a comparator is situated in the ALU.

The instruction in the instruction set that implements the operation 'compare' is the CMP instruction (acronym for compare). The contents of the 2 registers are *equal* if the *corresponding flip-flops* in both registers are in the same state. To compare the contents of both registers, the output signals of all corresponding flip-flops must be compared. If the outputs of register 1 are the same as those of register 2, the output of the comparator is 1. If the outputs differ, the output is 0.

SHIFT REGISTERS

In digital technology *shift registers* are second in importance only to counters. We can see from the name that a shift register is a register in which the data can shift. It has been explained that a register is formed by a series of flip-flops. Each flip-flop can store 1 bit. The same is true for shift registers. However, a shift register can shift the contents of the flip-flops to the left or to the right on the command of a clock pulse. The clock inputs are not included in the following figures. Shift registers are used, among other things, for multiplication or division in computers.

Input

There are two ways of entering data into a shift register: by *serial input* or by *parallel input*. In fig. 5-18 data is fed in serially. The initial state of all the flip-flops is 0. We first enter a 1 at the input of the 1st flip-flop. When a clock pulse is applied, the 1 is transferred to the output of flip-flop 1, the 0 on flip-flip 1 is shifted to flip-flop 2, and the 0 on flip-flop 2 to flip-flop 3.

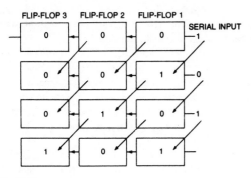

Fig. 5-18.

A 0 is then entered at the input. With the following clock pulse this is transferred to the output of flip-flop 1. The 1 in flip-flop 1 then shifts to flip-flop 2, and so forth. Another 1 is now entered. Again this is transferred to the output of flip-flop 1 and the other data shifts one place to the left. We have, as it were, read in the shift register by entering bits serially to the input and applying three clock pulses. Data is thus entered on one line.

The flip-flops shown in fig. 5-19 are fed with information simultaneously. When feeding in parallel, the word length (total number of bits) of the data is equal to the number of parallel inputs.

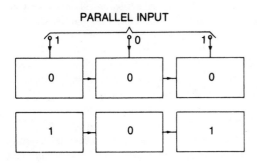

Fig. 5-19.

Output

How data stored in a shift register is read out is shown in fig. 5-20, where data is read out serially. With each clock pulse the data shifts one place to the left and flip-flop 3 releases it. The bits stored in the shift register are thus pushed—one after the other or in series—out of the register. Data can also be read out in parallel (fig. 5-21).

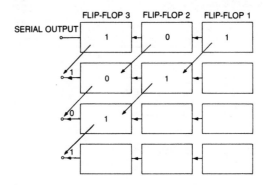

Fig. 5-20.

A clock pulse shifts the information in the flip-flops to the outputs of each flip-flop. This is the case, for example, with the instruction register of the microprocessor. When an instruction is fetched from memory, it is placed in the instruction register and then 'clocked through' to the instruction decoder, which decodes it and determines what must be done.

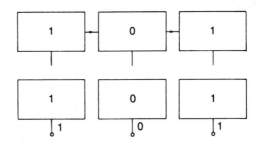

Fig. 5-21.

Multiplication and Division

Using a shift register it is quite easy to divide or to multiply in binary. If we want to multiply $A = 10100_2$ by $B = 10_2$, the answer is $C = 101000_2$.

$$\begin{array}{rl} 10100 & A \\ 10 & \times \ B \\ \hline 101000 & C \end{array}$$

If we write A as 0010100, it is easy to see that we obtain C by shifting all the bits 1 place to the left. Multiplying 10100 by $1000_2 = 8_{10}$, is performed by shifting 3 places to the left. To divide we must shift to the right, dividing being the opposite of multiplying. However, it is clear that by shifting from left to right or from right to left, we can only divide or multiply by powers of 2. Since all binary numbers are combinations of powers of 2, this is no problem.

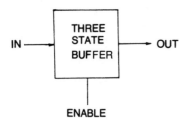

Fig. 5-22.

If we want to multiply a binary number by 5, we first shift the number 2 places to the left (= multiplying by 4). Then we add the number to be multiplied once to the result. $5 \times A$ is, of course, $(4 \times A) + A$. This method is used to multiply as well as to divide in the accumulator of the microcomputer. The contents of the accumulator can be shifted to the left or to the right by means of special instructions.

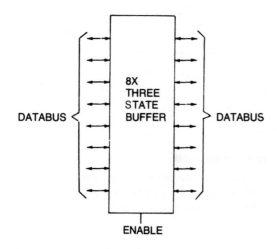

Fig. 5-23.

54

SPECIAL CIRCUITRY

Driver

A driver is a circuit which works as a current amplifier. Drivers are used to control numerical indicator tubes or 7-segment indicators. Drivers also serve to connect the logic circuits of one system to the circuitry of another which works at higher voltage levels. Drivers are also often applied in digital data transmission via cables. Two drivers used to control 7-segment indicators are shown in fig. 5-24. They are of type 238.

Three State Buffer

A three state buffer is a circuit which isolates certain parts of a microcomputer from each other. A three state buffer acts like a switch.

When the control or *enable* is made 0, the switch is blocked and the output produces a very high resistance (high impedance or floating). If the enable signal is 1, the switch is closed and the state of the input is the same as that of the output, that is, either a 1 or a 0. Thus the output of a three state buffer can be in 1 of 3 conditions; 0, 1, or high impedance.

In most cases the output of the three state buffer has an extra high *fan-out* (the fan-out is a figure indicating how many new inputs can be connected to one output). We can say, therefore, that the buffer also acts as a current amplifier. In such a case we refer to a *buffer-driver*.

A buffer circuit made up of 8 three state buffers in 1 IC is shown in fig. 5-23. In fig. 5-23 the buffer circuit is connected to the data bus and thus works in two directions (bi-directional). The data bus shown in fig. 5-24 is also buffered by a buffer-driver IC type 8228. This IC contains other functions as well, which we will not go into in this chapter.

In fig. 5-24 the enable signal for the buffer is indicated by BUSEN (BUS ENable), pin 22. The IC type 8212 shown in fig. 5-24 is a buffer as well. This one does not work bi-directionally, but serves as isolation between the data bus and the 7-segment displays. The enable signal is here indicated by STB (STroBe), pin 11.

When there are several memory ICs (RAMs or ROMs) in a microcomputer, the address bus is usually provided with one or more three state buffer-drivers. (This is not the case in fig. 5-24).

HARDWARE TK80

Figure 2-1 in Chapter 2 shows a diagram of a single-board microcomputer. Figure 5-24 is the same singleboard computer with the 8080A as CPU. Both figures are used merely as *examples* during this course. Several parts of fig. 5-24 will be discussed in the following sections.

We would like to emphasize that the microcomputer pictured here is only one of the many microcomputers in existence. The details discussed here are valid only for this microcomputer so, this section will not be included in the examination.

Reset

If a logic 1 is entered at the RESET input of the 8080 (CPU), the contents of the program counter become 0000_{16}. When the supply voltage of the CPU is turned on all registers, including the program counter, assume an arbitrary state. It is desirable, however, that the program counter assume a fixed state when the supply voltage is turned on, so that the first instruction to be executed is addressed.

If we choose the address 0000_{16}, a RESET pulse must be given to the 8080 after switching on. This is done automatically in most microcomputers by means of added hardware. Figure 5-25 shows that part of fig. 5-24 which deals with the automatic RESET.

Note

The diode in parallel with the resistor is to quickly discharge the capacitor should the supply voltage fail. In the event of a very short interruption to the supply voltage, the 8080 automatically receives a RESET pulse.

Supply Voltages

The 8080A requires 3 different supply voltages; e.g. +12V, +5V and −5V. In fig. 5-24 these are called V_{DD}, V_{CC}, and V_{BB}, respectively. The voltages V_{DD} and V_{CC} must be supplied from external, regulated power supplies. Only the CPU requires the supply voltage V_{BB} (−5V). The necessary current I_{BB} has a maximum of 1 mA, and is derived from the clock oscillator 8224. Figure 5-26 is a detail from fig. 5-24 showing the components used to obtain V_{BB}.

A signal with a frequency of approximately 18 MHz is present at the output OSC of the 8224. This signal is rectified and smoothed by the diode D_2 and the capacitor C_1.

Note

The capacitor C_2, the diode D_1 and the 1 KΩ resistor decouple the dc voltage level V_{BB} from the OSC output.

7-Segment Display

The eight 7-segment displays in fig. 5-24 display the following in hexadecimal display code:

- addresses
- the contents of memory words
- the contents of (general-purpose) registers.

A 7-segment display is represented in fig. 5-27. The segments and the decimal point are LEDs. The anodes of these LEDs are connected together. This is called a common anode circuit. The common point is connected to a positive supply voltage. If one of the cathodes is now connected to ground, the corresponding LED segment will light up. If the combination 00000111 is connected to the pins from a to dp, the decimal digit 3 becomes visible on the 7-segment display.

Because the LEDs need 10 to 40 mA in order to light up, drivers are required. Both drivers shown in fig. 5-24 are of the type 238 (SN 7438). Each chip contains 4 NAND gates with open-collector output. Each output can sink a maximum load of 48 mA, and the 51 ohm resistors are used to limit the current through the LEDs to about 40 mA.

Both inputs of the NAND gates are connected together, so that the NAND gates function as inverters. In order to display the decimal digit 3, the combination 11111000 must be applied to the buffer input lines. Table 5-7 gives the combinations needed to display the hexadecimal symbols 0 to F using the circuit shown in fig. 5-27a.

Note

If the cathodes of the LEDs are connected together, it is known as a common-cathode display. With these, another type of driver must be used.

Multiplexed Displays

To represent the digit 8 on a 7-segment display, a current of 7×40 mA = 280 mA is required. In the microcomputer discussed here, 8 of these displays are present. If each display is connected simultaneously, the maximum current required is 8×280 mA = 2.24 A.

Because a computer is so fast the segments need not be continually driven. The displays can be *multiplexed*, i.e. can be driven sequentially. Because of the speed, they appear to glow continually. The principle behind this is shown in fig. 5-28.

The oscillator 555 generates a square wave with a time period of between 1 and 2 ms. The counter 223 (SN 7493) consists of 4 J-K master-slave flip-flops, 3 of which are used to form a binary 8 counter. The outputs V_3, V_2

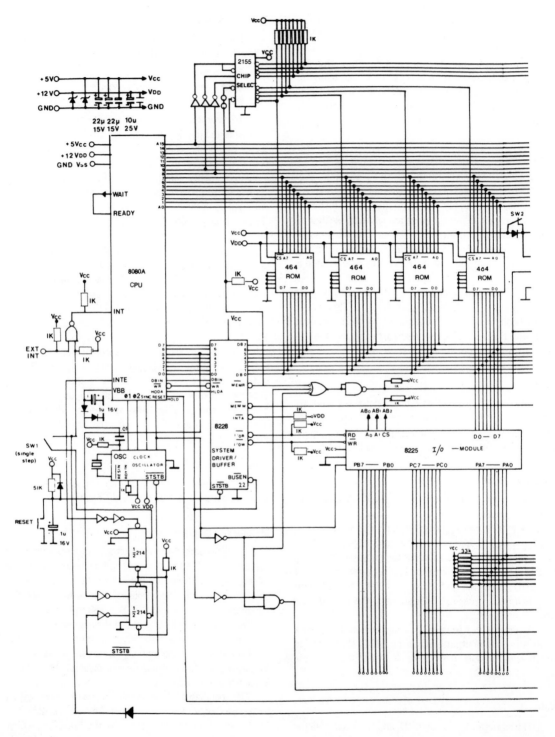

Fig. 5-24.

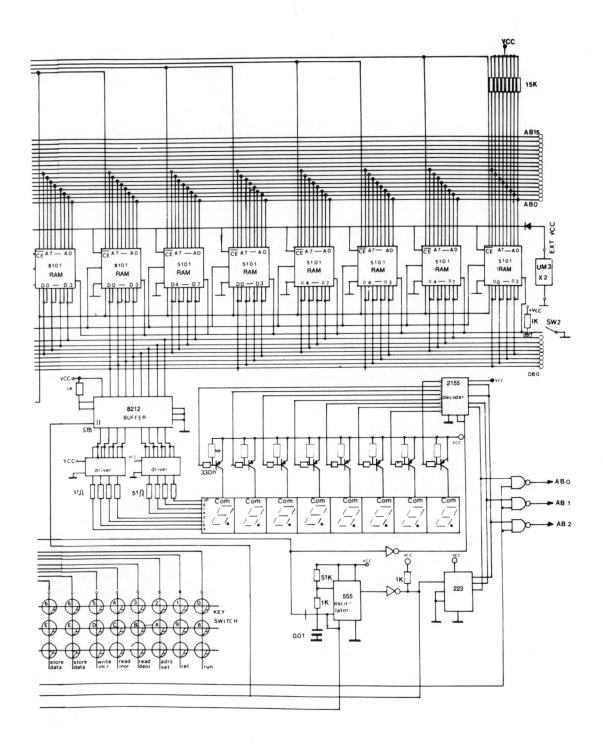

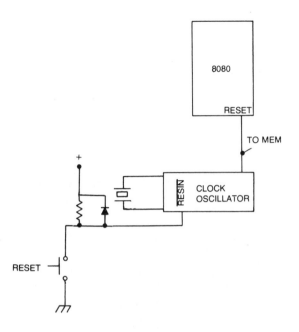

Fig. 5-25.

Table 5-7.

Hex	Display	Code (a-dp)
0		00100001
1		10101111
2		00010011
3		00000111
4		10001101
5		01000101
6		01000001
7		00101111
8		00000001
9		00001101
A		00001001
B(b)		11000001
C		01110001
D(d)		10000011
E		01010001
F		01011001

and V_1 count continually from 000_2 to 111_2. The decoder 2155 (SN 74155) converts this 3-bit information into 8 bits, Y_0 to Y_7. These 8 bits are used to sequentially turn on the transistors that operate as electronic switches so that only one common at a time is connected to the supply voltage.

Of course it is necessary to feed the data relating to a given display to the drivers. This is done via the data bus and buffer 8212 at the time that a display is switched on. Now it is possible to reproduce 8 symbols on the displays, apparently simultaneously. These symbols must be presented to the buffer 8212 in the code given in Table 5-7. The 8 codes which must be placed sequentially on the data bus are stored in the RAM memory at the addresses $83F9_{16}$ to $83FF_{16}$. The signals V_3, V_2 and V_1 indicate, in binary form, which display is selected. AB_2, AB_1 and AB_0, derived from these signals, form the last 3 bits of addresses 83F9 to 83FF. These indicate where the data for the selected display can be found.

Note

The remaining 13 bits of these addresses 83F8 to 83FF are placed on the address bus by the CPU.

SUMMARY

1. The output of an AND gate is one only if all inputs are 1.

2. The output of an OR gate is 1 only if one or more inputs are 1.

3. The output of a NOT gate is the opposite of the input.

4. The opposite of A, B and F is represented as $\overline{A}$, $\overline{B}$ and $\overline{F}$.

5. The NAND gate produces 0 only if all inputs are 1.

6. The NOR gate yields a 1 only if all inputs are 0.

7. The EXclusive OR yields a 1 at the output only if one of the inputs is 1.

8. In a D flip-flop the information at the D input shifts to the Q output when the clock signal goes from 0 to 1.

9. The J-K master-slave flip-flop can function both as memory and as divide-by-two circuit.

10. The J-K master-slave flip-flop operates as a divide-by-two circuit on the clock pulses if J = 1 and K = 1.

11. A J-K master-slave flip-flop is reset by making R = 0 and set by making S = 0.

12. Registers can be constructed with flip-flops acting as memories. A register is a circuit which can store a number.

13. In a register for storing binary numbers, one flip-flop per bit is required.

14. The contents of two registers can be compared by a comparator.

58

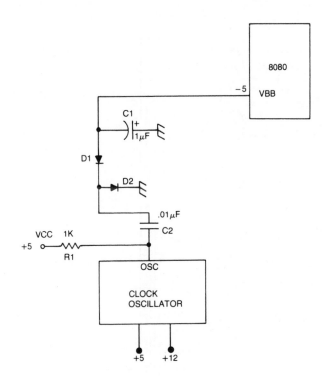

Fig. 5-26.

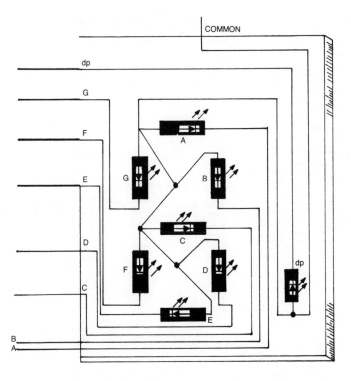

Fig. 5-27.

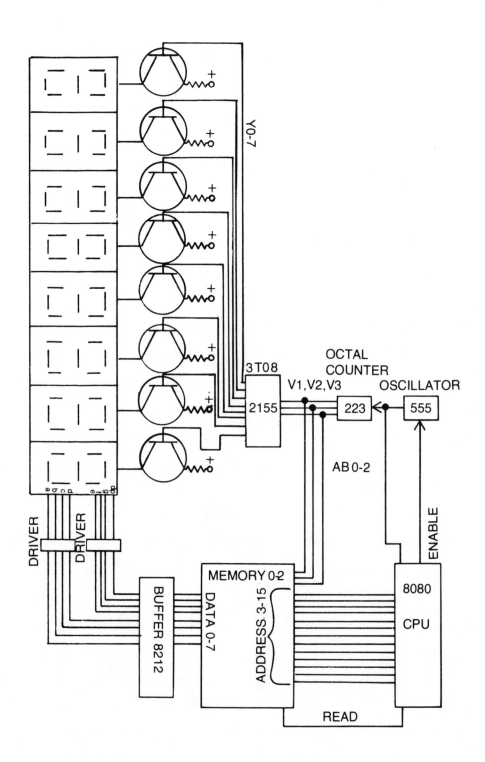

Fig. 5-28.

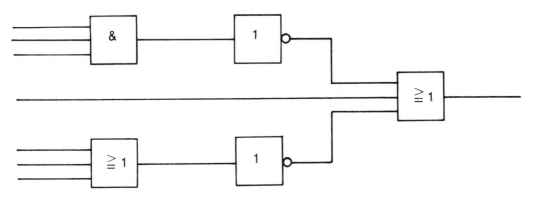

Fig. 5-29.

15. The data stored in shift registers can be shifted from left to right and vice versa at the command of the shift pulse, fed in to the clock input.

16. Data can be read into a shift register in series or in parallel.

17. The data stored in a shift register can be read out in series or in parallel.

18. Shift registers can be used as division or multiplication circuits.

REVIEW EXERCISES

1. Draw an AND gate with three inputs and indicate when a 1 appears at the output.

2. Draw an OR gate with three inputs and indicate when a 1 appears at the output.

3. Draw a NOT gate. What can be said about the output signal?

4. Draw a NAND gate. What can be said about the output signal?

5. Draw a NOR gate. What can be said about the output signal?

6. Draw an EXclusive OR. What can be said about the output signal?

7. Review the gates that have been dealt with up to this point on a separate piece of paper. Give old symbol, new symbol, truth table, and Boolean formula.

8. Draw fig. 5-4 according to the European norm.

9. When does the flip-flop shown in fig. 5-11 take over the condition of the D input?

10. Draw the diagram for a J-K master-slave flip-flop and show the corresponding truth table.

11. When does a J-K master-slave flip-flop act as a divide-by-two counter for the clock pulses?

12. How many flip-flops are needed to store an 8-bit word?

13. Give two examples of how a register can be used.

14. What is the function of a shift register?

15. Give some examples of the use of a shift register.

ANSWERS

1. See fig. 5-1 and the truth table.

2. See fig. 5-2 and the truth table.

3. See fig. 5-3. The output is the opposite of the input.

4. See fig. 5-6. A NAND gate only produces a 0 if all inputs are 1.

5. See fig. 5-8. A NOR gate produces a 1 only if all inputs are 0.

6. See fig. 5-9. A NOR gate produces a 1 at the output only if one of the inputs is 1.

7. See figures 5-1 through 5-9 and tables.

8. Figure 5-29.

9. During the leading edge of the clock pulse.

10. See fig. 5-13.

11. When J = 1 and K = 1.

12. 8 flip-flops.

13. Accumulator and general-purpose registers.

14. In a shift register the contents of the flip-flops can be shifted to left or right at the command of a shift pulse.

15. For multiplication or division in a computer.

Chapter 6

Main Memory

We have seen that the series of operations that the computer must execute, i.e. the program, are stored in a part of the main memory called the program memory. The data used in these operations is stored in the data memory.

The program and data memory are *not always* physically separate. In other words, data are not always stored in one part of memory and instructions in another. If a memory location contains an instruction, that location is part of the program memory, and if a memory-location contains data, that location is part of data memory, irrespective of its physical position in the computer. The instructions (the operations to be carried out) and the data are taken out of memory and offered, one by one, to the CPU during the execution of the program. Each memory location has its own address. One memory word of (in this case) 8 bits is found in each *address* in memory.

An address in memory refers not to the location of a *bit*, but of a *word*. As far as a computer is concerned, the *contents of a memory word* is only a series of ones and zeros—nothing more, nothing less. The contents of a memory word can be interpreted by the programmer in a variety of ways (fig. 6-1), i.e.:

1. Data, used to carry out an operation. If a memory word of 8 bits represents a piece of data, this can be:
    a. an 8-bit *number*
    b. a *portion of a number* longer than 8 bits
    c. a *character*, i.e. a digit, letter or symbol, in a code such as ASCII.

2. Instruction code, used to execute an operation or, in a multiple-byte instruction, a portion of an instruction code.

We will explain these points further in this chapter, and then discuss an example of a program which will once again show very clearly the interplay between the memory and the CPU.

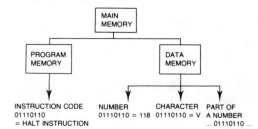

Fig. 6-1.

THE ORGANIZATION OF MEMORY

Every computer memory consists of a number of bi-stable elements. 1 bit (0 or 1) can be stored in each element. The various *types* of memory (RAM, ROM, etc.) will not be discussed again here, but if you'd like to review this information, refer to the chapter 'The Microcomputer in General'. We would, however, like to go over the difference between a volatile and a non-volatile memory once again (fig. 6-2a).

In a volatile memory, the information stored is lost when the power supply is turned off. This happens with

62

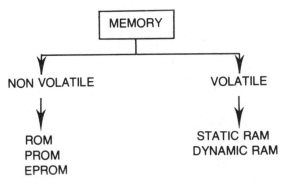

Fig. 6-2A.

Fig. 6-2C.

static as well as dynamic RAMs (with dynamic RAMs, the information must be continually refreshed even if the power supply is on).

In a non-volatile memory, the information is retained if the power supply is cut off. Examples of non-volatile memories are ROM, PROM, and EPROM.

An example of the so-called *Eurocard* is given in the photo below.

Fig. 6-2B.

A Eurocard is a printed circuit board with European standard dimensions, such as 10 × 16 cm. The windows, through which the memory is erased with ultraviolet light, are visible in the EPROMs. Using the EPROM programming device shown below, 2 EPROMs can be programmed at a time. To do this, the EPROMs are extracted from the Eurocard and put into the sockets.

WORD LENGTH

The *number* of different instructions a computer can carry out is in part determined by the *number* of bits which these instructions represent. Most microcom-

puters have 8 bits available to represent a maximum of 2^8, or 256 different instructions. This is usually enough.

In such a case the memory is so organized that *one* memory location comprises 8 bits, and we speak of a computer with a word length of 8 bits, or an *8-bit computer*. A unit of 8 bits is also known as a *byte*. In an 8-bit computer the word length is thus equal to 1 byte.

Some microcomputers work with a word length of 4 or 16 bits. These are, however, less common than 8-bit microcomputers. The word length of a 4-bit microcomputer is, a half-byte, also called a 'nybble'. A 16-bit microcomputer has a word length of 2 bytes.

Memory capacity, i.e. the maximum number of memory words that can be stored, is often expressed in 'kilobytes', abbreviated to K. If a memory has a capacity of 1K, it can store 1024 8-bit words. In computer technology the prefix *kilo* is not 1000 as in the metric system, but rather the power of 2 closest to 1000, which is $1024 = 2^{10}$.) In addition the number of bits contained in the memory word is sometimes given, and memory capacity is indicated, for example, as 1K × 4 or 1K × 8. This means 1024 4-bit words and 1024 8-bit words, respectively.

The microcomputer shown in fig. 2-1 of the chapter 'What is a Microcomputer' has a memory capacity of ¾K for the ROM and ½K for the RAM. The capacity can be raised to 1K for the ROM as well as for the RAM.

THE MEMORY MODULE

Apart from the length of the memory word, an important characteristic of a microcomputer is the number of bit places it has available for addressing these memory words. If it has, for example, 8 bit places available, i.e. 1 byte, it can then address $2^8 = 256$ different memory word addresses. In most cases this is not sufficient. Therefore, most 8-bit microcomputers have 2 bytes = 16 bits available so that $2^{16} = 65536$ memory words can be addressed. The lowest address would then be $0000000000000000_2 =$

63

0000_{16}. The highest address is $1111111111111111_2 = FFFF_{16}$. These addresses are represented in hexadecimal in fig. 6-3.

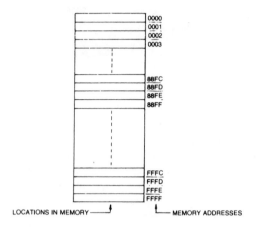

Fig. 6-3.

Often the bits in *one* memory word are divided among various chips (ICs). The chips, which *combined* form a memory word are called a *memory module*. Some memory modules that can store memory words with a length of 1 byte are shown in figs 6-4a—6-4c.

The example in fig. 6-4a is a memory module made up of 8 chips. 1 bit of each memory word is found on each

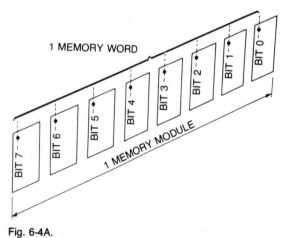

Fig. 6-4A.

chip. Figure 6-4b shows a memory module of 2 chips, each chip storing 4 bits of each memory word. A 1-chip memory word is represented in fig. 6-4c. All the bits of the memory word are contained on the same chip. The number of bits which can be stored on one chip is always a

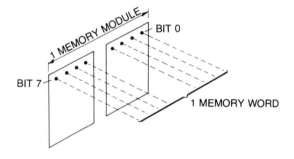

Fig. 6-4B.

power of 2. Values often seen are 1024, 4096 or 16384.

Modern semiconductor memories are usually organized according to fig. 6-4a, each chip containing one bit of each memory word. The number of memory *words* which can be stored on one memory *module*, following fig. 6-4a, is the same as the number of *bits* which can be stored on one *chip*.

In fig. 5-24 in the chapter "Circuitry in a Computer" we see that in ROMs all 8-bits of a word are stored on 1 chip. This becomes obvious when we realize that each chip has 8 connections to the data bus. (The type number of the ROMs is 464). However, with RAMs, only 4 bits of each word are stored on each chip; each chip has only 4 connections to the data bus. In this type of microcomputer each RAM module always consists of 2 chips. (The type number of the RAMs is 5101.)

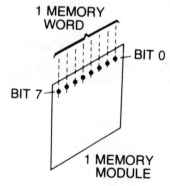

Fig. 6-4C.

ADDRESSING

The number of bits that make up a memory address depends on the memory capacity of the computer. If the capacity is 16K a memory address of 14 bits must be presented ($2^{14} = 16,384$).

64

If the main memory of a microcomputer contains more than one memory module, a part of the memory address must indicate in which memory module a given memory word can be found. This part is called *module select* or *chip select*. Module select is the better term, because we are selecting a module and not a chip. The part of the memory address which addresses a given memory word within the module is called the *word address*. An example of such a memory address is given in fig. 6-5.

The decoding of the word address takes place on the memory chips themselves. To decode a chip select, a separate IC is used. This can be seen in fig. 5-24 in the chapter "Circuitry in a Computer" as part of 2155 at the top of the diagram. *Which of the address bits are used for module select and which are used for word address depends upon the construction of main memory.* This is determined by the manufacturers of the microcomputer.

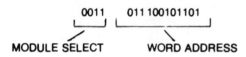

$$\underbrace{0011}_{\text{MODULE SELECT}} \quad \underbrace{011\,100101101}_{\text{WORD ADDRESS}}$$

Fig. 6-5.

Note

One may wonder why we call fig. 6-4c a memory module. Please bear in mind that a microcomputer can contain various memory forms, for example a RAM module (fig. 6-4a) and a ROM module (fig. 6-4c). Once we decide to address according to the module select and word address system, we must do it on every occasion, in which case the ROM in fig. 6-4c receives its own module select.

Example

Given that: the main memory of a microcomputer is made up of 4 memory modules (1 ROM module and 3 RAM modules), the ROM module has a capacity of $1K = 2^{10}$ words, the 3 RAM modules each have a capacity of $4K = 2^{12}$ words, and a memory address is represented by 16 bits in the microcomputer concerned;

Question: How do we address the memory word?

Possible solution: In order to select a memory word within the ROM module, we need 10 bits for the word address ($2^{10} = 1024 = 1K$) so that 6 bits are left for the module select.

If we choose 000000 as module select for this ROM module, the addresses within the ROM module run from $0000000000000000_2 = 0000_{16}$ to $0000001111111111_2 = 03FF_{16}$.

In order to select from a memory word within one of the RAM modules, we need 12 bits for the word address ($2^{12} = 4096 = 4K$). 4 bits are now left for the module select.

If we choose 0001 as module select for the first RAM module, the addresses within this module run from $0001\,000000000000_2 = 1000_{16}$ to $0001\,111111111111_2$. Within the second RAM module, for which we have chosen 0010 as module select, the addresses run from $00101\,000000000000_2 = 2000_{16}$ to $0010\,111111111111_2 = 2FFF_{16}$. Within the third RAM module, for which we have chosen $0011\,111111111111_2 = 3FFF_{16}$.

The addresses of all the memory words are represented schematically in fig. 6-6. Such a diagram is called a *memory map*.

Fig. 6-6.

CONTENTS OF THE MEMORY WORD

The contents of a memory word in an 8-bit microcomputer can be interpreted in various ways:

1. data - this can be:
   a. an 8-bit number
   b. part of a number larger than 8 bits
   c. a character
2. an instruction code.

An 8-Bit Number

When a microcomputer performs a calculation, the contents of the memory word are carried from the CPU to the Arithmetic and Logic Unit (ALU). The pattern of ones and zeros represents, in this case, a binary number.

Table 6-1 shows how a microcomputer distinguishes between positive and negative numbers. Negative numbers are represented as the 2's complement of the corresponding positive number. The binary representation of -125 can thus be found in the following way:

● The binary representation of $+125$ is 01111101_2.
● The 1's complement of this is 10000010_2.
● The 2's complement of 01111101_2 if the 1's complement $+ 1$.
● The binary representation of -125 is:

$$\begin{array}{r} 10000010_2 \\ 1_2 + \\ \hline -125_{10} = 10000011_2 \end{array}$$

Table 6-1.

Binary	Decimal	Hexadecimal
10000000	-128	80
10000001	-127	81
10000010	-126	82
10000011	-125	83
.	.	.
.	.	.
.	.	.
11111110	-2	FE
11111111	-1	FF
00000000	0	0
00000001	1	1
00000010	2	2
00000011	3	3
.	.	.
.	.	.
.	.	.
01111101	$+125$	7D
01111110	$+126$	7E
01111111	$+127$	7F

a) Table 1

b) binary

c) decimal

d) hexadecimal

It is clear from table 6-1 that an 8-bit number, when represented in this manner, lies between -128 and $+127$. The advantage of this kind of notation is that we can immediately see whether a number is positive or negative. In a positive number the MSB is 0. In a negative number the MSB is 1.

Part of a Number

With an 8-bit word we can represent positive numbers between 0 and 255. A computer must often process larger numbers, and thus uses more bits. One number is then constructed from several memory words. Using only two memory words we can produce any number between 0 and 65535_{10}. In principle the number of memory words used is unlimited. Figure 6-7 shows a number comprising 48 bits, made up of 6 memory words of 1 byte each.

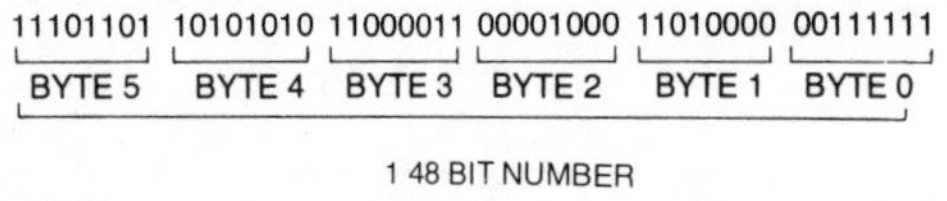

```
11101101  10101010  11000011  00001000  11010000  00111111
└─BYTE 5─┘ └─BYTE 4─┘ └─BYTE 3─┘ └─BYTE 2─┘ └─BYTE 1─┘ └─BYTE 0─┘
```

1 48 BIT NUMBER

Fig. 6-7.

Character

A computer would be of little use if we were only able to feed in the data as a series of zeros and ones or if the result were presented to the world as a similar series of ones and zeros. A computer must also be able to process letters and symbols, that is to say the series of ones and zeros encoded as letters and symbols. Therefore certain parts of the memory will contain binary information which represents numbers, while another part will interpret the memory words as letters or symbols - otherwise known as *characters*. We recognize the following characters:

- 26 capital letters;
- 26 lower-case letters;
- about 25 symbols such as ! ? , . /
- 10 digits (0 to 9).

To avoid the confusion which would arise from a multiplicity of codes, a few international codes have been standardized to translate bits into characters. The codes most frequently used are ASCII (American Standard

Code for Information Interchange) and EBCDIC (Extended Binary Coded Decimal Interchange Code). We have 87 different characters, so that 7 bits are needed for coding.

In an 8-bit microcomputer, which we always use as a starting point, 1 bit per word remains. This bit is used in the transfer of data between the CPU and the peripherals to check errors. This eighth bit is called the *parity bit*. The state of the parity bit (1 or 0) is such that the word, including the parity bit itself, contains either always an *even* or always an *odd* number of ones. This must, of course, be agreed upon beforehand. In this case we speak of even parity or odd parity.

If we wish to have odd parity, the state of the parity bit is such that the number of ones in the word is odd. Several examples of odd parity are:

10000000 - number of ones = 1
00000001 - number of ones = 1
11001011 - number of ones = 5
11011111 - number of ones = 7
01010100 - number of ones = 3

If we've chosen *odd* parity and come across a word which contains an *even* number of ones, we know that an error has been made somewhere.

A number of characters forming the word 'MICRO' and coded in ASCII is given below as an example. Even parity has been opted for (study this for yourself).

M   I   C   R   O
01001101 11001001 11000011 11010010 11001111

Instruction Code

In the foregoing we have interpreted the contents of the memory word as data in the form of numbers and characters. The contents of a memory word can also be a new instruction for the computer or, in other words, a command to execute an operation. In this case it is an instruction code.

EXAMPLE

We shall now investigate how a single instruction is carried out in a microcomputer and how the microcomputer is prepared to process the next instruction. As an example we will take the instruction ADD *r*, which means that the contents of register r, one of the general purpose registers, must be added to the contents of the accumulator and that the result must be stored in the accumulator.

The computer executes the instruction in 2 steps:

a. The *instruction fetch*, during which the instruction is fetched from memory and the program counter is incremented by 1.

b. The *instruction execution*, during which the instruction is executed.

There are two registers available in the control unit of the CPU to guide these steps. The first is the program counter which keeps track of the consecutive addresses of the instructions. The second register is the instruction register, which is used to temporarily store the instruction fetched from the program memory.

The control unit tests the contents of the instruction register to determine which operation must be carried out with which operands. In our example the operands are stored in general-purpose register r and in the accumulator (fig. 6-8). We now take the following (fig. 6-9):

a. The program counter stands at $0A30_{16}$, in other words, the instruction to be executed is present at the memory location with the address $0A30_{16}$.

b. The content of the memory word with the address $0A30_{16}$ is $10000010_2 = 82_{16}$; this is the instruction code for ADD r.

c. The contents of the general-purpose register r and the accumulator are, before execution of the instruction, $2F_{16}$ and $3A_{16}$ respectively.

Instruction Fetch

The content of the memory word, whose address is given in the program counter, is fetched. In our case this address is $0A30_{16}$. The content of the memory word having this address is 82_{16}. This information is put in the instruction register. The condition is now as is represented in fig. 6-9.

The contents of the program counter now incremented by 1 in order to prepare the computer for the execution of the next instruction, following execution of the instruction which has just been fetched. The contents of the program counter thus becomes $0A31_{16}$. The instruction fetch has now been completed.

Instruction Execution

The microcomputer now decodes the contents of the instruction register in the instruction decoder and at the same time determines the addresses of the operands. In our case the operands are located in general-purpose register r and in the accumulator. Following the operation code the operation (addition) is carried out. The instruction execution has now been completed and the sum stands in the accumulator (fig. 6-10).

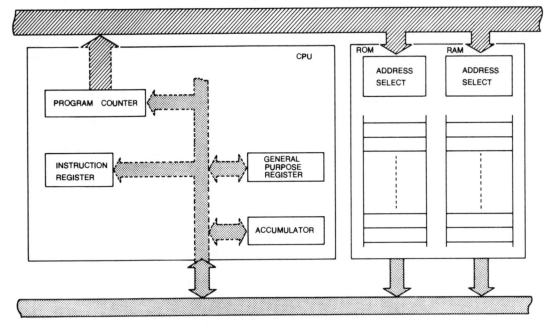

Fig. 6-8.

THE VON NEUMANN CONTROL CYCLE

The instruction fetch and the instruction execution are often described with the help of the so-called *von Neumann Control Cycle*. This is shown in fig. 6-11. Dur-ing the instruction fetch (1), the contents of the memory word, indicated by the program counter, is taken from memory and placed in the instruction register (IR). The instruction code goes from the instruction register to the

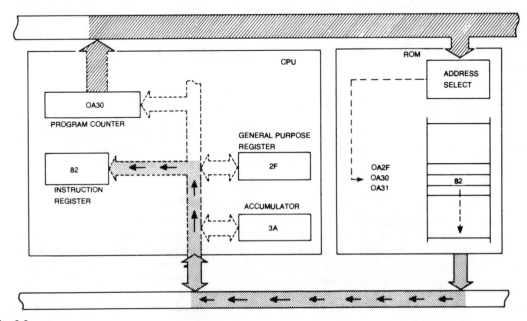

Fig. 6-9.

instruction decoder (2) where it is decoded. The program counter is then incremented by 1 (3).

If the instruction consists of several bytes, the process ((1), (2), and (3)) is repeated. We will refer to this again in the next chapter. If the instruction contains only one byte, we can immediately start with instruction execution (4). When the instruction has been executed, we return to (1) and the next instruction is fetched.

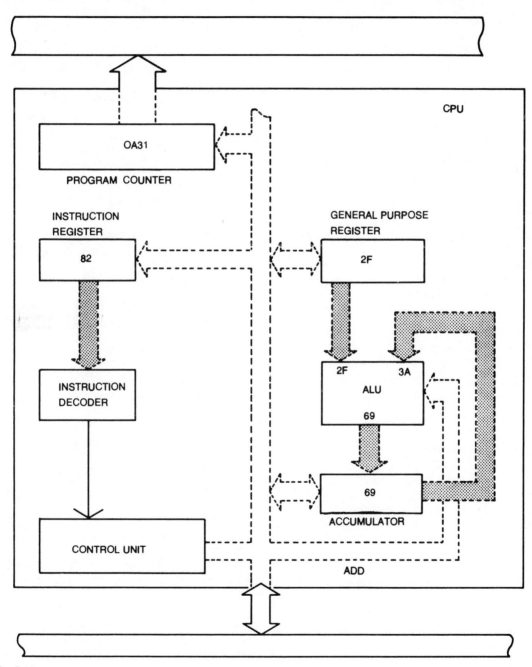

Fig. 6-10.

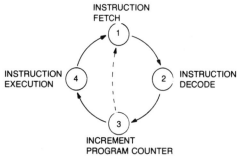

Fig. 6-11.

Note

(1), (2), and (3) combined form the instruction fetch. With a 2 or 3 byte instruction, the instruction fetch is repeated once or twice, respectively.

HARDWARE TK 80
Introduction

In this section we look more closely at several subjects which were discussed previously on the basis of fig. 5-24 of the chapter "Circuitry in a Computer". Figure 6-12 is a detail from fig. 5-24 showing the main memory. This section will not be covered in the review material.

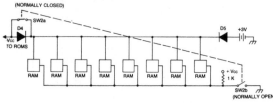

Fig. 6-12.

Memory Map /Chip Select

Figure 6-13 shows the memory map for fig. 6-12.

There are 4 ROM modules and 4 RAM modules. Each module contains 256 bytes. A word address within a module thus contains 8 bits ($2^8 = 256$). One RAM module is made up of 2 chips. Each chip in an 8-bit memory word contains 4 bits. Therefore, whenever a RAM module is selected, 2 chips are chosen at the same time. The ROM addresses are 0000 to 03FF, inclusive; the RAM addresses 8000-83FF. The first bit of an address within a ROM is thus always a 0, the first bit of an address within a RAM memory is always a 1. Therefore, the MSB of an address (A_{15}) is already one bit for the chip select. In addition to A_{15}, A_8 and A_9 are also used for this. These bits are fed to the inputs of the 3-line to 8-line decoder 2155 (= SN 74155) via three inverters.

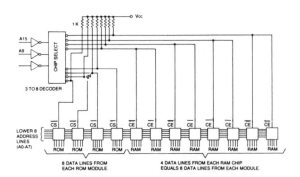

Fig. 6-13.

Table 6-2 shows which module is selected in this manner. In this table R, Q and P are the inverted signals of A_{15}, A_9 and A_8, respectively.

Table 6-2.

A 15	A 9	A 8	R	Q	P	ADDRESS RANGE	MODULE SELECTED
0	0	0	1	1	1	0000-00FF H	ROM 1
0	0	1	1	1	0	0100-01FF H	ROM 2
0	1	0	1	0	1	0200-02FF H	ROM 3
0	1	1	1	0	0	0300-03FF H	ROM 4
1	0	0	0	1	1	8000-80FF H	RAM 1
1	0	1	0	1	0	8100-81FF H	RAM 2
1	1	0	0	0	1	8200-82FF H	RAM 3
1	1	1	0	0	0	8300-83FF H	RAM 4

Note 1

A module is selected through a 0 at the input $\overline{CS}$ (= chip select) or $\overline{CE}$ (= chip enable).

Note 2

ROMs have no separate READ input. When a ROM is selected, information can only be placed on the data bus. Therefore the $\overline{CS}$ input at the same time functions as READ input.

Battery Back-Up

It is sometimes necessary to retain the contents of the RAMs when the power is turned off. This is done as shown in fig. 6-12 with diodes D_4 and D_5 and the switch SW2. A 3 V battery is connected between ground and the point EXT V_{CC}.

We now have 2 possibilities:

1. SW2 in the 'ENABLE' state, i.e. SW2a closed and SW2b open. The RAMs are connected to V_{CC}. If the supply voltage fails, the battery and D_5 assure that a voltage of about 3 V remains present. Because D_4 is

short-circuited by SW2a, the battery provides current to all the supply points V_{CC} in the circuit. Because this current is ± 1 A, the battery is quickly discharged.

2. SW2 in the 'PROTECT' state, i.e. SW2a open and SW2b closed. If the supply voltage V_{CC} is present, the RAMs are fed via D_4. If the supply voltage fails, *only* the RAMs receive a supply voltage of about 3 V via D_5. If the supply voltages V_{CC} and V_{DD} are turned off, short-term, undefined levels can appear at the address and control inputs of the RAMs, possibly affecting the contents.

In order to assure that the RAMs do not react to this, a second chip enable input (labeled 1K in fig. 6-12) is connected to ground of every RAM via SW2b. If this input is 0, the RAM will not react to control signals. Thus, if SW2 is in the 'PROTECT' state, we cannot communicate with the RAMs. This implies that we can only set the switch SW2 to the 'PROTECT' state just before turning off the supply voltage.

Note

A RAM is thus only selected on the following condition: CE and K = 1. If SW2b is open, all K inputs are set at 1 by the 1K resistor to supply V_{CC}.

SUMMARY

1. In a volatile memory, as opposed to a non-volatile memory, all the information which has been stored there is lost whenever the power is removed.

2. The word length of a microcomputer is equal to the number of bits which form a memory word.

3. 8 bits = 1 byte = 2 nybbles.

4. A capacity of 1 K means a capacity of 1024 memory words, of 8 bits each. A capacity of 1K × 4 means a capacity of 1024 memory words of 4 bits each.

5. Most microcomputers have 2 bytes = 16 bits available to address a memory word. So 2_{16} = 65536 words in memory can be addressed.

6. In memory organization using memory modules, part of the memory address consists of the module select and part of the word address.

7. A memory map is a diagram in which the addresses of the memory word are represented in ascending order.

8. The contents of the memory word are a pattern of ones and zeros. We can interpret this as:

1. data; this can be:
   a. an 8-bit number
   b. part of a number greater than 8 bits long
   c. a character
2. an instruction code.

9. A negative number is represented in micro-computers as the 2's complement of the corresponding positive number.

10. A number can be constructed from any number of memory words.

11. A character is a letter, digit or symbol coded according to a stated code.

12. When the contents of a memory word are described as the command for the execution of a new operation, we call it an instruction code.

13. The microcomputer executes an instruction in 2 steps.

   a. The instruction fetch, during which the instruction is fetched from the program memory.
   b. The instruction execution during which the instruction is executed.

14. The programmer must determine, and remember, where the numbers, characters and instruction codes are to be found in memory. As far as the microcomputer is concerned, the content of a memory word is nothing more than a pattern of ones and zeros.

REVIEW EXERCISES

1. When does a memory location form part of the data memory and when does it form part of the program memory?

2. What is the difference between a volatile and a nonvolatile memory?

3. What types of RAMs are there?

4. What is meant by the word length of a microcomputer?

5. What is a byte and what is a nybble?

6. What does it mean when we say that a memory has a capacity of 4K × 8?

7. How many bit places do most microcomputers have available for the addressing of memory addresses?

8. What is a memory module?

9. Given that a memory module is composed of 2 RAM chips, each with a capacity of 4K × 4. How many 8-bit memory words can we store in this memory module?

10. What are chip select, module select, and word address?

11. How many bits does an address contain if a memory module has a capacity of 2048 memory words?

12. Given that the memory addresses within a given ROM go from 0000_{16} to $03FF_{16}$, how large is the capacity of the memory?

13. How can the contents of a memory word with 8 bits be interpreted?

14. How are negative numbers represented in microcomputers?

15. In a microcomputer, what is the binary representation of -59_{10}?

16. What is a character?

17. How many different characters do we recognize and how many bits are needed to code them?

18. What is an instruction code?

19. In what stages does a computer execute an instruction?

ANSWERS

1. A memory location is part of the data memory if the contents of the memory place must be interpreted as a number of a character. If the contents must be interpreted as an instruction code, the location memory is part of the program memory.

2. A volatile memory loses all stored information if the power is removed, as opposed to a non-volatile memory.

3. Static and dynamic RAMs.

4. This is equal to the length of the memory word.

5. A byte is an 8-bit unit. A nybble is a 4-bit unit. In an 8-bit computer the word length is equal to 1 byte.

6. This means that we can store 4K = 4096 8-bit words in this memory.

7. 16 bit places, so that $2^{16} = 65536$ memory words can be addressed.

8. A memory module is a memory which is constructed from more than one chip. Together they contain the complete memory word.

9. 4K = 4096 4-bit memory words can be stored on each RAM chip. If we combine these two chips, we can then store 4K = 4096 8-bit memory words.

10. The chip select is the same as the module select, i.e. that part of the memory address that indicates in which memory module the memory word concerned is located. The word address indicates where the memory word is located within this memory module.

11. $2048 = 2^{11}$. The word address must thus comprise 11 bits.

12. The capacity of the ROM is $3FF_{16} = 1024_{10}$ memory words.

13. 1. As data, i.e.
   a. as a number
   b. as a portion of a number
   c. as a character
2. As an instruction code.

14. As the 2's complement of the corresponding positive number.

15. $+59_{10} = 00111011_2$.

The 1's complement of 00111011_2 is $\rightarrow 11000100_2$

The 2's complement of $00111011_2 \rightarrow$ $\underline{\qquad 1_+}$

is then $\quad 11000101_2 = -59_{10}$

16. A character is a letter, digit or symbol which has been coded according to a given code.

17. We recognize 26 lower-case letters, 26 capital letters, 10 digits and about 25 symbols. There are in total, 87 characters, which means that we need at least 7 bits in order to code them.

18. An instruction code is the contents of a memory word which must be interpreted as a command for the execution of a process.

19. 1. The instruction fetch, during which the instruction is brought from the memory to the CPU.

2. Instruction execution, during which the instruction is carried out.

Chapter 7
Simple Programming

This chapter will show you how information is processed in a computer and this will be illustrated by a simple addition program. Also you will see how data and program are fed in. Data may be digits, letters, punctuation marks, tight, sound, etc.

A program (fig. 7-1) is made up of *instructions*. An instruction consists of an *operation code,* which describes *what* must take place. This is followed by a code, which indicates where the subject of the operation is to be found. The operation code may, for example, mean "Bring to the accumulator." After the operation code an indication is required as to where the data concerned is located. In fig. 7-1 the information is located in a memory word. Thus, a memory address follows the operation code.

Program and data are stored in the main memory (fig. 7-2). The program is stored in a ROM and the data in a RAM. The memory consists of memory words. A memory word is an area in memory. A memory word has contents and an address. By indicating the address of a memory word, we can make the content available to us.

HEXADECIMAL NUMBERS

Figures 7-1 and 7-2 show the instructions, the contents of memory words and the addresses of memory words as combinations of zeros and ones. These combinations of zeros and ones are called *machine language*.

As you know, a computer works with circuits which do or do not output voltage. We indicate the presence or absence of voltage by 1 and 0. So, in this context, 1 and 0 are not digits, but rather indications of certain electrical states. Speaking or writing about instructions and addresses and content of memory words in a series of zeros and ones is not only time-consuming, but also creates opportunities for error. That is why we use an abbreviated system of notation when writing or speaking about binary numbers in a computer. The system used is the hexadecimal system of notation.

Hexadecimal notation comprises 16 symbols - 10 symbols are digits (0 - 9) and 6 symbols are letters (A to F). Each one stands for a combination of 4 bits in accordance with table 7-1. A binary number is encoded in hexadecimal by dividing the binary number into groups of 4 bits. If the number of bits is not a multiple of 4 bits, we make it so by placing zeros in front of it.

If we encode the address given in fig. 7-2 in hexadecimal, we come up with BC90. The contents of the RAM are 2A and 3F. Because the contents of a memory word are 8 bits, we can encode this using 2 hexadecimal symbols. If a memory address is 16 bits long, we need 4 hexadecimal symbols. If the memory addresses are shorter we naturally need fewer hexadecimal symbols.

A GENERALLY APPLICABLE PROGRAM

If we write a program, it should be generally applicable. If we write a program for performing addition, we must be able to use it for any set of numbers. This means that we cannot include the numbers in the program itself, because these will differ from case to case. This problem

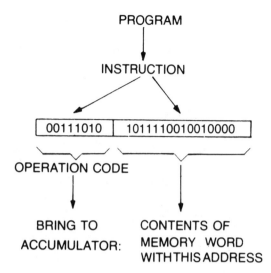

Fig. 7-1.

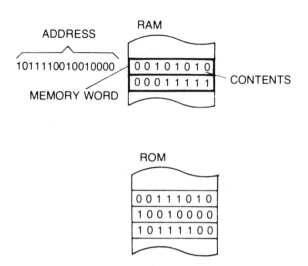

Fig. 7-2.

is solved by including the memory location where the numbers required can be found in the program.

We can agree that in our addition program the two numbers to be added together will be placed in the addresses BC90 and BC91 in memory and the sum in address BC92. If we now want to perform an operation on the first of the numbers to be added, we indicate what must be done with the operation code for that instruction; for example, 'Bring to the accumulator'. We then indicate

Table 7-1.

Binary	Hexadecimal
0000	0
0001	1
0010	2
0011	3
0100	4
0101	5
0110	6
0111	7
1000	8
1001	9
1010	A
1011	B
1100	C
1101	D
1110	E
1111	F

where the number can be found; in this case in address BC90. In this case the instruction is 3 bytes long. The operation code takes up 1 byte and the address is 2 bytes long. Thus we speak of a *3-byte instruction*.

This instruction is stored in the ROM as in fig. 7-3. The first memory word contains the operation code. The second memory word contains the lowest 8 bits of the address where the first of the numbers to be added is located. The third memory word contains the 8 highest bits of this address.

EXECUTION OF A PROGRAM FOR ADDITION

As illustrated in fig. 7-4, we shall describe how a program for the addition of two numbers is carried out by the microcomputer. The numbers to be added are placed in the addresses BC90 and BC91 in the data memory, the RAM. The sum is placed in address BC92. We use the above when formulating the instructions. We assume that the numbers to be added together are 2A and 3F.

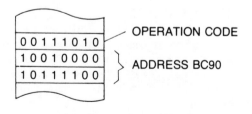

Fig. 7-3.

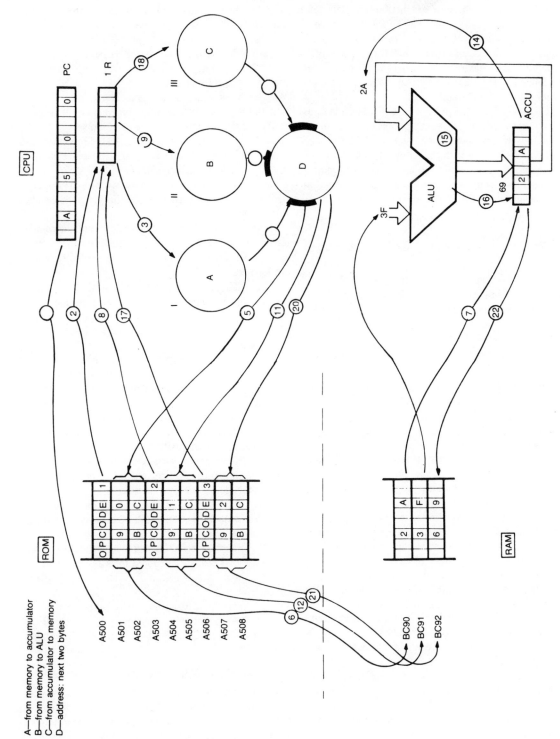

A—from memory to accumulator
B—from memory to ALU
C—from accumulator to memory
D—address: next two bytes

Fig. 7-4.

The program's sequential instructions are placed in the program memory, the ROM. The instructions are taken from the microprocessor's instruction set. In our example, the addition can be performed with the help of 3 instructions. Each instruction consists of an operation code, followed by an address where the data can be found or where it is to be placed.

The processing takes place in the CPU. The addition is done in the ALU. Before we can perform the addition, one of the two numbers must be placed in the accumulator. We do this with the following instruction:

Bring the contents of the memory word, whose address is formed by the following 2 bytes, to the accumulator.

The operation code of this instruction is defined as op-code 1.

The addition takes place using the following instruction:

Bring the contents of the memory word, of which the next 2 bytes form the address, to the ALU and add this to the contents of the accumulator in the ALU.

Put the sum in the accumulator.

The operation code of this instruction is defined as op-code 2.

The sum is placed in memory using the following instruction:

Bring the contents of the accumulator to the memory word, of which the next 2 bytes form the address.

The operation code of this instruction is defined as op-code 3.

The sequential bytes in the program are placed in ascending sequential order, beginning with address A500. The program counter, called the PC, ensures that the program is carried out step-by-step. The program counter is a sort of schoolmaster who tells you in what sequence the events must take place.

Before processing the program, the program counter (fig. 7-4) is set to A500. It then holds the memory address of the first instruction.

1. As soon as we puch the RUN button, the program is processed and the following happens:

2. The contents of address A500 is copied. The copy is put in the instruction register.

3. The program counter is incremented while the content of the instruction register—op code 1—"settles."

4. Then it is decoded, and the computer now knows that instruction 1 must be carried out.

5. The contents of the following 2 bytes form the address BC90. These are fetched into a temporary register.

6. Address BC90 is then addressed.

7. The contents of address BC90 are copied and placed in the accumulator.

With this, instruction 1 has been carried out.

In the meantime, the program counter has become A503 and the program continues as follows:

8. The contents of address A503 are copied and placed in the instruction register. The old content—operation code 1—is *over-written.*

9. The content of the instruction register—operation code 2—settles while the program counter increments.

10. Then the instruction is decoded, and the computer now knows that instruction 2 must be carried out.

11. The next 2 bytes form the address BC91. These are fetched.

12. Address BC91 is then addressed.

13. The contents of address BC91 are brought to the ALU.

14. The contents of the accumulator are also brought to the ALU.

15. Addition is performed in the ALU.

16. The sum—69 in hexadecimal—is now placed in the accumulator. The old contents—2A—are over-written.

With this, instruction 2 has been carried out.

In the meantime, the program counter has become A506 and we continue with:

17. The contents of address A506 are copied and placed in the instruction register. The old contents—operation code 2—are over-written.

18. The content of the instruction register—operation code 3—settles while the program counter increments.

19. Then the instruction is decoded and the computer now knows that instruction 3 must be carried out.

20. The next 2 bytes form the address BC92. These are fetched.

21. Address BC92 is then addressed.

22. The contents of the accumulator are copied and placed in address BC92. With this, instruction 3 has been carried out.

INPUTTING THE PROGRAM AND DATA

In the previous sections we have seen how information is processed following a given program. The question to be considered now is how we can fill main memory with a program and data? The data is fed into RAM. In most cases, the program is stored in a ROM, where it is permanently fixed. A ROM is usually programmed by the manufacturer, but there are also ROMs which the user can program himself. The program could, of course, also be placed in a RAM, but with the disadvantage that it would be lost if the power were to fail.

If we want to fill a memory with a given quantity, we must indicate two things:

a. the address of the memory word to be filled

b. the contents the memory word must have.

A memory word can be filled in three different ways on simple microcomputers:

a. in binary form with switches

b. using a hexadecimal keyboard

c. with punched tape.

We will discuss the first two methods mentioned in this section. In the chapter System Software we will discuss input by means of a punched tape.

INPUTTING USING SWITCHES

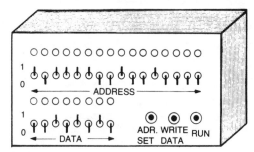

Fig. 7-5.

Lamps

The Lamps have, at first sight, nothing to do with inputting. The memory word being processed by the computer is indicated by a row of 16 lamps. A row of 8 lamps indicates what its contents are. When a program is running, addresses and contents change very quickly. Whenever a program is processed step-by-step using a *single-step* switch, the lamps allow main memory to be viewed word-by-word.

Switches

The memory word which has to be filled is indicated by the 16 address switches. If the 'address set' button is depressed, the memory word concerned is indicated. The contents intended for the addressed memory word are set with the 8 word switches. If the 'write data' button is depressed, these contents are entered in the appropriate

address. In this way we can fill the memory word by word.

To execute the program we use the switches to set the address of the memory word where the first byte of the program can be found. Then depress the 'run' button and the program runs.

Inputting with switches is a lot of work. Moreover, we have to be very careful, since it is easy to confuse ones and zeros.

Inputting with a Hex Keyboard

Inputting takes less time and allows less margin for error if we use a hexadecimal keyboard and if we read out the addresses and the contents of the memory words in hexadecimal. An example of this can be seen in fig. 2-1 in the chapter "What is a Microcomputer?" Figure 7-6 is a picture from this.

Fig. 7-6.

If we depress one of the buttons 0 to 9 or A to F, the appropriate pattern of 4 bits is activated. Inputting is as follows:

a. We type in the address of the first memory word.

b. We then depress the 'address set' button. The address which has been typed in is then indicated.

c. Now we type in the data which must fill the memory word.

d. We can use the display to check if we have presented the correct address and the correct contents. The 4 displays at the left indicate the address. The 2 displays at the right indicate the contents of this address. The remaining 2 displays indicate the contents of the previous address.

e. We input by depressing the 'write increment' button. The stated memory word is filled (write), and the next address is indicated (increment). We thus only have to indicate the first address.

f. After we have input program and data in this manner, we can check our work once again by depressing the 'read increment' and 'read decrement' keys. When we depress the 'read decrement' key, we address the previous address. When we depress the 'read increment' key, we address the next address.

g. If it transpires that we have made no typing errors when inputting, we type in the address of the first byte of the program, depress the 'address set' key and next the 'run' key. The program then runs.

h. When we have depressed the 'run' button, the keyboard is no longer in control. To regain control of the system, we depress the 'reset' key, which is directly connected to the CPU. This fills the program counter with 0000. This address contains the first instruction of a special program in the ROM to scan the keyboard. After depressing the 'reset' key the keyboard again takes over control.

i. If we want to retain our program we can store it on a regular audio-cassette recorder. The 'store data' and 'load data' keys serve to store data on a cassette and to return it to main memory, respectively. These instructions are written from the viewpoint of the computer. 'Store data' thus means 'bring data from main memory to the cassette recorder', 'Load data' means 'bring data from the cassette recorder to main memory'.
The cassette recorder is connected via a circuit which is mounted next to the keyboard on the printed circuit board.

Note

We will not discuss the function of the 'RET' key (return) in this chapter. This deals with the 'single step' function and will be dealt with in a later chapter.

HOW THE KEYBOARD AND DISPLAYS WORK

As can be seen in fig. 5-24 in the chapter 'Circuitry in a Computer', a special program is entered in the ROM of the microprocessor by the manufacturer. This program controls the computer system during the input of the work program. This control program is called the *monitor*.

The monitor ensures that the information present at input gates PA and PC is fetched and brought into the CPU every 1 ms. Whenever a key is depressed, a combination of zeros and ones is presented to the input gates, so that the microcomputer knows which key has been depressed. If we depress key 7, PA_7 is connected to PC_{13}, a '1' appears at both inputs. If one of the command keys has been depressed, for example *write data* or *read decrement,* the monitor sees that this command is executed. If one of the keys from 0 to F is depressed, this combination of bits is brought to a given memory word in the RAM and the monitor translates this combination of bits into a code for the 7-segment displays.

This code is now sent to the 7-segment displays via the buffer 8212 and the drivers 238. The 7-segment displays are turned on sequentially so as to limit the current used. Furthermore, at any given moment only 1 combination of 8 bits is offered, so that only 1 driver circuit need be used. The IC2155, a decoder, determines which display this combination of ones and zeros must process. The 7-segment displays are driven sequentially so quickly that it appears that each displays continuously. However, this is not the case.

The 8212 and the 2155 must drive the displays synchronously, because otherwise symbols could appear on the wrong display. This synchronization is taken care of by a separate clock generator built around the 555.

SUMMARY

1. An instruction comprises an operation code, which indicates which operation a microcomputer must perform and a part which indicates where, or with what, this process must be performed.

2. A computer works with 2-state circuitry, which either does or does not output voltage. These states are coded as 1 and 0.

3. When speaking of or writing about the contents and addresses of memory words and instructions, we use the hexadecimal code. A group of 4 bits is represented by a hexadecimal symbol.

4. To make a program applicable for any values, we state in the program the addresses of the memory words where the data is located.

5. The instruction whereby a process is performed on data from the data memory takes up 3 bytes; 1 byte is used for the operation code and 2 bytes for the memory address.

6. The data to be processed is stored in the RAM. The instructions making up the program are stored in the ROM.

7. The operations are carried out by the ALU. One of the operands must be placed in the accumulator. The result of the operation can be found in the accumulator.

8. The program counter addresses the memory words of the program memory in ascending sequential order.

9. The operation code of an instruction is found in the instruction register. The operation code is decoded. From the result, the computer concludes what must be done.

10. Main memory can be filled using:
   a. switches
   b. hexadecimal keyboard
   c. punched tape.

11. Filling main memory using switches not only takes time, but gives opportunity for errors.

12. The contents and addresses of memory words can be displayed by lamps (binary) or 7-segment displays (hexadecimal).

REVIEW EXERCISES

1. What does a program consist of?
2. What does an instruction consist of?
3. What is the first part of an instruction called?
4. Where is the program stored?
5. Where is the information stored?

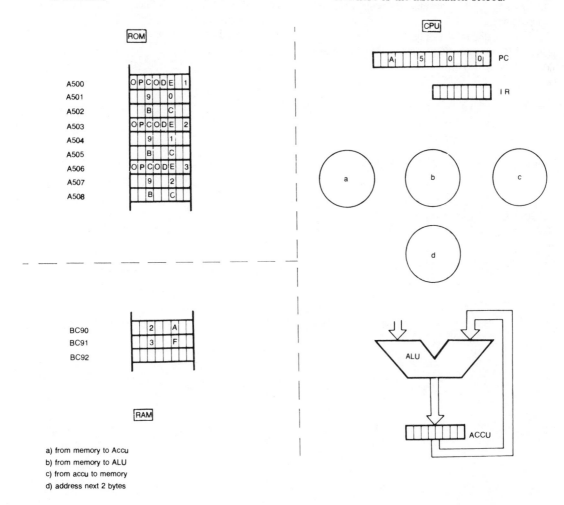

a) from memory to Accu
b) from memory to ALU
c) from accu to memory
d) address next 2 bytes

Fig. 7-7.

79

6. What is the advantage of coding in hexadecimal in relation to the use of machine language?

7. How is an instruction code which addresses a memory word made up?

8. What is an instruction set?

9. Compose a table which shows how groups of 4 bits can be coded into symbols using hexadecimal notation.

10. How many memory words are needed to store a 16-bit memory address in memory in an 8-bit microcomputer?

11. How does one ensure that a program is usable for data with any values?

12. How many bytes does an instruction take up when the memory address is given?

13. In what way(s) can we input the program and data to a microcomputer?

14. Use the diagrams in Fig. 7-7 to help explain a program written by yourself or another. Do it in pencil so that you can make corrections later.

ANSWERS

1. A number of instructions.

2. An operation code which indicates *which* operation must be carried out, *where* and *with what* the operation must take place.

3. Operation code.

4. Usually in a ROM.

5. In a RAM.

6. It takes less time and there is less chance of error.

7. An operation code (1 byte) and a memory address (2 bytes).

8. A list of the possible operations which the microcomputer can carry out. The instruction set also gives the bit patterns from which the operation codes are made up.

9. See table 7-1.

10. In an 8-bit microcomputer, the length of a memory word is also 8 bits. You thus need 2 memory words in order to store 16 bits.

11. By giving the memory-word address where the information is stored.

12. Three - 1 byte for the operation code and 2 bytes for the address.

13. a. Using switches.

    b. Using a hexadecimal keyboard.

    c. Using a punched tape.

14. See fig. 7-4.

Chapter 8

CPU Architecture-1

To program efficiently, we must be familiar with the architecture, i.e., the functional construction of the microprocessor. With fig. 8-2 as a guide we will analyze this construction in detail in this chapter.

Figure 8-2 shows that in an 8-bit microcomputer the microprocessor is composed mainly of 8-bit registers and 8-bit data paths. The registers may contain the data from a previous operation. They can also be used to store data temporarily during the execution of an instruction.

Before discussing the functions of the various registers, we will review what happens during an instruction cycle (fig. 8-1).

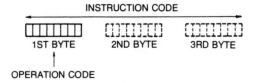

INSTRUCTION CODE

1ST BYTE   2ND BYTE   3RD BYTE

OPERATION CODE

Fig. 8-1.

The purpose of an instruction is to process data. An instruction is made up of 1, 2, or 3 bytes which are stored in memory in sequential positions. During the previous instruction, the program counter is filled with a value corresponding to the address of the memory word where the first byte of the next instruction to be carried out is located. The first byte of an instruction contains the operation code. The operation code indicates which operation must be carried out and which data are to be used.

We start by fetching the first instruction byte from memory, the one containing the operation code. If the operation code indicates that the second and third bytes of the instruction together form the address of the data to be processed, these two must be transferred to the CPU. After this, the CPU 'knows' where the data is to be found.

If the operation code indicates directly where the data are located, processing can start once the first byte has been fetched. The operation code may indicate, for instance, that the data to be processed is the second byte of the instruction code.

The instruction determines where the data to be processed is located and what operations must be applied. The transportation of the first instruction byte from memory to the CPU is part of the instruction fetch because the first byte contains the operation code. If the second and third byte contain an address, fetching the address bytes from memory to the CPU is also part of the instruction fetch.

The processing of the data is called the *instruction execution*. This also includes the transportation of data— for example, from an input device to the CPU.

ARITHMETIC AND LOGIC UNIT

Every microprocessor contains an Arithmetic and Logic Unit (ALU), where arithmetic and logic operations take place.

Arithmetic Operations

Which arithmetic operations can be handled depends upon the type of ALU. There are, for example, microprocessors with ALUs which can only perform addition and shift operations. With these basic steps we can program any arithmetic process, such as multiplication and division.

Logical Operations

In almost all microprocessors the ALU can perform the logic functions AND, OR and EXOR. The advantage of this can be seen from the following.

Suppose a value is in the accumulator and we need to know if b3 is 0 or 1. We do this by using the AND function to comapre the bits of the number with the corresponding bits of 00001000. We allocate the value 1 only to the comparsion bit of this so called *mask*. All the remaining bits are 0. For bits b0 to b2 and b4 to b7 the comparison must result in 0s. If the result is 00001000, bit 3 has the value 1. If the result is 00000000, bit 3 has the value 0.

With this method we can pick out 1 bit from a word by masking out the other bits. In the chapter 'Description of the Instructions' we will study this logic operation more closely.

Registers Around the CPU

The ALU receives data to be processed (operands) from various locations simultaneously. The following operations are possible (fig. 8-2):

a. From the accumulator and from a general-purpose register—D, for instance.

b. From the accumulator and from memory (via the data bus buffer).

In addition, the ALU can be fed data from the *status flag register*.

The block diagram of a CPU in fig. 8-2 is that of a one-address machine. In other words, one of the operands that is fed to the ALU comes from the accumulator. The other operand is fed to the ALU from one of the general-purpose registers B, C, D, E, H or L, or from memory. So if we want to add the contents of two general-purpose registers, we must first feed the contents of one of them to the accumulator.

STATUS FLAGS

The result of an operation may be required to carry out the succeeding one. This is the case, for example, with an addition involving a carry. To make the result of a calculation available, the ALU is connected to a number of flip-flops which are set or reset after the calculation, depending on the result. Such a flip-flop is called a *status flag*. Together these flip-flops form the status flag register (fig. 8-3).

Note 1

Because the results of all operations carried out by the ALU are sent to the accumulator, one can say that the status flag register indicates something about the data transferred from the ALU to the accumulator.

Note 2

The contents of the status flag is only used with certain types of instructions, with others it is ignored.

Note 3

Different types of microprocessors have different numbers of status flags.

CARRY STATUS FLAG

A very important status flag is the *carry status flag*. When adding two 8-bit numbers in the ALU it indicates when a carry must be made to the LSB of the following byte. This is similar to 'normal' addition when we carry a one.

Example 1

$$\begin{array}{r} 10111000 \\ 11011010 + \\ \hline \text{carry flag (1)} \quad 10010010 \end{array}$$

The carry status flag also indicates when a bit must be borrowed in subtracting two 8-bit numbers. It depends on the instructions available in the instruction set how a programmer realizes a subtraction, and these in turn depend on the construction of the ALU. If the ALU has a hardware function which makes direct subtraction possible, the instruction will contain a SUB-instruction. An example of direct subtraction is given below.

$$\begin{array}{ll} 11011111 & \text{direct} \\ 10111001 - & \text{subtraction} \\ \hline 00100110 \end{array}$$

If the ALU does not have the hardware function 'subtract', the programmer must first derive the 2's complement in the ALU and then add, using, for instance, an ADD instruction.

Example 2

$$\begin{array}{ll} 11011111 & \text{1's complement} = 01000110 \\ 01000111 + & 1 + \\ \hline (1)\ 00100110 & \text{2's complement} = 01000111 \end{array}$$

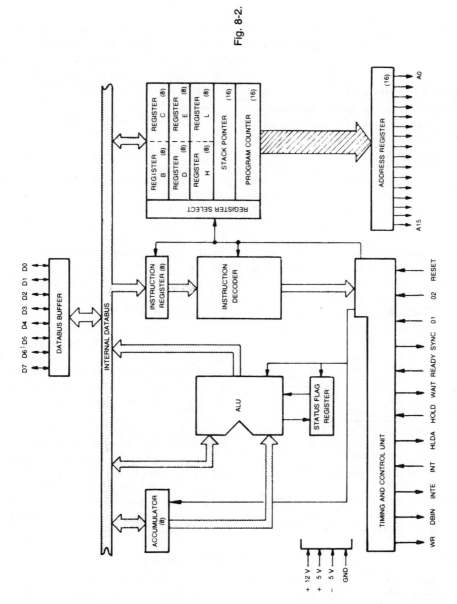

Fig. 8-2.

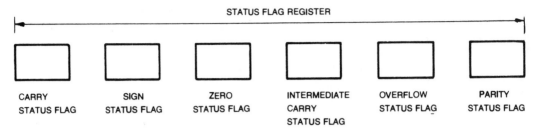

CARRY STATUS FLAG   SIGN STATUS FLAG   ZERO STATUS FLAG   INTERMEDIATE CARRY STATUS FLAG   OVERFLOW STATUS FLAG   PARITY STATUS FLAG

Fig. 8-3.

In this case the instruction 'subtraction' is carried out in two steps, i.e., by taking the 2's complement and then adding.

INTERMEDIATE CARRY STATUS FLAG

A variant of the carry status flag is the *intermediate carry status flag,* which is always set if a carry from b3 to b4 occurs in the ALU. The intermediate carry status flag is used when adding numbers coded in BCD. Whenever a carry occurs from b3 to b4 we must apply the decimal adjust (+6 correction). Thus, whenever BCD coded numbers are processed, the programmer must indicate in his instructions that the intermediary carry status flag is to be used. If he fails to do this, the flag is automatically ignored.

Below we can see an example of how 19 and 09 are added when encoded in BCD. In the addition a carry from b3 to b4 occurs which is handled in the normal way. The carry is passed to the intermediate carry status flag, which is set accordingly. This means that a decimal adjust must be applied, which occurs automatically if it has been indicated in the instruction.

$$
\begin{array}{rll}
19 = 000 & 1001 \\
09 = 0000 & 1001 \, + \\
\hline
0010\,(1) & 0010 \\
0000 & 0110 \, + \\
\hline
\text{decimal adjust} \quad 28 = 0010 & 1000
\end{array}
$$

Note

A decimal adjust might also be applied should one of the combinations 1010 through 1111 appear. As you know, these combinations are undefined in BCD.

ZERO STATUS FLAG

The *zero status flag* indicates when a given operation produces 00000000_2 in the ALU. For example, this flag can be used if we want the computer to wait for a certain time before continuing the execution of the program. We use an instruction to enter a number (say 100) in the register. The next instruction causes 1 to be successively subtracted until the result is zero and the zero status flag is set. Only then the processing of the program continues. In this manner we can form a *wait loop.*

SIGN STATUS FLAG

In the chapter "How Does a Computer Compute?" we have seen that a negative number is represented in a computer using the 2's complement method. In this case the MSB of a number represents not only a value but also the sign of a number. If the MSB is 1, the number is negative. If the MSB is 0, the number is positive. We can see that the MSB determines the sign of a number. Because of this the MSB of the result of an ALU operation is stored in the *sign status flag* for later use.

OVERFLOW STATUS FLAG

When we perform a calculation using the 2's complement, we choose a certain word length. If, during the calculation we get a result that does not fit in this word length, a signal must be given expanding the word length. If this is not possible, the calculation must be stopped. The facility indicating this is called the *overflow status flag.*

We will not discuss here how the ALU decides that another byte must be added. When working with microcomputers without an overflow status flag one must choose a word length that will not only accommodate the number being manipulated, but also the result. If one is not sure of this, the program must be written in such a way that the likelihood that the word length will need adapting is tested automatically.

PARITY STATUS FLAG

This status flag is set if in the result of an operation the number of ones is even. If the result of a computation is, for example, 01101010, the parity status flag is set because there is an even number of ones. The parity status flag is most often used to control the parity of data during transfer. This way we can check whether an error occurred during transport.

INSTRUCTION REGISTER AND DECODER

Every operation that a microcomputer performs originates from an instruction code presented to it. If a microcomputer has 8 bit places available to indicate the operation code, it can distinguish a maximum of $2^8 = 256$ operation codes. In most cases this is more than sufficient.

The number of bytes which make up an instruction depends on the operation to be carried out (fig. 8-4). In

GENERAL-PURPOSE REGISTERS

Several 8-bit general-purpose registers are visible in the block diagram of the CPU in fig. 8-2 where operands can be stored for fast accessibility. To address these general-purpose registers and the accumulator, an *abbreviated address* of 3 bits is used. With these we can choose from a maximum of $2^3 = 8$ different general-purpose registers.

The general-purpose registers in fig. 8-2 are represented by the letters B, C, D, E, H and L. From fig. 8-2 we see that these registers are arranged in pairs and can be used alone (8 bits) or in pairs (16 bits). The latter applies if we wish to store a memory address in the registers or calculate with 2-byte numbers.

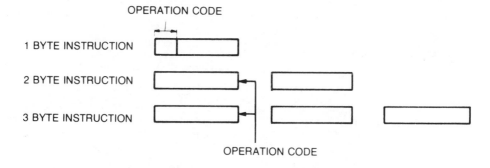

Fig. 8-4.

microcomputers, the maximum number of bytes is usually 3. The operation code indicating which operation has to be carried out is always located in the first byte. In 1-byte instructions the operation code takes up only a part of the first byte (for example, 2 bits). In 3-byte instructions, the operation code usually uses the entire first byte. The entire first byte of the instruction code is fetched from memory and fed to the instruction register during the instruction fetch, regardless of which part of the operation code is used. This first byte is decoded and shows:

a. how many bytes the instruction comprises.

b. if the second and third bytes combined contain the address of the memory location where the data to be processed is stored.

c. which operation must be carried out.

The first byte is transferred from the instruction register to the instruction decoder which, together with timing unit, activates new control commands. These fetch the second and third bytes from memory, if necessary, and attend to the execution of the instruction.

THE PROGRAM COUNTER

The program counter indicates where the instruction bytes are located in memory. The control unit increments the program counter by 1 each time a byte of the instruction code is transferred from memory to the CPU. If an instruction code has 2 bytes, the instruction fetch takes place in 2 steps. The program counter already contains the address of the first byte of the current instruction, because the program counter was incremented by one at the end of the fetch in the previous instruction. After the previous instruction has been executed, this first byte can be carried to the CPU and the program counter incremented by 1. The program counter now contains the address of the second byte of the instruction. This second byte is brought to the CPU and the program counter is again incremented by 1 and now contains the address of the first byte of the following instruction.

THE STACK POINTER

To explain the term 'stack pointer' we must describe the jump instruction, briefly touched on in the chapter "What is a Microcomputer?", and the subroutine.

Jump Instruction

The instructions which form the program are placed in ascending sequence in memory and are thus addressed in the same order. The programmer can break this sequence by applying a *jump instruction*.

During the fetch of a jump instruction, the program counter is incremented by 1 three times. During instruction execution the entire contents of the program counter are replaced by the address indicated in the jump instruction.

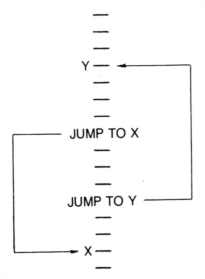

Fig. 8-5.

Two jump instructions are shown in fig. 8-5. Sometimes it depends on the condition of one of the status flags whether the jumps concerned are performed or not. For example, the jump instruction might be carried out if the result of a given operation were 0, but not if it were 1, in which case the next instruction in the programs is executed. Jumps which depend on the state or condition of a flag are called *conditional jumps* or *branches*. If the jump is always executed, it is called an *unconditional jump*.

Subroutines

A special kind of jump is that which is executed when a *subroutine* is called. A subroutine is a sub-program which is run through several times during the course of the main program. For example, a program might require the multiplication of two numbers more than once. The numbers change, but the multiplication operation is the same. It would be inefficient to write the program and store the instruction separately for each occasion. Be-

cause the operation is the same, the instruction can be stored in a single memory location to be called upon as necessary—in other words a subroutine (fig. 8-6a).

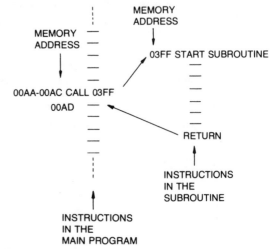

Fig. 8-6A.

We give a CALL instruction whenever we want to multiply during the main program. This instruction contains the address of the first instruction of the subroutine to be executed ($03FF_{16}$) and takes up 3 bytes.

The processor has a special facility whereby it returns to the main program after the execution of the subroutine. Whenever the processor receives a CALL instruction, the program counter is incremented and the contents are stored ($00AD_{16}$) in a memory location reserved by the programmer for this purpose, known as the *stack*. The stack contains the address of the instruction to be executed after the CPU has completed the subroutine. The CPU also substitutes the contents of the program counter with the address of the subroutine specified in the CALL instruction ($00FF_{16}$). This means that the next instruction fetched from memory by the processor is the first instruction of the subroutine. The last instruction of a subroutine is always a RETURN instruction. No address is given in this instruction. The return instruction assures that the address stored in the stack ($00AD_{16}$) is returned to the program counter. The main program then continues from the point where the subroutine was called.

Subroutines are often nested (fig. 8-6b). That is to say, one subroutine often calls a second, which in turn calls a third, and so forth. If a stack can store 3 return addresses, we can nest twice. We can nest one time less than the number of return addresses the stack can contain.

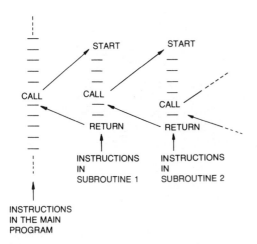

INSTRUCTIONS
IN THE MAIN
PROGRAM

Fig. 8-6B.

Note

In some microprocessors the stack is not part of main memory, but is formed by a separate RAM connected to the microprocessor proper.

Stack Pointer

A special 16-bit register in the CPU is reserved to address stack memory locations—the *stack pointer*. The stack pointer contains the address of the stack where the requisite return address can be found.

ADDRESS REGISTER

Writing and reading of a memory word takes place under the control of a memory address. This memory address indicates the memory location where an instruction byte or data byte must either be transferred to or from. The CPU transfers the address from a register to memory via the address bus. A memory has a certain access time, so that a period of time elapses before the memory word concerned can be activated. Because of this delay, the address generated by the CPU must be present for some specific time. To do this, most microcomputers have a built-it register to store the address. This register is called the *address register*.

SUMMARY

1. Arithmetic and logic operations can take place in the ALU.

2. The ALUs of most microprocessors can perform the following arithmetic operations: addition, and shifting. With these basic function, a programmer can write a program for, for example, multiplication or division.

3. In almost all ALUs, two 8-bit numbers can be compared to each other using the AND, OR or EXOR functions.

4. A flip-flop which is set or reset depending upon the result of an operation in the ALU is called a status flag. A number of these flags form the status flag register.

5. The carry status flag indicates when a carry or borrow 1 must be performed when two numbers are added or subtracted.

6. The intermediate carry status flag indicates when, during addition, a carry occurs from b3 to b4. This flag is used when calculating in BCD code and indicates when a decimal adjust must be made.

7. The zero status flag indicates when the result of a calculation in the ALU is 00000000_2.

8. The sign status flag is a copy of the MSB of the result of a calculation in the 2's complement system and indicates whether the result is positive or negative.

9. The overflow status flag is a facility indicating if the word length must be extended to accommodate the result of a calculation.

10. The parity status flag indicates whether the result of an operation contains an even or odd number of ones.

11. The byte of the instruction code which contains the operation code is always placed in the instruction register.

12. The number of bytes comprising an instruction code depends upon the operation to be carried out. In an 8-bit microcomputer an instruction code is 1, 2 or 3 bytes long.

13. The general-purpose registers in the CPU serve to make the operands quickly accessible, without having first to fetch them from memory.

14. A jump instruction contains the address of the next instruction to be executed. It is therefore possible to store this instruction at a random memory location.

15. A subroutine is a part of a program which may be used more than once during the course of the main program.

16. A subroutine is called using a CALL instruction. This instruction contains the address of the first instruction to be executed in the subroutine. The last instruction of a subroutine is a return instruction.

17. The stack is a part of memory which stores the return addresses from subroutines, for example.

18. The stack pointer is a 16-bit register in the CPU that indicates memory locations in the stack.

19. The address register in the CPU is a register which temporarily stores addresses until they are decoded by memory.

REVIEW EXERCISES

1. What is the instruction fetch?
2. What is the instruction execution?
3. How many bytes does an instruction code take up?
4. Which 2 types of operation can take place in the ALU?
5. Which arithmetic operations can take place in an ALU?
6. Which logic operations can take place in an ALU?
7. What does masking mean?
8. From which sources does an ALU get data to be processed?
9. What is the function of the status flag register?
10. Which (5) status flags do you know?
11. What does the carry status flag indicate?
12. If the ALU does not have the hardware function *SUB*tract, how can a programmer execute a subtraction?
13. What does the intermediate carry status flag indicate?
14. Give another name for the +6 correction.
15. What does the zero status flag indicate?
16. How are negative numbers represented?
17. What does the sign status flag indicate?
18. What does the overflow status flag indicate?
19. In which register is the first byte of an instruction stored?
20. What does the instruction decoder do?
21. How are general-purpose registers and the accumulator addressed?
22. When do we use two 8-bit general-purpose registers in pairs?
23. When is the program counter incremented by 1?
24. What is a jump instruction?
25. What is a subroutine?
26. What is the advantage of a subroutine?
27. What does a CALL instruction contain?
28. What is the last instruction of a subroutine called and what does this instruction do?
29. What is nesting? How often can one nest?
30. What is a stack?
31. What is a stack pointer?
32. What is the purpose of an address register?

ANSWERS

1. The means by which operations that are to be performed are put into the instruction decoder.

2. Instruction execution is the execution of the operation given in the operation code.
3. 1, 2 or 3.
4. Arithmetic and logic operations.
5. a. addition
   b. deriving the 2's complement.
6. AND, OR and EXOR.
7. Ignoring specific bits so that the state (condition) of a single bit can be examined.
8. a. From the general purpose registers.
   b. From the accumulator.
   c. From memory.
   d. From the status flag register.
9. It stores the result of an operation for use in a succeeding operation.
10. a. Carry status flag.
    b. Sign status flag
    c. Zero status flag
    d. Intermediate carry status flag
    e. Overflow status flag
    f. Parity status flag.
11. The carry status flag indicates whether a carry must be made during addition, or if the ALU can subtract a borrow during subtraction.
12. By using the 2's complement method and then adding.
13. This is a carry status flag indicating when a carry must be made from b3 to b4. It is used when adding numbers coded in BCD. If there is a carry, the decimal adjust must be applied.
14. Decimal adjust.
15. The zero status flag is set when the result of an ALU operation is 0.
16. As the 2's complement of the corresponding positive number.
17. We can determine the MSB of a number by looking at the sign status flag. In the 2's complement it indicates the sign of a number.
18. When working with the 2's complement system the overflow status indicates whether an extra byte must be added or if the operation must be stopped.
19. In the instruction register.
20. The instruction decoder decodes the operation code which is stored in the instruction register and activates the control commands that take care of the execution of the instruction.
21. With an abbreviated 3-bit address.
22. If we want to store a memory address temporarily or if we want to perform calculations using 2-byte numbers.
23. Each time that a byte is fetched from the program memory.

24. In a jump instruction the ascending sequential address order of the program is broken. A jump may be forwards or backwards. Whether or not a jump is made may depend on the result of the previous calculation.

25. A subroutine is a sub-program which is used more than once during the course of the main program.

26. The advantage of a subroutine is that memory space is saved.

27. A CALL instruction indicates the address of the first instruction in the subroutine to be executed.

28. Return instruction. This instruction assures that the program counter receives the address that was stored in the stack at the start of the subroutine. The program then resumes at the point the subroutine was called.

29. The calling of a new subroutine while a subroutine is being executed. The number of times nesting is possible, is one less than the number of return addresses the stack can contain.

30. A memory where return addresses are stored during the execution of a subroutine.

31. A register indicating which return address must be called.

32. To store a memory address.

Chapter 9

CPU Architecture—2

In the last chapter we saw what was in the CPU, now let's look at how everything is controlled.

TIMING UNIT

The sequence and coordination of events in a microcomputer require time control just like any other digital apparatus. A clock generator, usually based on a crystal, takes care of this time control. The circuits associated with the crystal are often contained on the microprocessor chip. In the microcomputer shown in fig. 2-1 of the chapter "What is a Microcomputer?" these circuits are not located on the microprocessor chip, but on a separate IC, the 8224. (See also fig. 5-24 of the chapter "Circuitry in a Computer".) The clock signal, generally indicated by 0, can be a square wave like the one shown in fig. 9-1a. In most cases the clock signal consists of a combination of two non-overlapping square waves 01 and 02, where 02 and 01 are derived from the same square wave (see fig. 9-1b).

Before we can say any more about the purpose of the clock signal, we must first explain the meaning of the concepts *instruction cycle, machine cycle,* and *state*. An instruction cycle is the time necessary for the execution of the instruction fetch and the execution of the instruction itself. Each instruction cycle takes 1 to 5 machine cycles, depending upon the type of instruction. The number of machine cycles is equal to the number of times that the CPU addresses memory or one of the I/O devices. Therefore we can state that the number of machine cycles equals the number of times the data bus is used.

Each instruction cycle consists of a minimum of 1 machine cycle, because at least 1 instruction byte must always be taken from memory and delivered to the CPU. Each machine cycle itself is made up of various basic actions or *states*. For example, in an instruction fetch the memory address concerned must first be indicated and decoded. Only then can the first instruction byte be transferred to the CPU and stored in the instruction register. So a state is the smallest possible action which can take place in a microcomputer. A state is executed during one period of the clock signal. One machine cycle consists of 3 to 5 states. To work out how long the execution of an instruction will take, we need to know the number of states comprising the instruction cycle. The period of the clock signal must also be known.

Fig. 9-1A.

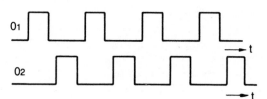

Fig. 9-1B.

The ADD instruction in the chapter "What is a Computer?" has 4 states. If the period of the clock signal is 500 ns, the instruction cycle takes 2 μs. In this way the duration of each instruction cycle can be calculated, as well as the time required for the execution of a program. Figure 9-1c shows an example of timing signals which may occur in a particular instruction cycle.

To understand this diagram we must first know the contents of the input instruction exactly. This takes up 2 bytes. The first byte contains the operation code and indicates which operation must take place (get data from an input port). The second byte indicates the operand, i.e. from which port the data must be obtained. Figure 9-2 shows:

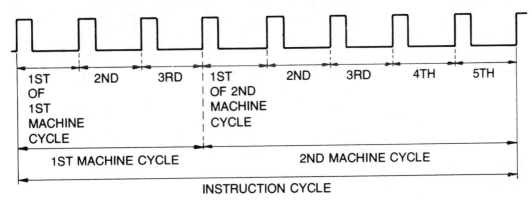

Fig. 9-1C.

CONTROL UNIT

The control unit is one of the most important units within the CPU. Together with the clock generator, the control unit assures the proper completion of the sequential events. After an instruction has been taken from memory and decoded, the control unit generates the signals necessary for the execution of the instruction.

In many microcomputer the control unit also can react independently on external signals. For example, in the event of an interrupt request from a teletype wanting to feed in data, the control unit will interrupt the execution of the main program and allow a given subroutine to be executed. A ready signal from memory or an I/O port also arrives via the control unit. The ready signal is used if memory or an I/O device is slower than the CPU. The CPU must then wait until memory or an I/O port has the data available.

TIMING DIAGRAMS

All manufacturers publish the characteristics of their microprocessors in the form of a timing diagram. Such a diagram represents a sequence of events as a function of time. A timing diagram can be drawn up for every operation a microcomputer performs. To illustrate this we will use the timing diagram of an input instruction (fig. 9-2).

a. The clock signal 01.

b. The clock signal 02 derived from 01.

c. A synchronization signal SYNC - derived from 02. Among other things, the synchronization signal indicates the start of a machine cycle.

d. The absence or presence of signals A_0 to A_{15} on the address bus. Because the signals on the address lines A_0 to A_{15} are usually different, we indicate only their presence. This we do thus:

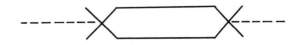

If no signals are present on the address bus, this is indicated by a dotted line (see above).

e. The absence or presence of signals D_0 to D_7 on the data bus.

In fig. 9-2 three machine cycles, M1 to M3, are shown. The operation code is fetched during M1. During M2 the operand address is fetched from memory, and during M3 the instruction is executed, i.e. the input port

91

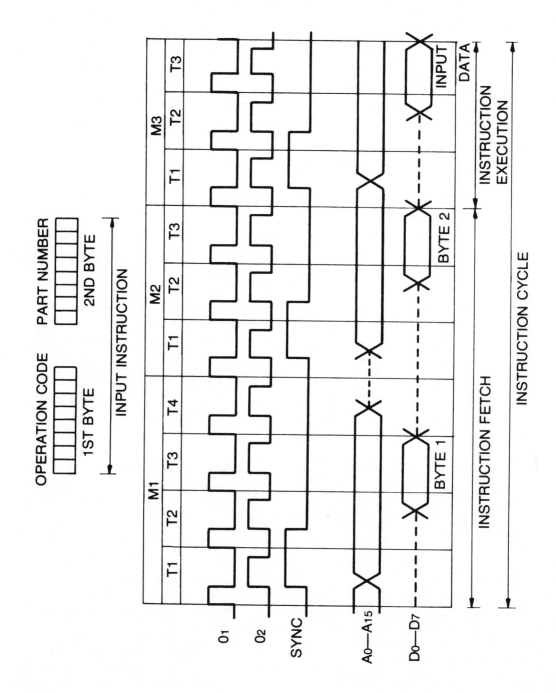

Fig. 9-2.

is addressed and the data transferred to the CPU. Instruction fetch takes place during M1 and M2, and instruction execution during M3. Each machine cycle comprises a number of states. An address is placed on the address lines A0 to A15 during state T2 of every machine cycle. In M1 this is the memory address of the operation code; in M2 the memory address of the operand (port number); and in M3 the port number of the input port concerned.

During state T2 of each machine cycle, a check is made to see if there is any reason why execution of the machine cycle should be delayed. A reason for this could be a difference in speed between the CPU and an I/O port, or between the CPU and memory. If there is cause to wait, the CPU switches to the *wait state*. If there is no cause to wait, the first and second byte of the instruction are fetched from memory during the states (T3) of machine cycles M1 and M2. These are then brought to the CPU via the data lines D0 to D7. During state T3 of machine cycle M3, the instruction is executed and the data is entered.

In the figure we can also see that machine cycle M1 consists not of 3, but of 4 states. This fourth state is used for such operations within the CPU as decoding the operation code.

A separate machine cycle is needed for the execution of an input instruction, because an I/O port is involved. If, however, the execution of an instruction takes place within the CPU, where no memory or I/O device is accessed, the instruction execution takes place during the fourth or possibly the fifth state of the previous machine cycle. So it is possible that an instruction takes only a single machine cycle. An example is the ADD r instruction from one of the previous chapters.

The ADD r instruction comprises 1 byte and is executed within the CPU. It requires that the contents of the general-purpose register r be added to the contents of the accumulator. This takes place within the CPU. Memory is accessed only once, namely when the instruction is fetched, involving, therefore, only one machine cycle.

PIN CONFIGURATION

There is very little difference in the pin configuration of the microprocessors supplied by the various manufacturers (fig. 9-3). Here we will consider one brand, and indicate the difference between this and other brands as they appear.

All microprocessors must be able to access the address bus which is used to transfer addresses to the memory or to an I/O device. Most microprocessors operate with 16-bit addresses, which means that the CPU usually has 16 pins at its disposal, viz. A_0 to A_{15}.

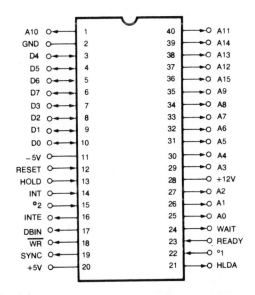

Fig. 9-3.

In some microprocessors some pins have a double function. One moment they may indicate the state of an address bit, while at another they may contain information about reading or writing in the memory. Sometimes 8 address pins also serve as connectors to the data bus. Using these techniques is called multiplexing.

D_0 to D_7 (IN/OUT)

Every 8-bit microprocessor has 8 pins to connect to the data bus. These connections are bi-directional, i.e. data is transferred both to and from the CPU via these pins.

01 and 02 (Inputs)

In fig. 9-3, pin 22 and 15 are the inputs for the clock signals 01 and 02. In this microprocessor the clock signals are generated by external logic. Some microprocessors only require the clock signal 01, 02 then being derived from 01 within the microprocessor.

SYNC (Output)

The synchronization signal in fig. 9-3 is available on pin 19. This tells memory and the I/O device that the CPU has begun a new machine cycle, so that they remain in synchronism with the CPU.

+12V, −5V, +5V, GND (Inputs)

Every microprocessor needs a supply voltage. In the CPU shown in fig. 9-3 this is +12 V, −5 V, +5 V and GND (ground). Other microprocessors only need +5 V and GND.

RESET (Input)

The RESET input enables us to set the contents of the program counter to 0000_{16}. In fig. 5-24 (19 to 21), a RESET pulse is automatically generated by an RC circuit when the supply voltage is turned on. This ensures that the address of the first instruction to be executed is correctly defined. The contents of the remaining CPU registers remain undefined after the application of a RESET signal.

WR (Output)

Data is transported over the data bus in two directions, i.e. from CPU to either memory or I/O port, or vice versa. The CPU must inform the memory or I/O port as to whether it wants to write in (WRITE operation) or read out (READ operation). The CPU indicates a write operation with a low or a high signal at the WR (write) output. Some microprocessors continually issue a WRP (write pulse) during a memory write or output operation, which synchronizes the memory or the I/O device.

READY (Input)

When a data transfer must take place between the memory or an input device and the CPU, it must first send an address to indicate where the data must be sent to or taken from. This address is first decoded in memory or in an I/O port and then the destination or source is selected. Some time therefore elapses before the actual exchange of data can take place. This time is called *access time*. When the access time has elapsed, the memory or input port indicates this by sending a signal to the ready input of the microprocessor. The CPU then knows that the data exchange can take place.

WAIT (Output)

The CPU indicates that it is in the *wait* state, for example during access time, by a signal on the WAIT output.

DBIN (Output)

When the CPU accepts data through a memory read or an Input operation, it indicates this by a signal at the DBIN (Data Bus IN) Output.

HOLD (Input) and HLDA (Output)

A large quantity of data originating, for example, from a floppy disc can be entered into main memory from the microcomputer without the intervention of the CPU. This is called Direct Memory Access or DMA. In DMA the CPU must, however, be disconnected from the address bus and the data bus. In other words, the in- and outputs D_0 to D_7 and the outputs A_0 to A_{15} of the CPU must be high impedance or floating. This is done by a signal to the HOLD input of the CPU. If the CPU accepts a HOLD request and has disconnected itself from the data bus and the address bus, it indicates this by a signal at the HLDA output (Hold Acknowledge output).

In some microprocessors the HOLD Input is called the *pause input* and the HLDA Output the *run/wait output*.

INT (Input) and INTE (Output)

An interrupt request from, for example, an input device wishing to transfer data comes into the CPU on the interrupt input. In the 8080 microprocessor (fig. 9-3) an instruction can be used forbidding the CPU to answer an interrupt request. The microprocessor indicates this by a signal on the INTE (INTerrupt-Enable) Output.

If the INTE signal is 1, an interrupt request can be accepted. If the INTE signal is 0, the I/O device knows an interrupt request to the CPU is unacceptable. Some microprocessors indicate acceptance of an interrupr request by a signal at the INTA (INTerrupt Acknowledge) Output.

HARDWARE TK80

In this section we will discuss in more detail several of the subjects earlier touched upon using fig. 5-24 in the chapter "Circuitry in a Computer". This section will not be included in the examination.

Clock Oscillator 8224

We discussed how the 8224 is used in the RESETing and supplying the voltage V_{BB} in the chapter "Circuitry in a Computer". The main function of this clock oscillator is really supplying clock pulses 01 and 02 to the CPU. Figure 9-4a shows a part of the 8224 that generates the signals 01 and 02 using an external crystal. A crystal is connected to the points 14 and 15. The oscillator generates a signal F with a frequency determined by the crystal. In the microcomputer under discussion here this is about 18 MHz. The digital divide-by-nine circuit converts this into 2 clock signals 01 and 02 (see fig. 9-4b). The pulses of the divide-by-nine circuit are at TTL levels ("1" = 3.3 V, "0" = 0 V). Two buffers convert this into the voltage levels required for the 8080 ('1' = 8 V, '0' = 1 V).

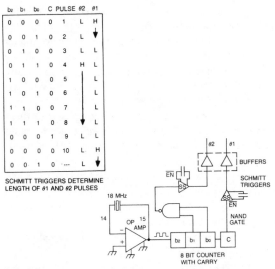

Fig. 9-4A.

The frequency of 01 and 02 is thus $1/9 \times 18$ MHz = 2 MHz.

Note 1

In addition the 8224 makes the signal 02 available at TTL levels. This signal is not used in the microcomputer shown in fig. 5-24. It is used, however, within the 8224 to obtain the fixed pulse width of the RESET 1-shot (see figs. 5-24 and 5-25 of the chapter "Circuitry in a Computer).

Note 2

Figure 9-4a also illustrates how the Output signal OSC for V_{BB} is obtained from the signal F via a buffer. (See the chapter "Circuitry in a Computer".)

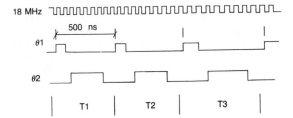

Fig. 9-4B.

SUMMARY

1. An instruction cycle is the time required for the execution of the instruction fetch and the instruction execution.

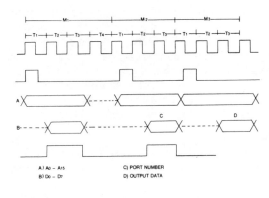

| A) A0 – A15 | C) PORT NUMBER |
| B) D0 – D7 | D) OUTPUT DATA |

Fig. 9-4C.

2. An instruction cycle comprises 1 to 5 machine cycles. A machine cycle comprises 3 to 5 states.

3. The number of machine cycles equals the number of times that the CPU must address memory or an I/O device.

4. A state is the smallest possible action a microcompter can perform. A state is executed during one period of the clock signal.

5. The control unit ensures the proper completion of sequential events. The timing of these events is regulated by the timing unit.

6. The characteristics of a microprocessor can be illustrated by a timing diagram. A timing diagram represents a sequence of events as a function of time.

7. An 8-bit microprocessor has 8 pins for connections to the data bus. Most 8-bit microprocessors have 16 pins for connections to the address bus. In some of these microprocessors some pins have a double function.

8. Every microprocessor has, in addition to pins for connections to address and data bus, a number of control inputs and outputs.

REVIEW EXERCISES

1. What is the timing unit used for?
2. How is the clock signal for a microprocessor usually constructed?
3. Which 2 cycles comprise an instruction cycle?
4. What is the function of the control unit?
5. What determines the number of machine cycles?
6. What happens during the first machine cycle of each instruction cycle?

7. What is a state?

8. What is checked during the second state of each machine cycle?

9. What reason could there be for interrupting the execution of a machine cycle for a short period of time?

10. What can be read from a timing diagram?

11. Why does one need a separate machine cycle for the instruction execution of an output instruction?

12. What is the RESET input used for?

13. What does the WR output indicate?

14. What is the READY input used for?

ANSWERS

1. The timing unit serves to regulate the sequence and combined action of events in the microcomputer.

2. From two non-overlapping square waves 01 and 02.

3. The instruction cycle comprises the instruction fetch and instruction execution.

4. The control unit, together with the clock generator, takes care of the proper completion of sequential events.

5. The number of machine cycles is equal to the number of times that the CPU must access the memory or an I/O device.

6. The operation code is taken from memory during M1 of each instruction cycle.

7. A state is the smallest possible action that a microcomputer can perform.

8. During state T2 of each machine cycle, a check is made to see if there is any reason for breaking off the further execution of the machine cycle.

9. One reason for temporarily stopping the execution of a machine cycle would be a difference in speed between the CPU and an I/O port or the CPU and memory.

10. One can see from a timing diagram the sequence of events.

11. Because an I/O port is accessed during execution of an output instruction.

12. The RESET Input is used to set the contents of the program counter to zero.

13. The WR output is used to indicate that the information from the data bus must be entered in the memory word indicated by the address on the address bus.

14. When memory or an I/O port has decoded an address that the CPU has placed on the address bus, the READY input sends a signal to the CPU indicating that a location can be written or read out.

Chapter 10

Microcomputer Architecture

A microcomputer consists of 4 parts:

- The CPU
- main memory, made up of 1 or more memory modules
- I/O ports
- the bus system.

In this chapter we will discuss the schematic construction of these units. We will not discuss the block diagram of the CPU in detail as it has been covered extensively in previous chapters. At the end of the chapter the block diagrams of the above-mentioned components will be put together to form a block diagram of the microcomputer as a whole. With this block diagram we will examine the data flow for some instructions.

BLOCK DIAGRAM OF THE CPU

The block diagram we have seen in the chapter "CPU Architecture 1" is shown again in fig. 10-1. We see, however, several additions:

a. A temporary register (TEM) which temporarily stores data until taken over by one of the CPU registers or the ALU.

b. A temporary general-purpose register—W, Z—to store data temporarily during the execution of an instruction.

These temporary registers were purposely omitted in the chapter "CPU Architecture 1", since they cannot be accessed by the programmer. However, we need them when discussing data flow during the execution of the instructions.

BLOCK DIAGRAM OF MEMORY

The block diagram of a memory is shown in fig. 10-2. Each memory is made up of a large number of memory cells. 1 bit can be stored in each memory cell. In an 8-bit microcomputer, 8 cells are combined to make 1 memory word where one byte can be stored.

The number of memory words which can be addressed (and also used) is determined by the word length of the memory address. If a CPU can handle memory addresses of 16 bits as in fig. 10-2, no purpose is served by combining it with a memory of more than $2^{16} = 65536$ memory words.

The address-selection circuit shown in fig. 10-2 connects the memory word associated with a given memory address to the data bus. Each of the 8 memory cells of a memory word is connected to the related line of the data bus. Together with the memory address, the CPU sends a control signal to memory via a line of the control bus. This indicates whether data must be entered in the memory (WRITE) or read from the memory (READ). When an address has been selected, the memory indicates this by putting a signal on the ready line of the control bus. A signal on the ready line in a memory write operation indicates that the data can be entered into the memory, or in a memory read operation that the CPU can accept the data.

BLOCK DIAGRAM OF AN I/O MODULE

The CPU can exchange data with the outside world via I/O modules. An I/O module (fig. 10-3) comprises the following parts:

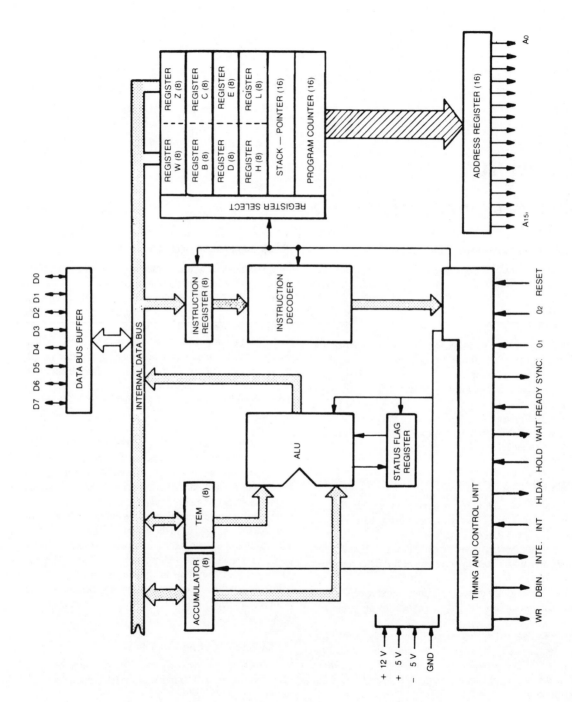

Fig. 10-1.

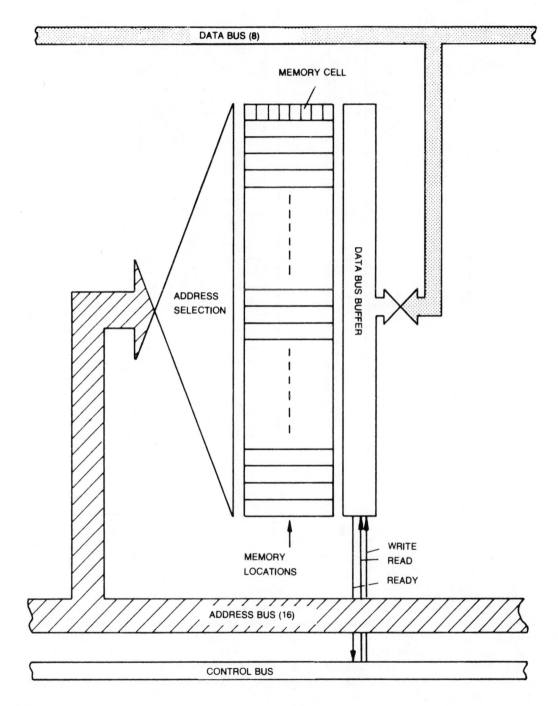

Fig. 10-2.

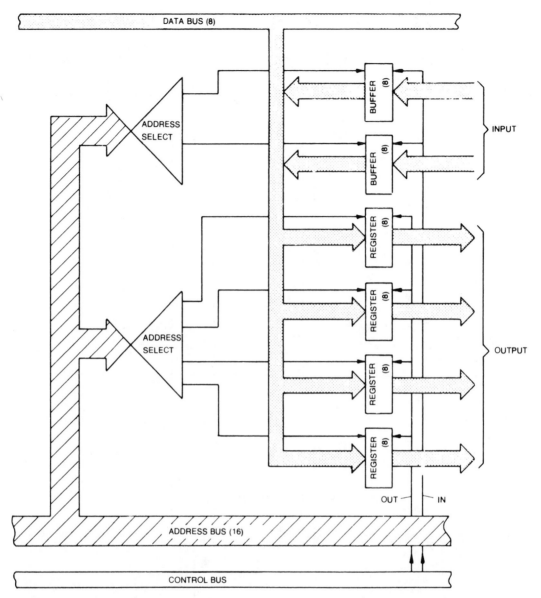

Fig. 10-3.

a. A selection mechanism which decodes the address (port number) given by the CPU and thus indicates the correct Input or Output port;

b. A number of Output ports; these are registers in which data is stored so that it can be accepted by an Output device. The information is retained in an Output port until it is changed by a new Output operation;

c. A number of Input ports (buffers), through which the data is transferred to the CPU. During an Input operation these Input ports are sampled. In other words, the signal is let through for only an instant.

To output information, the I/O logic must perform the following operations:

a. The Output register that will receive the data presented by the CPU is selected. This is done by an address (port number) from the CPU.

100

b. An OUT command indicates when the data presented by the CPU can be accepted by the Output register.

c. The Output register must take over the data and make it available to the outside world.

In order to input information the following operations must be performed by the I/O logic:

a. The Input buffer must be selected.

b. An IN command indicates at which instant the buffer must sample the signal connected to the input port and transfer it to the CPU.

The I/O module shown in fig. 10-3 contains 4 Output ports and 2 Input ports. Other combinations of Input and Output ports are, of course, possible. The number of bits the CPU has available to indicate a port number determines the maximum number of Input and Output ports which can be addressed. With 8 bits the maximum number of input and output ports which can be addressed is $2^8 = 256$. This does not mean, however, that 256 I/O devices can be connected to the microcomputer. One I/O device often needs more than one port.

SYNCHRONIZATION

When the CPU needs data from memory it transmits a memory address and a ready signal to memory. Memory decodes the memory address, looks for the memory word requested and puts the contents of it on the data bus from which the CPU can take it over.

It is clear that memory cannot immediately produce the data requested when it receives an address and a read command. This takes a certain amount of time, known as the access time. Memory indicates when the access time has elapsed by transmitting a ready signal. Until the CPU has received the ready signal it must wait. The CPU is then in a wait state. The process of waiting until the access time has elapsed and the CPU has received the ready signal is called a ready wait cycle. A ready wait cycle takes place not only in a memory read operation, but also when the CPU accesses memory or an I/O device—in other words, whenever the CPU transmits an address and must then wait until it is decoded, either in memory or in an I/O module. A ready wait cycle is a part of the machine cycle.

The ready signal and wait state can also be used in other ways. By making the presence or absence of the ready signal dependent on a switch or pushbutton on the computer console, as well as on the memory or I/O module, one can extend the WAIT state as long as desired. The state of the computer, as shown by lamps can thus be examined step-by-step. Each time the pushbutton

is depressed, the ready signal is momentarily present. The processor can, in this way, run through exactly *one* ready cycle and stop again at the ready wait cycle of the next machine cycle. This method of letting the CPU run through one cycle on the command of a pushbutton on the console is called *single step.* It is an aid in checking the operation of a computer and in looking for mistakes in a program.

DATA FLOW

The three block diagrams just discussed are combined in fig. 10-4 to form a block diagram of the microcomputer. The connection between the CPU, memory and the I/O module is the bus system which comprises the following parts:

a. the address bus (16 lines), to bring an address from the CPU to memory or an I/O module

b. the data bus (8 lines) to transport data

c. The control bus, to transport the control signals, such as *READY, READ, WRITE,* etc.

On the basis of the block diagram in fig. 10-4 we will now discuss how the flow of data takes place during the execution of an instruction cycle. First we discuss the data flow during the instruction fetch of a 1 byte instruction and then the data flow during the instruction fetch of the following instructions.

Register to Register Transfer

This is an instruction which transfers data from one general-purpose register to another. The general form of this instruction is MOV r_1, r_2, MOV is the mnemonic for the operation code "move." The associated general-purpose registers are indicated by r_1 and r_2.

Memory to Register Transfer

This instruction transfers the contents of a memory word to one of the general-purpose registers in the CPU. The general form of this instruction is MOV r, M. The letter M here means the memory word, the address of which is in registers H and L.

Input

This one transfers data from an Input port to the accumulator. The general form of this instruction is IN port. #. IN is the mnemonic of the operation code 'input'. By "port" we mean the port number, i.e. the address of the Input port where the data comes from.

Instruction Fetch

The instruction fetch is a part of every instruction cycle. With it the instruction code is obtained from mem-

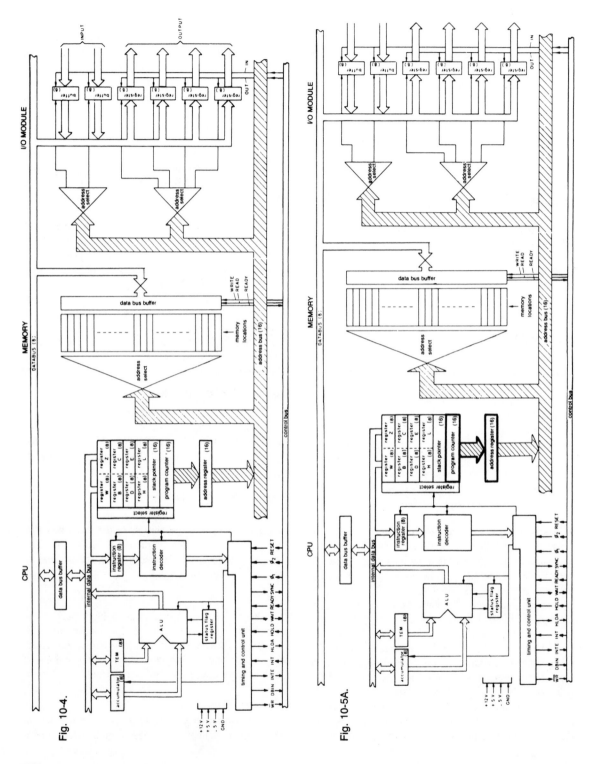

Fig. 10-4.

Fig. 10-5A.

102

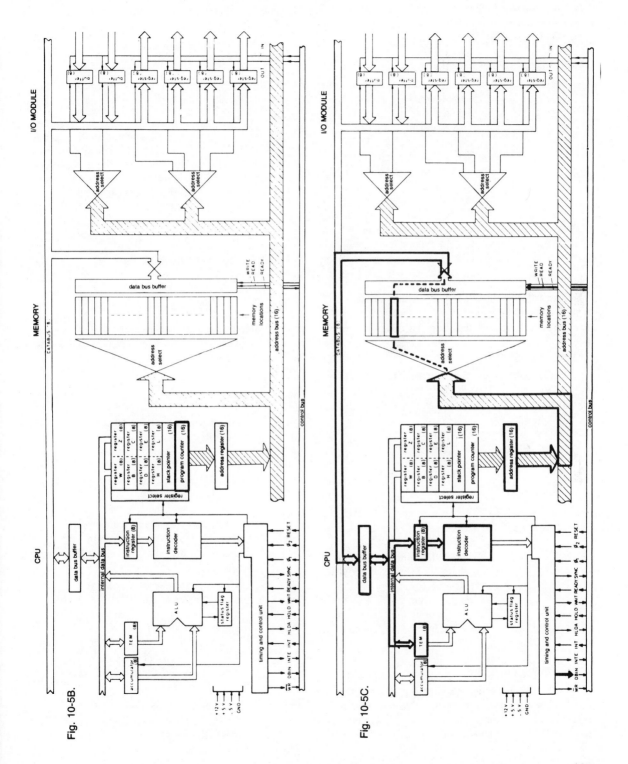

Fig. 10-5B.

Fig. 10-5C.

ory and transferred to the CPU. The instruction fetch in a 1 byte instruction (which we will be discussing) takes up 1 machine cycle (M).

Machine cycle	State	Description
M_1	T_1	The contents of the program counter is placed in the address register (fig. 10-5a)
M_1	T_2	The program counter is incremented by 1 (fig. 10-5b)
M_1	T_3	The instruction code is taken from memory and stored in the instruction register and in the temporary auxiliary register TEM. The instruction decoder next takes over control (fig. 10-5c). Everything that takes place thereafter depends wholly upon the operation code just fetched.

The instruction fetch (in a 1 byte instruction) takes up 3 states. With a clock frequency of 2 MHz, 1 state lasts 500 ns. The instruction fetch thus lasts 3×500 ns or $1.5\ \mu s$.

Register to Register Transfer

With this instruction the contents of r_2 is transferred to r. An example is; MOV E, B. In this case registers E and B, respectively, are chosen as r_1 and r_2.

Machine cycle	State	Description
M_1	T_1	Instruction fetch
M_1	T_2	
M_1	T_3	
M_1	T_4	The contents of register B (r_2) is transferred to the temporary register TEM (fig. 10-6a)
M_1	T_5	The contents of the temporary register TEM is transferred to register E (r_1). See fig. 10-6b.

The total time necessary for this instruction amounts to 5 states of 500 ns each = $2.5\ \mu s$.

Memory to Register Transfer

With this instruction register r is filled with the contents of the memory word M, whose address is in register H,L. An example is; MOV D, M. In this case register D has been chosen for register r.

Machine cycle	State	Description
M_1	T_1	Instruction fetch
M_1	T_2	
M_1	T_3	
M_1	T_4	Instruction is decoded
M_2	T_1	The address register is filled with the contents of the register pair H, L (fig. 10-7a)
M_2	$T_{2,3}$	The contents of the address register is transferred to memory and decoded. The data from the selected memory location is transferred to register D (fig. 10-7b).

The total time necessary for this instruction is 7 states of 500 ns each = $3.5\ \mu s$.

Input

With this instruction, data is transferred from an Input port to the accumulator. Because this instruction comprises 2 bytes, the memory is accessed twice during the instruction fetch.

Mach. cycle	State	
M_1	T_1	first part of the instruction fetch (operation code)
M_1	T_2	
M_1	T_3	
M_1	T_4	Instruction is decoded
M_2	T_1	The address of the second byte of the instruction (port number) travels from the program counter to the address register (fig. 10-8a)
M_2	T_2	The program counter is incremented by 1 (fig. 10-8b)
M_2	T_3	The second byte of the instruction (the port number) is taken from memory and placed in registers W and Z (fig. 10-8c)
M_3	T_1	The address register is filled with the contents of registers W and Z (fig. 10-8d)

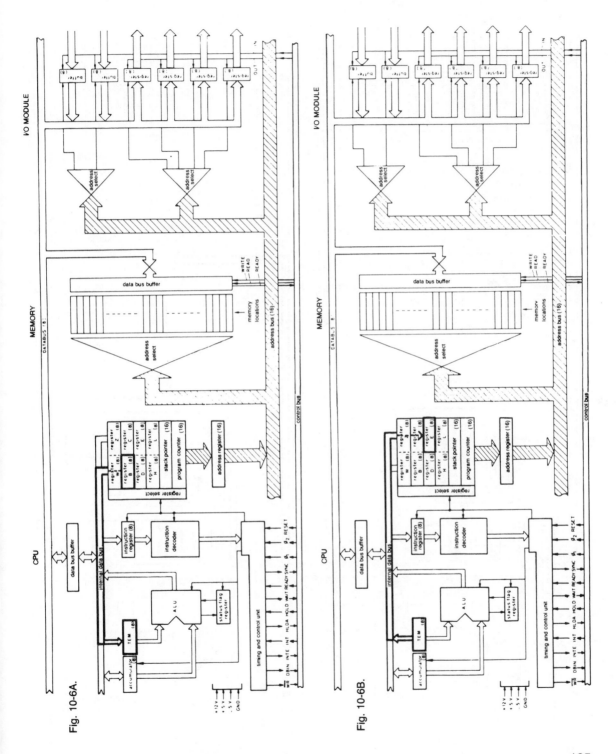

Fig. 10-6A.

Fig. 10-6B.

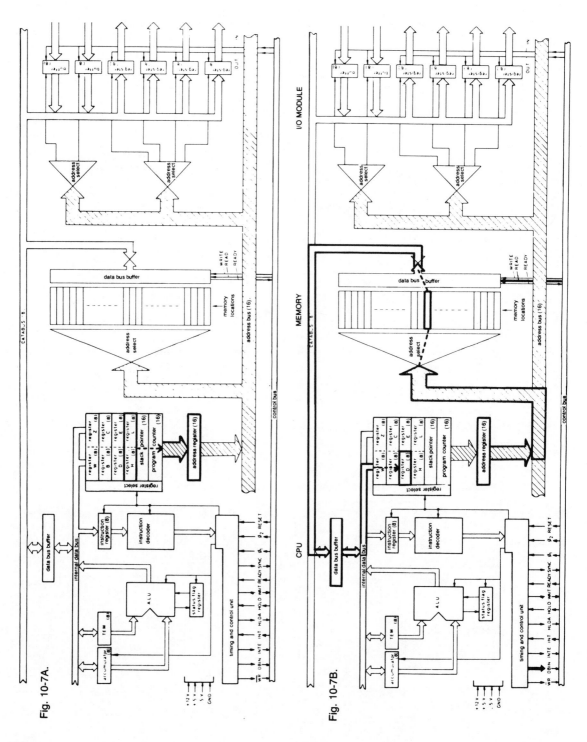

Fig. 10-7A.

Fig. 10-7B.

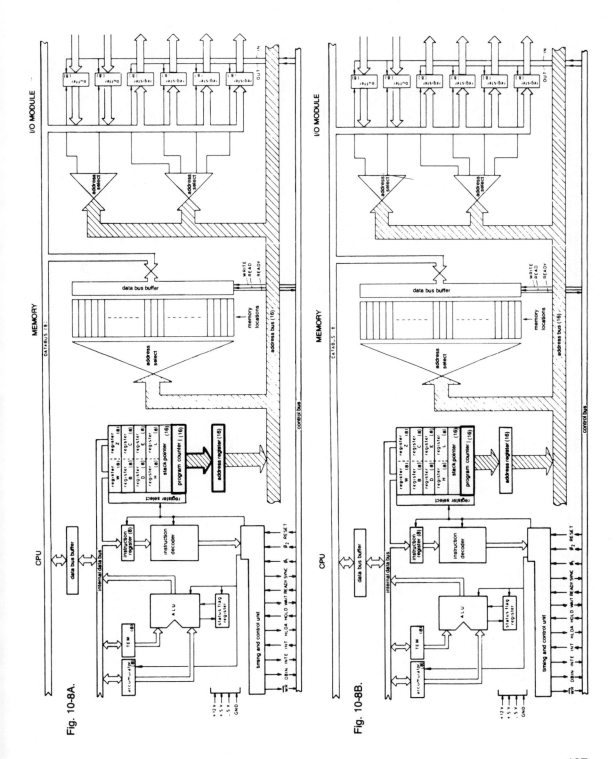

Fig. 10-8A.

Fig. 10-8B.

107

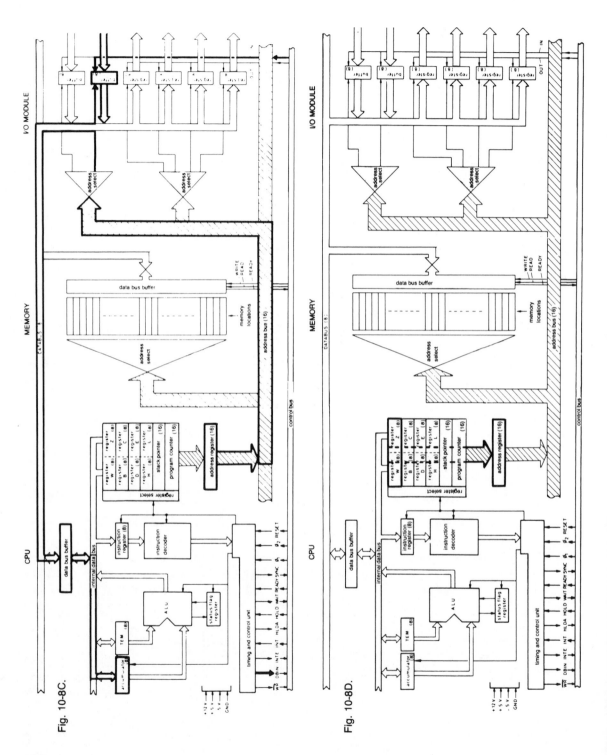

Fig. 10-8C.

Fig. 10-8D.

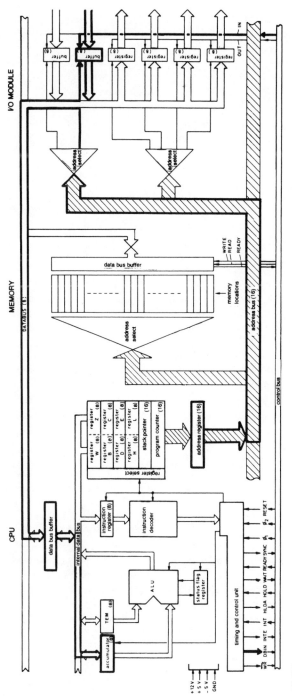

Fig. 10-8E.

Mach. State
cycle

M_3 $T_{2,3}$ contents of the address register are transferred to the I/O
module, where the address
selection takes place. The contents of the selected input port is
then transferred to the accumulator (fig. 10-8e)

$\Big\}$ instruction execution

The total time necessary for this instruction is 10 states of 500 ns = 5 μs.

SUMMARY

1. A computer comprises:

● the CPU
● main memory
● I/O ports
● the bus system

2. A memory is made up of a large number of memory cells, each of which can contain 1 bit. In an 8-bit microcomputer, 8 memory cells make one memory word.

3. The CPU sends, along with the memory address, a read or write signal to memory to indicate whether data has to be taken from the CPU and brought to memory or taken from memory and brought to the CPU.

4. Memory indicates when the address selection has taken place by means of a ready signal.

5. An I/O module comprises an address selection mechanism and a number of Input and Output ports.

6. An Output port is a register than stores data until it is taken over by an output device. The data is retained in an Output port until it is changed by a new Output operation.

7. An Input port is a buffer that, during an input operation, samples the signal offered to it.

8. The *access time* is the time necessary for the decoding of a memory address or a port number.

9. The process of waiting until access time is over and the CPU receives a *ready* signal, is called the *ready wait* cycle.

10. The *single step* is a method of letting the CPU run through one machine cycle at a time on the command of a pushbutton on the console.

REVIEW EXERCISES

1. Which circuit assures that the correct memory word is accessed at the related memory address?

2. How does memory indicate that the address selection has taken place?

3. What is an I/O module made up of?

4. What operations must be performed by the I/O logic in order to be able to output data?

5. If a channel number contains 8 bits, what is the maximum number of input and output ports which can be addressed?

6. What is access time?

7. What is a ready wait cycle?

8. What is the connection between a ready wait cycle and a machine cycle?

9. How is the single-step method realized?

10. What is the single-step method used for?

ANSWERS

1. The address selection circuit.

2. With the help of a signal of the ready line.

3. a. A selection mechanism.
   b. A number of output ports (registers)
   c. A number of input ports (buffers)

4. a. The output register must be selected.
   b. The OUT command indicates when the data sent out by the CPU is on the data bus.
   c. The output register must accept the data.

5. $2^8 = 256$ input and output ports.

6. This is the time that memory needs to produce or receive the correct data after getting an address and a read or write command.

7. This is the process of waiting until the access time has elapsed and the CPU has received a READY signal.

8. A READY WAIT cycle is a part of the machine cycle.

9. Through making the absence or presence of a ready signal not only dependent upon memory or an I/O module, but also on a switch or pushbutton on the computer console.

10. For checking the operation of the computer and looking for mistakes in a program.

Chapter 11
Description of
the Instructions

A computer needs a program before it can execute a series of sequential operations. If the program is written in a high-level programming language, such as PL/M, we do not have to concern ourselves with the characteristics of the particular microcomputer. We only need to know the language. If we write the series of operations to be executed in assembly language, however, we must first know which operations the microcomputer can perform. In other words, we must know its instruction set.

An instruction set can be divided into 5 groups:

a. Transfer instructions that, for example, transport data from memory to the CPU.

b. Arithmetic instructions, such as addition and subtraction.

c. Logic instructions, e.g. processing 2 bytes with an AND function.

d. Jump instructions, i.e., JUMP, CALL, RETURN.

e. Special instructions; for example HALT.

We will now examine several instructions from each group in more detail. We shall base our discussion on the instruction set of the Intel 8080 given in Appendix A. These give the general form of each instruction. For example, the letter r means one of the general-purpose registers or the accumulator in the 8080, and the letters rp one of the register pairs. When the letters "addr" are given, a 16-bit address must be filled in and for "data" a given 8-bit number.

TRANSPORT INSTRUCTIONS

A transfer instruction commands the microprocessor to transfer data from one place to another. A transfer instruction must always have a *source* and a *destination*. The following rules must be adhered to:

a. In an instruction we first mention the destination and then the source.

b. *If the source or the destination of the instruction is the memory word M, the address of this memory word can always be found in the general-purpose registers H and L.*

The high-order byte of the address is always in register H, while register L contains the low-order byte. Applying this to address $3F4A_{16}$, register H contains $3F_{16}$, register L contains $4A_{16}$.

MOV

In a MOV (move) instruction the source and the destination can be:

a. a register and a memory word

b. a memory word and a register word

c. a register and another register

For example, MOV A, B. A stands for accumulator. B is a general-purpose register in the CPU. This instruction means that the contents of register B must be placed in the accumulator. The former contents of the accumulator are erased. After the execution of the instruction, the contents of register B remains unchanged, they have simply been copied.

In MOV M,D, M is a memory word. D is a general-purpose register in the CPU. The instruction means that the contents of register D must be transferred to a memory word, the address of which is indicated in registers H and L.

The MOV instruction takes up 1 byte. The highest 2 bits indicate the operation code (01), the remaining 6 bits the source and destination. In the instruction MOV M,D, for example, the 3rd to 5th bits indicate that the destination is a memory word, the address of which is given in registers H and L. The zero to second bit indicate that the source is register D.

MVI

The MVI instruction (*MoVe Immediate*) differs from the MOV instruction in that the source is an 8-bit constant which immediately follows the MVI instruction. The destination is a register or a memory word. MVI M, 10111001B means that the value 10111001_2 must be transferred to the memory address, the address of which is in registers H and L. The letter B following 10111001 indicates that this is a binary number. The constant could also have been input in the form of a decimal or hexadecimal number. In which case we must place a D or an H immediately after the number when writing a program. The assembly translation program converts this number into a binary number.

MVI A, 'D' means that the letter D—coded in ASCII—must be taken to the accumulator. Here the assembly translation program makes the necessary translation. The fact that 'D' is placed between inverted commas shows that 'D' is a character. These quotation marks must not be forgotten when entering a program. If they are, the computer will recognize this letter D as something else; for example a hexadecimal number.

Note

In this context the word 'immediate' indicates that the operand immediately follows the operation code.

LDA

The LDA instruction (*LoaD Accumulator*) loads the accumulator with the contents of the memory address, the address of which follows the operation code (LDA). LDA 2FFFH means that the contents of the memory word with the address $2FFF_{16}$ must be transferred to the accumulator. The LDA instruction takes up 3 bytes—one for the operation code (LDA) and two for the address $(2FFF_{16})$.

LXI

The LXI instruction (Load register pair Immediate) can be used to fill the register pairs BC, DE or HL with a 16-bit number in one step. This number is indicated immediately following the operation code. The LXI instruction is, in a way, a variant of the MVI instruction, but in the MVI instruction we use an 8-bit number.

Example

Given: Load register pair H, L with the value $3FF4_{16}$.

Solution 1: MVI H,3FH
MVI L,F4H

Solution 2: LXI H,3FF4H

Solution 2 takes up 3 bytes. Solution 1 takes up 4 bytes. In this case solution 2 is the better solution because it takes up less memory space.

OUT/IN

The OUT and IN instructions regulate the traffic with the I/O device. *In an OUT instruction the source is always the accumulator. In an IN instruction the destination is always the accumulator.* Only the *port number* needs to be stated after an IN or OUT operation code, in other words the address of the I/O device where information must be transferred to or from. OUT 03H means that the contents of the accumulator must be transferred to the output port numbered 03_{16}.

IN 06H
MOV M,A

The first instruction transfers the data from input port 06_{16} to the accumulator. It is stored in memory with the second instruction. The address of the memory word concerned is in registers H and L.

Note

In the chapter "Subroutines and Syntax" we shall discuss two more important transfer instructions, namely the PUSH and POP instructions.

ARITHMETIC INSTRUCTIONS

The arithmetic operations a microprocessor can perform take place in the ALU. The commands to process arithmetic operations are given using arithmetic instructions. The 8080 microprocessor, whose instruction set we are considering, can carry out the following arithmetic operations:
- addition
- subtraction

ADD

This instruction set has a 1-address structure. In other words, one of the operands is always located in the accumulator, so no address for it is needed. We must indicate, following the operation code, where the other operand is located. The result (the sum) is placed in the accumulator. The operand which was previously located in the accumulator is erased. ADD H means that the contents of register H must be added to the contents of the accumulator. The sum is placed in the accumulator. An ADD M takes the contents of a memory word, the address of which is in registers H and L, must be added to the contents of the accumulator. The result is placed in the accumulator.

Example

Given: Add the numbers 12_{10} and 84_{10} and bring the result to the memory location $2AA3_{16}$.

Solution: MVI A,12D   Load the accumulator with the number 12_{10}.

MVI B,84D   Load register B with the number 84_{10}.

ADD B   Add the contents of register B to the contents of the accumulator and place the sum in the accumulator.

LXI H, 2AA3H   Load the register pair H,L with $2AA3_{16}$ (the address where the sum must go).

MOV M,A   Bring the contents of the accumulator (the sum) to the memory word M ($2AA3_{16}$).

ADC

A variation of the ADD instruction is the ADC (*AD*d with *C*arry) instruction. Not only are the 2 operands added in the ADC instruction, but also the carry remaining from a prior operation is added to the result in the accumulator. For example, ADC M adds the contents of a memory word, the address of which is in registers H and L, and the contents of the carry status flag to the contents of the accumulator.

ADI /ACI

With the ADI instruction (*AD*d *I*mmediate) we can add a number that immediately follows the instruction to the contents of the accumulator. ADI 16D adds the decimal number 16 to the contents of the accumulator. The sum is placed in the accumulator. If we also wish to add the contents of the status carry flag to the contents of the accumulator we can do this with the ACI (*A*dd with *C*arry *I*mmediate) instruction.

INR

The INR (*IN*c*R*ement) instruction is a variation on the ADD instruction. It tells the microprocessor to increment by one the contents of one of the general-purpose registers, the accumulator or the memory word M. INR C increments the contents of register C.

SUB

The SUB (SUBtract) instruction allows the microprocessor to directly subtract the contents of one of the general-purpose registers or the memory word M from the contents of the accumulator, in other words, without first taking the 2's complement and adding. Also, in this instruction, the result of the calculation is placed in the accumulator.

SBB/SUI/SBI

The SUB instruction has the same variants as the ADD instruction.

SBB = *SuB*tract with *B*orrow

SUI = *SU*btract *I*mmediate

SBI = *S*ubtract with *B*orrow *I*mmediate

SBB H means that not only the content of register H, but also a borrow, if there is one, are subtracted from the contents of the accumulator. The borrow arose out of a prior subtraction and is stored in the carry status flag. SUI 3AH subtracts the hexadecimal number 3A from the contents of the accumulator. The result is put in the accumulator. If we had also wanted to subtract a borrow from the contents of the accumulator, we would have used the instruction SBI 3AH.

DCR

This instruction is used to decrement the contents of one of the general-purpose registers, the accumulator, or a memory word M by 1.

LOGIC INSTRUCTIONS

The following operations can be performed using the logic instructions:

a. The corresponding bits of 2 operands can be processed according to the AND, OR and EXOR functions. One of the operands is always located in the accumulator. The result of the operation is placed in the accumulator. The truth tables representing these functions are shown in fig. 11-1.

b. The 1's complement of a number in the accumulator can be taken.

c. Comparing 2 numbers. The ALU acts as if the numbers are subtracted from each other and the positive, negative, or zero flags are set. The contents of the registers do not change.

d. Shifting the contents of the accumulator to the left or right. This is used to multiply or divide numbers. Shifting all bits in a number 1 place to the left is the same as multiplying that number by 2. Shifting right divides.

AND function		
X	Y	f
0	0	0
0	1	0
1	0	0
1	1	1

OR function		
X	Y	f
0	0	0
0	1	1
1	0	1
1	1	1

EXOR function		
X	Y	f
0	0	0
0	1	1
1	0	1
1	1	0

Fig. 11-1.

ANA

The ANA (*AN*d with *A*ccumulator) instruction is used to process the contents of one of the general-purpose registers or a memory word M with the contents of the accumulator according to the AND function. ANA M means that the contents of the memory word, the address of which is in registers H and L is processed with the content of the accumulator using the AND function. The result of this operation is placed in the accumulator.

ORA

The ORA instruction (OR with Accumulator) is used to process the contents of one of the general-purpose registers or a memory word M with the contents of the accumulator following the OR function. ORA B causes the contents of register B to be processed with the contents of the accumulator using the OR function. The result is placed in the accumulator.

XRA

The XRA (e*X*clusive o*R* with *A*ccumulator) instruction is used to process the contents of one of the general-purpose registers or a memory word M with the contents of the accumulator using the EXOR function.

The ANA, ORA and XRA instructions also have an immediate form. The contents of the accumulator are then processed with the next number after the instruction. These instructions have the mnemonics; ANI, ORI, and XRI.

There are two ways to check the condition of the third bit (b_2) of the contents of register B.

MOV A,B   The content of register B is brought to the accumulator. (All logic operations take place here).

ANI 00000100B   Process the content of the accumulator with the value 00000100_2 using the AND function. If b_2 in register B has the value 0, the result is 00000000_2 and the zero status flag is set. If b_2 in register B has the value 1, the result is 00000100_2 and the zero status flag is *not* set. From the content of the zero status flag we can see whether b_2 of register B is 0 or 1.
Or

MVI A,00000100B ANA B   Fill the accumulator with 00000100_2. Process the contents of register B with the contents of the accumulator.

We might now ask ourselves which solution is the better one. Both solutions use 3 memory locations. Solution 2 is preferred because it is faster. The time required to execute an operation can be determined by checking how many states each instruction uses. The number of states each instruction takes up is given in the instruction set. For solution 1 the total is 12 states. For solution 2 the total is 11 states.

Change b_5 of the contents of the memory word with address 0400_{16}. Assume that the content of this memory word is 01110100_2.

LXI H,0400H   Load registers H and L with the value 0400_{16}.

MVI A,00100000B   Put the number 00100000 in the accumulator.

XRA M   Process the contents of the memory word, the address of which is in registers H and L with the content of the accumulator using the EXOR function. This results in only b_5 changing.

CMA

The microprocessor uses the CMA (*C*o*M*plement *A*ccumulator) instruction to take the 1's complement of the contents of the accumulator. If we want to find the 1's complement of the contents of one of the general-purpose registers or a memory word, we must first bring it to the accumulator. For example, to replace the contents of the memory address with address 0200_{16} by it's 2's complement:

LXI H,0200H   Load registers H and L with the value 0200_{16}.

MOV A,M   Bring the contents of memory place M to the accumulator.

CMA   Take the 1's complement of the contents of the accumulator.

INR A   Increase the contents of the accumulator by 1 (2's complement = 1's complement + 1).

MOV M,A   Bring the contents of the accumulator to the memory place with address 0200_{16}.

CMP

As the mnemonic implies, the CMP (*CoMP*are) instruction can be used to compare 2 numbers. One of the numbers is always located in the accumulator. In this comparison a simulated subtraction is performed and the result checked to see if it is positive, negative or zero. This can be seen from the contents of the carry status flag and the zero status flag. *The only difference between a CMP and a SUB instruction is that, in a CMP instruction, the result is not put in the accumulator* and the contents of the accumulator is thus *not* erased. A variation of the CMP instruction is the CPI (*ComP*are *I*mmediate) instruction. Now the contents of the accumulator are compared with the number immediately following the operation code.

RLC

The RLC (*R*otate *L*eft in *C*arry) instruction causes the contents of the accumulator to rotate one bit to the left. In other words, all bits are shifted one place to the left. At the same time the eighth bit is placed in the carry status flag *and* in position b_0 (see fig 11-2).

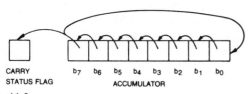

CARRY STATUS FLAG   ACCUMULATOR

Fig. 11-2.

If we want to move the contents of a memory word or one of the general-purpose registers, we must first bring the contents to the accumulator which is the only place where this operation can be performed. To load the carry status flag with b_6 of the contents of register L:

MOV A,L   Bring the contents of register L to the accumulator.

RLC   The contents of the accumulator rotated 1 bit to the left. B_7 goes to the carry status flag and b_6 becomes b_7.

RLC   The contents of the accumulator are again shifted 1 bit to the left. B_6 is now in the carry status flag.

RAL

The RAL (*R*otate *A*ccumulator *L*eft) instruction is also used to rotate the contents of the accumulator 1 bit to the left. The eighth (b_7) bit only goes to the carry status flag. The first bit position in the accumulator (b_0 is loaded with the old contents of the carry status flag (fig. 11-3)

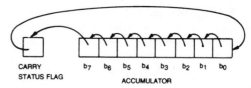

CARRY STATUS FLAG   ACCUMULATOR

Fig. 11-3.

RRC/RAR

With the RRC (*R*otate accumulator *R*ight in *C*arry) instruction the contents of the accumulator rotates 1 bit to the right. The contents of b_0 travel to the carry status flag *and* to bit position b_7 in the accumulator (fig. 11-4a)

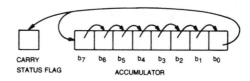

CARRY STATUS FLAG   ACCUMULATOR

Fig. 11-4A.

The RAR (*R*otate *A*ccumulator *R*ight through carry) instruction rotates the contents of the accumulator 1 bit to the right. B_0 goes to the carry status flag. The old contents of the carry status flag become b_7 in the accumulator (see fig. 11-4b).

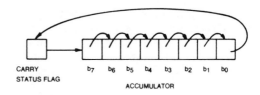

CARRY STATUS FLAG   ACCUMULATOR

Fig. 11-4B.

JUMP INSTRUCTIONS

Instructions are stored in consecutive locations in memory and are transferred to the CPU and executed in ascending sequential order of address. This sequence can be interrupted by one of the jump instructions. The jump instruction includes the address of the next instruction to be carried out. There are unconditional and conditional jump instructions.

Unconditional Jump Instructions

The program always jumps to the address which follows the instruction.

Conditional Jump Instructions

A jump is only made if the contents of one of the status flags conforms to a certain condition. The instruction determines which status flags must answer to which condition (0 or 1). If the condition is not satisfied, the jump is not performed and the program continues executing the instructions succeeding the jump instruction. A conditional jump can take place in reference to the contents of:

● the carry status flag
● the sign status flag
● the zero status flag
● the parity status flag.

JC

A JC (*J*ump on *C*arry) instruction is carried out only if a previous operation resulted in a carry—in other words, if the carry status flag is set.

JNC

A JNC (*J*ump *N*o *C*arry) instruction is performed only if the contents of the carry status flag is 0.

    BEGIN: ADI 01H
             JNC BEGIN
             MOV B,A

The first 2 instructions increment the contents of the accumulator by 1 (ADI 01H) until a carry appears. The JNC instruction ensures that, if no carry appears, a jump is made to the memory address with the symbolic name BEGIN. This is the address of the instruction ADI 01H. When a carry *does* appear the jump instruction is not performed. The program continues with the next instruction given; in this case MOV B,A. (The meaning of the colon (:) following BEGIN will be explained in the next chapter).

JZ/JNZ

The JZ (*J*ump on *Z*ero) instruction is a conditional instruction which is only carried out if the result of the previous operation was 0—in other words, if the zero status flag is set. The JNZ (*J*ump on *N*o *Z*ero) instruction is only carried out if the result was *not* 0—if the zero status flag is not set. Load the contents of memory word 0800_{16} with 100_{10} and then decrement by 1 until the result is zero.

LXI H,0800H   Registers H and L are loaded with the value 0800_{16}.

MVI M,100D   Memory word 0800_{16} is loaded with the value 100_{10}.

MIN:

DCR M   The contents of memory address 0800_{16} decremented by 1.

JNZ MIN   Jump to memory address MIN if the zero status flag is not yet set, i.e. if the contents of memory location 0800_{16} are not equal to zero.

JM/JP

The JM (*J*ump on *M*inus) instruction is only performed if the result of the previous operation is a negative number, i.e. if the contents of the sign status flag is 1. The JP (*J*ump on *P*ositive) instruction is only carried out if the result of the previous operation is a positive number, i.e. if the contents of the sign status flag is 0. Subtract the contents of memory word 0310_{16} from the contents of memory address 0311_{16} and jump to address NEG if the result is negative.

LXI H,0311H   Registers H and L are loaded with the value 0311_{16}.

MOV A,M   The accumulator is loaded with the contents of memory word 0311_{16}.

DCR L The contents of register L are decremented by 1.

SUB M   Subtract the contents of memory location 0310_{16} from the contents of the accumulator.

JM NEG   Jump to address NEG if the result is negative.

—

—

NEG:

—

JPE/JPO

A JPE (*J*ump on *P*arity *E*ven) instruction is carried out if the result of a previous operation contains an even number of ones. A JPO (*J*ump on *P*arity *O*dd) instruction is carried out if the result of a previous operation contains an odd number of ones. Examples of even parity are 01100011, 11101000, 11111111, etc. Examples of odd parity are 11111110, 00001000, 10101000, etc.

CALL/RET

The CALL and RET instructions are also jump instructions and the conditions given above apply to these instructions as well. For example, a CNZ (Call on No Zero) instruction is only carried out if the zero status flag is not set at that moment. In an RC (Return on Carry) instruction a return is made only if the carry status flag is set. We will study the CALL and RET instructions more closely in the chapter "Syntax and Subroutines".

SPECIAL INSTRUCTIONS

Every microprocessor recognizes a number of special instructions. They do not transfer or process data, but are used for internal control of the microprocessor.

HLT/DI/EI

The HLT (HaLT) instruction stops the program running until an interrupt request arrives from an I/O device. If the microcomputer receives a DI (Disable Interrupt) instruction, interrupt requests are ignored until an EI (Enable Interrupt) resets the interrupt flag.

SUMMARY

1. The instructions in all instruction sets can be divided into:
- a. transfer instructions
- b. arithmetic instructions
- c. logic instructions
- d. jump instructions
- e. special instructions.

2. When a source and a destination occur in an instruction, the destination is given first and then the source.

3. If the source or the destination of an instruction is the memory word M, the address of this memory word appears in registers H and L.

4. Traffic with the outside world is regulated by the OUT and IN instructions and always takes place via the accumulator.

5. Every arithmetic operation which a microprocessor performs takes place in the ALU.

6. In a one-address machine one of the operands is always located in the accumulator.

7. The result of an arithmetic operation performed in the ALU is placed in the accumulator.

8. All logical operations a microprocessor can perform takes place in the ALU.

9. In a logic operation one of the operands is always located in the accumulator.

10. Not only processing 2 numbers using logic functions, but also the taking of a 1's complement, comparing 2 numbers and rotating the contents of the accumulator are considered logic operations.

11. Jump instructions are sub-divided into conditional and unconditional jump instructions.

12. With conditional jump instructions, the jump is performed depending on the status of:
- a. the carry status flag
- b. the sign status flag
- c. the zero status flag
- d. the parity status flag.

13. If, in a conditional jump instruction, the condition is not met, the jump does not take place and the program continues with the execution of the next instruction.

REVIEW QUESTIONS

1. What is the disadvantage of assembly language when compared to one of the high-level programming languages?

2. What is an instruction set?

3. What 5 groups can every instruction set be divided into?

4. In transfer instructions we recognize a source and a destination. Which must be mentioned first?

5. In an assembly instruction, how are the differences between binary, hexadecimal and decimal values represented?

6. How is an ASCII character represented in an assembly instruction?

7. What does IN 03 mean?

8. Data transfer between the CPU and the I/O device takes place via which register?

9. Where is one of the operands in an ADD instruction located in a one-address machine?

10. Where is the result of an arithmetic operation in the ALU transferred to?

11. Where is the operand in an "immediate" instruction located?

12. What is the only difference between a subtraction and a compare instruction?

13. Draw truth tables for the AND, OR and EXOR functions.

14. How can we calculate how long the execution of a program takes?

15. Which logic instruction can we use to determine the condition of one bit in a word?

16. Which logic instruction can we use to change one bit in a word?

17. What is the difference between shifting and rotating?

18. What types of jump instructions do we know?

19. What must we consider in a conditional jump instruction?

20. What happens if certain conditions are not satisfied in a jump instruction?

ANSWERS

1. The disadvantage of assembly language is that one must first know the instruction set of the given microcomputer.

2. A list of the possible operations which the microcomputer can carry out.

3. a Transfer instructions
   b Arithmetic instructions
   c Logic instructions
   d Jump instructions
   e Special instructions.

4. The destination is stated first and then the source.

5. B is written following a binary value, an H after a hexadecimal value and D after a decimal value.

6. Between inverted commas.

7. In 03 means that data, originating from the I/O device with port number 03, must be brought to the accumulator.

8. Via the accumulator.

9. In the accumulator.

10. To the accumulator.

11. This is an instruction where the operand is stated directly after the operation code. This means that the operand does not need to be obtained first from data memory or a register.

12. In a compare instruction the result of the subtraction is not stored in the accumulator.

13. See fig. 11-1 in the chapter.

14. By adding up all the states of all the instructions in the program and then multiplying by the time taken by 1 state.

15. The AND function.

16. The EXOR function.

17. No bits are lost in rotation as they are in shifting.

18. Conditional and unconditional jump instructions.

19. From the content of one of the status flags.

20. The jump does not take place and the program continues with the next instruction to be executed.

Chapter 12
Syntax and Subroutines

In the chapter "What Is a Computer?" we explained the reasons for using assembly language when writing a program for a microcomputer instead of a series of zeros and ones. Because assembly language is machine oriented and because microcomputers vary, the assembly languages will differ. These differences exist mainly in the terms used in the instructions and in the way the operands are specified. The rest of the assembly language is designed to suit the specific features of the microprocessor. There is, of course, a great difference between a 1-address and a 2-address machine. Whether or not a machine has general-purpose registers is also an important factor.

The differences between various assembly languages have a number of consequences:

a. A program must be written in the assembly language for the type of microprocessor for which it is intended.

b. When a source program written in assembly language is converted into an object program, the translation program (assembler) used must suit that type of microprocessor. This does not necessarily mean that the translation must take place on that specific microcomputer. It can also be done on a large computer which has this assembly translating program as a part of its software. The assembly translating program is then written in the large computer's language, but it processes a source program written in the assembly language of the microcomputer.

The first part of this chapter is concerned with the similarities between all assembly languages - the *syntax*. This is the general construction and method of notation used in an assembly instruction.

The second half is a continuation of "Description of the Instructions", but then concentrated on the instructions used when including a *subroutine* in the program.

CONSTRUCTION OF AN ASSEMBLY INSTRUCTION

Although the letter coding for an instruction often differs from one microcomputer to another, the construction and notation (also called syntax) of an assembly instruction is the same for all assembly languages. An assembly instruction can be divided into 4 parts (called fields):

LABEL   MNEMONIC   OPERAND   COMMENT

Taken in order of importance, these terms have the following meanings.

Mnemonic

In the mnemonic or operator field of an instruction, a letter code is used to write the operation code. This letter code is usually an abbreviation of the type of operation defined by the operation code. Examples:

ADD this instruction is self-explanatory
SUB subtract
JMP jump
JNC jump on no carry
RRC rotate to the right through the carry status flag.

Operand

We use the operand field of an assembly instruction to specify which data (operands) are to be used in carrying out a given operation. Depending upon the type of instruction, the operand field may contain:

	MNEMONIC	OPERAND
a. the operand itself, e.g.	ANI	35H
b. the address of the operand, e.g.	LDA	03FFH
c. an operand address and an operand	MVI	A,11000101B
d. the addresses of 2 operands, e.g.	MOV	A,B

If 2 operands are specified in the operand field, they must be separated by a *comma*.

Label

When writing a program, we must specify the memory addresses where the sequential instruction bytes are located. This is done as shown in fig. 12-1. Assume that we have a part of a program consisting of 5 instructions—each of 1, 2 or 3 bytes. The consecutive bytes are placed in memory addresses 01_{10} to 12_{10} in consecutive order. The fifth instruction is a jump instruction. The address we must jump back to is given the mnemonic JMP. The way in which we enter the program determines whether we have to calculate these addresses ourselves or if it is done automatically for us by the assembly translation program.

When program entering with switches, we must calculate the addresses for ourselves. We then enter the addresses and instruction bytes in ones and zeros. This is done via switches. The address switches (there are usually 16) and the data switches (usually 8) are set to the requisite state (0 or 1) and a button is pushed which enters the data to the proper memory location, in parallel. Because only binary numbers can be entered, we must also translate the mnemonic into the proper operation code. All register numbers and hexadecimal numbers (e.g. memory addresses) must also be converted into their binary equivalents. We are, in fact, assuming the role of the assembly translation program (the assembler).

When inputting using the Assembly Translation Program, addresses need not be calculated. The assembly translation program does this for us and couples them to consecutive instruction bytes. We must, however, instruct the assembler as to the address of the first byte of the first instruction to be executed. Because we calculate no addresses ourselves, we can only define an address *symbolically in the instruction*. A jump instruction always contains an address. We must ensure that the address to which the jump must be made is clearly stated. The address to be jumped to is made clear by giving it a symbolic name or *label*. The label is written in the *label field*. A label is thus not a number, but a word (name). This label is placed after the jump mnemonic. The as-

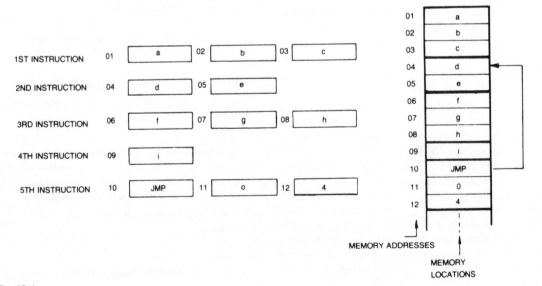

Fig. 12-1.

sembly translation program replaces the label by the proper address.

LABEL	MNEMONIC	OPERAND
FORWARD:	MOV	A,B
	ADD	D
	-	
	-	
	-	
	-	
	JMP	FORWARD

The label FORWARD is associated with the instruction MOV A,B. Because the assembler keeps track of the addressing while the program is entered, it knows which address we mean by FORWARD. If the instruction JMP FORWARD were now entered, the assembler could fill in the address value for the symbolic name FORWARD in the jump instruction.

Comment

The programmer can use this field for explanations in the instruction. The comment field is nothing more than an aid to the programmer and is completely ignored by the assembly translation program. If the program is typed using a teletype fitted with paper tape punch, each character that we type is converted into ASCII code on paper tape. This tape is called the source tape. This tape also contains the comment field.

TYPING IN ASSEMBLY INSTRUCTIONS

A teletype (usually abbreviated to TTY) is the device most often used to enter a program written in assembly language. A TTY can be used as a:

keyboard
print mechanism
paper tape punch
paper tape reader.

To convert a hand-written assembly program into a program that is stored in the memory of the microcomputer, the following steps are needed (fig. 12-2);

1. The TTY is turned on.

2. The microcomputer starts the assembly translation program. There are two possibilities:

a. This translation program is stored in a ROM located in the microcomputer;

b. The translation program is stored in a floppy disc, magnetic tape or paper tape. In this case the microcomputer must be connected to the equipment that feeds in the translation program.

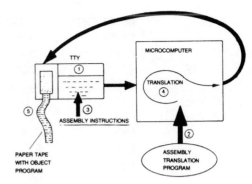

Fig. 12-2.

3. The program is typed in line-for-line following the rules that relate to the particular microprocessor. The TTY converts the numbers and letters to ASCII-coded characters and feeds them to the microcomputer in the form of electronic pulses. The program as printed by the line-printer of the TTY is checked for typing mistakes. If there are typing mistakes, these can be corrected by the use of an auxiliary program—the editor.

4. In the microcomputer the source program is converted to an object program. This is controlled by the assembly translation program. The object program is stored in memory.

5. The program stored in memory is put on paper tape by the TTY to be saved "for posterity".

There are other methods for translating a source program into an object program. These will be dealt with later in the chapter "System Software" and "Development Systems".

We must adhere to certain rules when typing in an assembly instruction with a TTY. These are:

a. One line must be reserved for every instruction. We depress the keys "line feed" and/or "carriage return" at the end of each instruction. This causes the TTY to return to the start of the next line. (If the TTY is connected to a paper tape reader, a certain hole combination is punched that indicates the end of the line).

b. The fields in the assembly instruction are divided by 1 or more spaces. This spacing must be consistent so that the respective fields always appear directly below one another. Spacing makes it more legible.

c. If there is no label, the first letter space is left blank.

d. In some assembly translation programs the end of a label is indicated by a colon (:). In other assemblers a space between the label and the mnemonic field is suffi-

LABEL	MNEMONIC	OPERAND	COMMENT
	ORG	1100H	
ETX	EQU	03H	
STORE	EQU	1200H	
CI	EQU	1009H	
STORE:	LXI	H,STORE	; INITIALIZE MEMORY POINTER
READ:	CALL	CI	; CHARACTER IN FROM CONSOLE
	MOV	M,A	; STORE CHARACTER
	CPI	ETX	
	RZ		; RETURN IF ETX
	INX	H	; INCREMENT POINTER
	JMP	READ	
	END		

Fig. 12-3.

cient. A label can consist of any combination of letters, numbers or characters, but must start with a letter. In some assembly translation programs certain restrictions are placed upon the construction of the label; for instance, a label must not be the same as an assembly instruction.

e. In some assembly translation programs the comment field must begin with a semi-colon (;). In others, a space between the operand field and the comment field is sufficient.

Figure 12-3 gives several examples of the construction of a line in a program.

ASSEMBLER DIRECTIVES

The assembly translation program (assembler) translates source programs, written in the assembly language, into object programs which the microcomputer can read. Although the assembly translation program takes over many of the programmer's tasks, such as addressing, conversion of numbers, etc., the programmer must still supply some specifications. For example, the assembler does not know in which memory location the first instruction in the program must be placed. Neither does it know when the program is completed. The programmer can give the assembly translation program this information through an *assembler directive*. An assembler directive does not produce a machine code in the object program, but is merely an instruction for the assembler to do something. Several examples of assembler directives are:

LABEL	MNEMONIC	OPERAND	COMMENT
	ORG	0400H	
CONS	EQU	05H	
	END		

The ORG origin directive gives the assembler the memory address of the first instruction in the program to be translated. The ORG 0400H directive assures that the first instruction in the program to be carried out is put at address 0400_{16}.

The assembler directive EQU (equate) is used when we have allotted a symbolic name to a given operand while writing the program. The EQU directive assigns specific value to this symbolic name. For example:

LABEL	MNEMONIC	OPERAND
CONS	EQU	05H
	MVI	A,CONS

The operand CONS is replaced by the value 05_{16} during assembly (translation) of the MVI instruction. The programmer uses the assembler directive END to indicate that the source program has ended.

Note

When we assign a symbolic name to the memory address of a specific instruction we do not have to inform the assembler of the actual value of this address by way of a EQU directive. The assembler does this using a *location counter* that is part of the assembly translating program. We have already informed the assembler of the location of the first instruction of the program using an ORG directive. After each instruction has been translated, the location counter is incremented by the number of bytes that instruction takes up.

SUBROUTINES

Quite often the same group of instructions, such as a multiplication routine, must be repeated in various places in the program. It would be a definite waste of memory space if these routines were to be entered separately as they occur in the program, especially if there are many of them. In such a case it is better to write this series of instructions as a "sub-program" and place them somewhere in the memory apart from the main program (fig. 12-4). By so doing we create a *subroutine* that can be called up as needed by means of a special instruction. We shall now discuss the instructions that arise with subroutines.

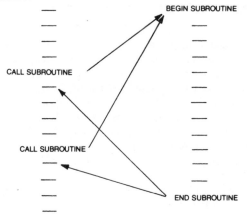

Fig. 12-4.

THE CALL INSTRUCTION

The CALL instruction calls up a subroutine. The CALL instruction comprises 3 bytes: 1 for the operation code (CALL) and 2 to indicate the address of the first instruction to be executed in the subroutine. This address is usually specified by a symbolic name. For example:

MNEMONIC	OPERAND
CALL	MULTI

The CALL instruction also ensures that once the subroutine has been executed a return is made to the proper point in the main program. The CALL instruction ensures that:

a. The program counter indicates the address of the instruction to follow the CALL instruction in the main program.

b. The contents of the program counter are transferred to the stack.

c. The increment of the stack pointer.

d. The program counter is loaded with the address specified in the CALL instruction.

Only then can the execution of the subroutine begin.

THE RET INSTRUCTION

The RET instruction is the last instruction in the subroutine. This instruction causes the actual return to the main program as prepared for in the CALL instruction. The RET instruction comprises only an operation code and ensures that:

a. The program counter receives from the stack the address of the instruction that succeeds the CALL instruction in the main program.

b. The contents of the stack pointer are accordingly decremented.

THE PUSH AND POP INSTRUCTION

It often happens that one or more of the general-purpose registers in the CPU are needed when executing a subroutine. However, these registers may contain data that is needed later in the main program. So data must be stored before the subroutine is started. This is done by using a PUSH instruction to store it in the stack. A POP instruction is used to retrieve the data after the subroutine has been executed. The storing and retrieving of information using the PUSh and POP instructions always involves register pairs. The available register pairs are:

● registers B and C
● registers D and E
● registers H and L
● the accumulator and the status flag register.

The content of the accumulator and the status flag register together form the *Program Status Word* or PSW. The length of the memory words in the stack is 8 bits. Therefore, storing the contents of a register pair (16 bits) in the stack requires 2 steps, assuming that the stack pointer indicates the last address in the stack at which data was stored. (In some microprocessors, though, the stack pointer indicates the first free location in the stack.) A PUSH instruction causes the following actions:

● The contents of the stack pointer are first decremented by 1.

● The first 8 bits are brought to the stack.

● The contents of the stack pointer are again decremented by 1.

● The following 8 bits are brought to the stack.

The reverse takes place with a POP instruction. The second byte is first brought from the stack to the CPU and the contents of the stack pointer are incremented by 1. The first byte is then brought from the stack to the CPU and the stack pointer is again incremented by 1. It will be

—	MULTI:	PUSH PSW	PUSH PSW and registers D,E and H,L in to stack
—		PUSH D	
—		PUSH H	
0100 CALL MULTI		—	
0103 —		—	
—		POP H	PULL registers H,L and D,E and the
—		POP D	PSW from the stack, then PULL the
—		POP PSW	address 0103_{16} and put it in the PC.
—		RET	

Fig. 12-5A.

clear that we must instruct the computer as to which part of memory we are reserving for the stack before we can begin executing our program. In other words, we must first load the stack pointer with the highest address in the stack + 1. (Since the stack pointer is decremented by 1 before the information is brought to the stack.) We can illustrate this by the following example:

Part of a program is shown in fig. 12-5a. In this program a subroutine is called up at a certain moment using the CALL MULTI instruction. The CALL MULTI instruction consists of 3 bytes, 1 for the operation code and 2 to specify the address of the first instruction in the subroutine to be executed. We have given this address the symbolic name MULTI. We often choose a symbolic name for a subroutine which gives a clue to the action performed in the subroutine itself. We have chosen MULTI since this is a subroutine to perform multiplication. The CALL MULTI instruction consists of 3 bytes and thus takes up 3 memory words. The operation code (CALL) is located at address 0100_{16} (fig. 12-5a). The 2 bytes of the address (MULTI) of the first two instructions of the subroutine to be executed are located at addresses 0101_{16} and 0102_{16}, respectively. Therefore the next instruction in the main program to be carried out is at address 0103_{16}. It follows that this must be stored in the program counter *after* the instruction fetch of the CALL MULTI instruction has taken place. Before the instruction execution of the CALL MULTI instruction can take place, i.e. before the program counter can be loaded with the MULTI value, its old contents (0103_{16}) must be transferred to the stack. This is done by the CALL instruction. The CALL instruction decrements the stack pointer by 1 and the first byte of 0103 is entered in the stack. The stack pointer is then decremented by 1 again and the next byte is transferred to the stack. Figure 12-5b shows the situation in the stack. As fig. 12-5b shows, memory locations 0500_{16} to $05FF_{16}$ are reserved for the stack.

When writing a value in the stack we must take care not to exceed this area, as otherwise we might mutilate the program itself, which is also in memory. Before starting the actual execution of the subroutine we must first store the contents of the PSW and registers D,E and H,L. This is done by the instructions PUSH PSW, PUSH D and PUSH H (fig. 12-5a). (Because the PUSH instruction always uses register pairs, we only need to mention the first register in the pair. PUSH H means, PUSH H and L).

Figure 12-5c shows the stack after the execution of the 3 PUSH instructions.

(acc) means: contents of the accumulator.
(flags) means: contents of the status flag register, etc.

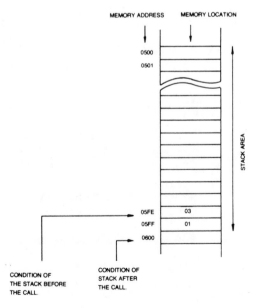

Fig. 12-5B.

124

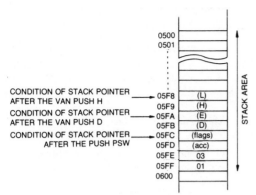

	0500
	0501
CONDITION OF STACK POINTER AFTER THE VAN PUSH H	05F8 (L)
	05F9 (H)
CONDITION OF STACK POINTER AFTER THE VAN PUSH D	05FA (E)
	05FB (D)
CONDITION OF STACK POINTER AFTER THE PUSH PSW	05FC (flags)
	05FD (acc)
	05FE 03
	05FF 01
	0600

Fig. 12-5C.

Now the actual execution of the subroutine can take place. When this has ended, the contents of the register pairs D,E and H,L, as well as the PSW, must be brought to the CPU again. Because the stack pointer is continually decremented by 1 when storing information in the stack (PUSH) and is incremented by 1 when retrieving information (POP), *that which was stored last must be retrieved first.* This principle is often called LIFO (*Last In First Out*). The sequence in a POP instruction must thus be the reverse of that in a PUSH instruction. If the programmer fails to remember this, the information that was in register pair H,L before execution of the subroutine could, for example, end up in register pair D,E after execution. After the information in the stack is placed in the registers of the CPU, a RET (return) command is given. This is done so that address 0103 in the stack will be placed in the program counter and the execution of the main program can be resumed.

SUMMARY

1. The general layout of an assembly instruction is:

LABEL   MNEMONIC   OPERAND   COMMENT

2. The mnemonic field contains the letter coding for the operation code.

3. The operand field is used to specify the subject of the operation.

4. The label field is used by the programmer to symbolically represent a memory address which must be jumped to.

5. The comment field gives further information on an assembly instruction.

6. A TTY is the device most often used to enter a program in assembly language.

7. One line is reserved for each assembly instruction. The fields of an assembly instruction are separated from each other by a space (or spaces). In some cases the label field ends with (:). In some cases the comment field begins with (;).

8. An assembler directive is a specification given to the assembly translation program by the programmer.

9. An assembler directive does not yield a machine code in the object program.

10. A subroutine is a part of a program which can be called up as often as necessary during the execution of the main program.

11. A subroutine is called up using a CALL instruction. This instruction also prepares for the return to the correct point in the main program after the subroutine has been executed.

12. The RET instruction is the last instruction in the subroutine and causes the return to the main program.

13. We can store the contents of a register pair in the stack by using a PUSH instruction.

14. The POP instruction causes the information in the stack to be returned to the registers in the CPU.

REVIEW EXERCISES

1. What is the same in every assembly language?

2. What is the general format of an assembly instruction?

3. What is the mnemonic of an assembly instruction?

4. What can the operand field contain?

5. How are the fields in an assembly instruction separated from each other?

6. How must a program line begin if there is no label?

7. What is the purpose of the "carriage return" and "line feed" keys on a TTY?

8. How must the beginning of the comment field be indicated in some assembly translation programs?

9. In which method of entering must we calculate the memory addresses ourselves?

10. How is the end of a label specified in some cases?

11. What is a source tape?

12. What is an assembly directive?

13. What are the ORG, EQU and END directives for?

14. What can a TTY be used for?

15. Which medium is most often used for storing the assembly translation program?

125

16. What is a subroutine?

17. Which instruction is used to call up a subroutine?

18. How does the CALL instruction prepare for the correct return to the main program from a subroutine?

19. What does the RET instruction take care of?

20. What happens in a PUSH instruction?

21. What happens in a POP instruction?

22. Which register pairs can be used?

23. What is the program status word?

24. How many bytes comprise a CALL instruction?

25. Why must that which was last stored in the stack be the first to be retrieved?

ANSWERS

1. The construction and notation, also called syntax.

2. LABEL   MNEMONIC   OPERAND   COMMENT.

3. A letter coding of the operation to be carried out.

4. ● An operand.
   ● An operand address.
   ● An operand and an operand address.
   ● Two operands.

5. By a space (or spaces).

6. By a space (or spaces).

7. To return the carriage to a new line.

8. By a semi-colon.

9. When we enter the program using switches. We then assume the role of the assembly translation program.

10. By a colon.

11. This is a tape on which all characters in the source program are represented in ASCII coded characters.

12. An indication for the assembly translation program. An assembly directive does not result in a machine code in the object program.

13. To indicate starting address, assign memory locations values, and indicate the end of the program.

14. A TTY can be used as:

   ● A keyboard.
   ● Print mechanism.
   ● Paper tape punch.
   ● Paper tape reader.

15. A floppy disc, magnetic tape, paper tape, or in a ROM.

16. A subroutine is a part of a program which can be called up as needed during execution of the main program.

17. The CALL instruction.

18. The CALL instruction ensures that:

   ● The program counter specifies the address of the instruction which follows the CALL instruction in the main program.
   ● The content of the program counter is brought to the stack.
   ● The content of the stack pointer is adjusted accordingly.
   ● The program counter is loaded with the address of the first instruction in the sub-program to be executed.

19. The RET instruction ensures that:

   ● The program counter in the stack is loaded with the address of the next instruction to be executed in the main program.
   ● The contents of the stack pointer are adjusted accordingly.

20. The contents of the stack pointer are first decremented by 1 and then the first 8 bits are transferred to the stack. The contents of the stack pointer are again decremented by 1 and the next 8 bits are transferred to the stack.

21. The second 8 bits are transferred from the stack to the CPU and the contents of the stack pointer are incremented by 1. The first 8 bits are then transferred from the stack to the CPU and the contents of the stack pointer are again incremented by 1.

22. B and C; D and E; H and L; PSW.

23. The program status word is formed by the contents of the accumulator and the status flag register.

24. The CALL instruction takes up 3 bytes. One byte is for the operation code and the other 2 for the address of the first instruction in the subroutine to be executed.

25. Because the stack pointer is decremented by 1 in a PUSH instruction and incremented by 1 in a POP instruction.

Chapter 13

Addressing Techniques

Addressing techniques describe the way we specify the operands or operand addresses in the instructions. In this chapter we will deal with the most common addressing techniques used with microcomputers. It is most important to choose an addressing technique that uses the least memory space in storing the program and the least time when executing it. Since an addressing technique rarely satisfies both of these conditions we will normally have to settle for a compromise. The addressing technique chosen is, of course, also determined by the instruction set a particular microprocessor has to offer.

IMMEDIATE ADDRESSING

In immediate addressing, the operand directly follows the operation code. See fig. 13-1. When the operation code has been entered in the CPU, the program counter indicates the operand. Because the operand itself—and not an operand address—follows the operation code, no addressing in the real sense of the word takes place. The operands are stored in memory in the location immediately succeeding the location where the operation code is stored.

Many immediate addressing instructions are two bytes long. The first byte contains the operation code and the second byte the operand. Immediate addressing is used if the operand is known when the program is written. In this case we speak of an immediate operand. Immediate addressing is indicated in the mnemonic by an I. Several examples are:

MVI A,01101010B	Move immediate to accumulator	Put the immediate operand in the accumulator
ADI 01101010B	Add immediate to accumulator	Add the immediate operand to the accumulator
ANI 01101010B	And immediate with accumulator	Process the contents of the accumulator with the immediate operand using the AND function.

DIRECT ADDRESSING

We speak of direct addressing when the address of the data required to carry out the operation follows the operation code. This address could be:

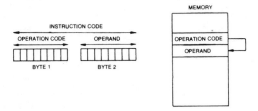

Fig. 13-1.

- a memory address
- a register number
- a port number.

Memory Address

This type of instruction comprises 3 bytes, since a memory address is 2 bytes long (see fig. 13-2).

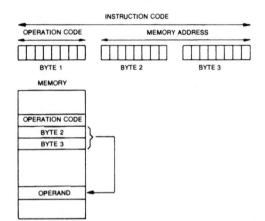

Fig. 13-2.

Some examples are:

LDA 2FFFH	Load accumulator direct	Load accumulator with contents of memory word with address $2FFF_{16}$
STA 0300H	Store accumulator direct	Bring contents of accumulator to memory word with address 0330_{16}

Register Number

This type of instruction only takes up 1 byte because the operation code is 2 bits and a register number, 3 bits long. If necessary, 2 register numbers could be contained in such an instruction, as would be the case if data were transferred from one register to another (fig. 13-3).

Examples

INR B	Increment register	Increment contents of register B by 1
MOV A,B	Move register to register	Bring the contents of register B to the accumulator

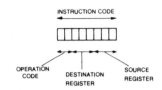

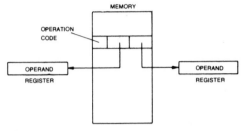

Fig. 13-3.

Port Number

This instruction type is two bytes long since we need 8 bits (1 byte) to indicate a port number (fig. 13-4).

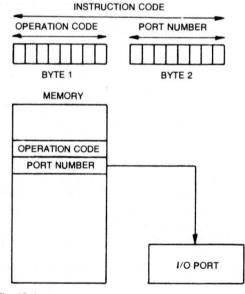

Fig. 13-4.

Examples

IN 06H	input	Bring the contents of the input port with the number 06_{16} to the accumulator

OUT 12H	output	Bring the contents of the accumulator to the output port with the number 12_{16}

Note

Direct addressing as well as immediate addressing may occur in the same instruction. It is also very common for immediate addressing to be combined with indirect addressing, which we will deal with in the following section. In that case the length of the instruction differs. Several examples of the combination of direct and immediate addressing are:

MVI B,12H	Move immediate register	Load register B with the immediate operand 12_{16}
LXI H,2A49H	Load register pair immediate	Load register pair H and L with the immediate operand $2A49_{16}$

INDIRECT ADDRESSING

This method uses two addresses. The first address is included in the instruction and is usually a register number. However, that register (or register pair) does not contain the operand, as with direct addressing, but rather a memory address. The operand is located in that memory address (fig. 13-5). Because 16 bits are needed for a memory address, the address must be divided between two 8-bit registers (register pair). Only the

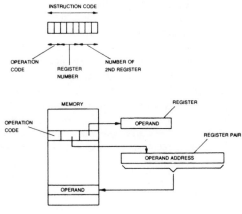

Fig. 13-5.

number of the first (high order) is given in the instruction code, since the operation code has already indicated that we are working with a register pair. The instruction length depends upon the way in which the other operand is addressed. For example, if the 2nd operand is located in a register, the instruction takes up 1 byte (fig. 13-5).

Examples

ADD M	Add memory to accumulator	The contents of the memory word, the address of which is in register pair H,L is added to contents of the accumulator.
INR M	Increment memory	Increment the contents of the memory address, the address of which is in register pair H,L.

Examples of combining indirect addressing with other addressing techniques:

MOV B,M	Move memory to register	Bring contents of the memory word with its address in register pair H,L to register B.
MVI M,2AH	Move immediate to register	Load memory word with its address in register pair H,L with immediate operand $2A_{16}$

IMPLIED ADDRESSING

In this addressing method, also known as implicit addressing, the address of one or both operands is implicit in the operation code. The instruction concerned can, for example, work only with the contents of the accumulator. The accumulator is then implicitly addressed and does not have to be specifically named. In the 8080 this is the case for all instructions using the AND, OR and EXOR functions. The first operand is always located in the accumulator. The second operand can be directly, indirectly or immediately addressed. This also determines the instruction length.

129

Examples

ANA B	And register with accumulator	Process the contents of the accumulator with the contents of register B using the AND function
ADD M	Add memory to accumulator	Add the contents of the memory word, the address of which is in registers H and L to the contents of the accumulator

RELATIVE ADDRESSING

Relative addressing is a collective name for a number of techniques which have one principle in common. In relative addressing the memory address of the operand is equal to the sum of the basic value and a *displacement*. The concept of displacement can be readily understood if one studies fig. 13-6. Assume that a table is stored in the memory shown in fig. 13-6 and that each item in the table takes up 2 bytes. The address of the first byte (b) of the first item is regarded as the basic value. The displacement of an item is the number (of bytes) that must be added to address b in order to locate the desired item. In our case, it is 2 for the second item, 4 for the third, etc. We will now cover several forms of relative addressing.

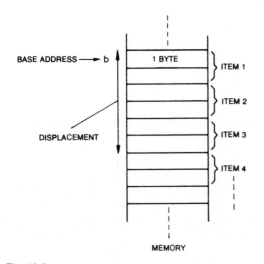

BASE ADDRESS ⟶ b

1 BYTE } ITEM 1
} ITEM 2
DISPLACEMENT } ITEM 3
} ITEM 4

MEMORY

Fig. 13-6.

Paging

Some microcomputers use what is called the *paging technique*. This means that memory is divided into blocks—each containing a given number of memory words. Such a block is called a page. It can be divided in such a way that the first byte of the address is the same for all memory words in a page. When the instruction code and its operand are in the same page, the first byte of the contents of the program counter can be used as the first byte of the memory address. Thus, the instruction only has to state the value of the second byte of the memory address. The example given in fig. 13-7 is based on pages containing 256 memory words. Thus, the maximum value of the second byte of the operand address is FF_{16}. The program counter contains the address $07A7_{16}$; this is the address of the operation code. Only the value of the 2nd byte of the operand address (FC_{16}) follows the operation code. The value of the first byte of the operand address is taken from the first byte of the contents of the program counter (07_{16}). The operand address is thus $07FC_{16}$.

Note

With this method we can only specify operand addresses which are located on the same page as the operation code. Whenever we want to address outside this page we must use another addressing method—direct addressing for example.

Indexed Addressing

In indexed addressing the operand address is found by adding the number that follows the operation code to the number in the *index register* (fig. 13-8). The address $08D4_{16}$ —given in the instruction—is added to address $421A_{16}$ from the index register. The sum is $4AEE_{16}$. It is evident from the operation code that this memory location must be accessed. Indexed addressing is applied when we want to read in or read out a large number of sequential memory locations. This is the case, for example, with a large number of measurement values in consecutive memory locations. We could access each memory location using direct addressing. However, each address would then take up 3 bytes. Moreover, a new instruction code would have to be added to the program (and thus also in the memory) every time a memory location was accessed. Indexed addressing requires less time (in programming) and takes up less space. We make the basic value equal the address of the first measure-

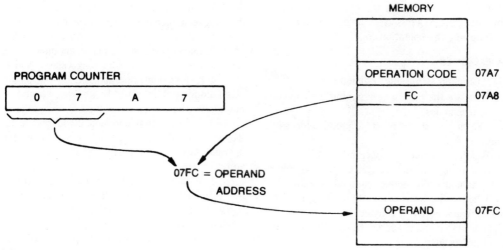

Fig. 13-7.

ment and set the index register to 0. We then enter an instruction that reads out of memory using the above-mentioned technique of indexed addressing. The first measurement will then be read out. Next the index register is incremented by 1 and the previous instruction is repeated. The second measurement is then read out. These instruction can be repeated until all the measurements have been read out.

SUMMARY

1. In immediate addressing the operand immediate follows the operation code.

2. In instructions using direct addressing the operand address immediately follows the operation code.

The operand address can be a memory address, a register number, or a port number.

3. Relative addressing is a collective name for a number of techniques which have the common principle that the memory address of the operand of an instruction is equal to the sum of a basic value and a displacement.

4. Two types of relative addressing are paging and indexed addressing.

5. In paging, memory is divided into blocks containing a certain number of memory words. When the instruction code and the operand of the instruction are on the same page, the operand address is found from the first byte of the program counter and the byte following the operation code.

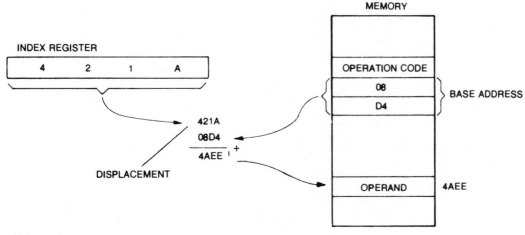

Fig. 13-8.

131

6. In indexed addressing the operand address is found by adding the contents of the index register to the address following the operation code.

REVIEW EXERCISES

1. What is an addressing technique?

2. What are the factors determining the choice of addressing techniques?

3. Which are the 5 most common addressing techniques?

4. What is an immediate operand?

5. What is the construction of an immediate addressing instruction and how is the mnemonic specified?

6. When is the instruction 2 bytes long in direct addressing? When is it 1 or 3 bytes?

7. How can a memory address be specified in 1 byte in indirect addressing?

8. Where is one of the operands always located in implied addressing.

9. What determines the instruction length in implied addressing?

10. Name 2 types of relative addressing.

11. On what is paging based?

12. When is indexed addressing applied?

ANSWERS

1. An addressing technique is the way in which the operands and operand addresses are specified in the instruction.

2. With microcomputers one should choose an addressing technique that requires the least memory space to store a program and the least time to execute it.

3. Immediate addressing; direct addressing; indirect addressing; implied addressing; relative addressing.

4. An immediate operand directly follows the operation code and is already known when the program is written.

5. An instruction in immediate addressing takes up 2 bytes—1 for the operation code and 1 for specifying the operand. All mnemonics in immediate addressing contain an I.

6. If the operand is located in an I/O port, the instruction takes up 2 bytes. If the operand is located in a register, it takes up 1 byte. If the operand is in memory it takes up 3 bytes.

7. The number of a register pair in which a 16-bit memory address is located is specified using 3 bits.

8. One of the operands is always located in the accumulator.

9. The length of the instruction is determined by the manner in which the second operand is specified.

10. Paging; indexed addressing.

11. In paging the first byte is the same as the first byte of the contents of the program counter. The second byte of the operand address is given following the operation code.

12. When we want to read in or read out a large number of consecutive memory places.

Chapter 14

Flowcharts

Defining the problem is always the starting point when we wish to apply a device in executing a job. Before a computer can be given the task of solving a problem, the problem must be fully analyzed. This analysis must be such that a program can be written on the basis of it. Once a problem has been analyzed, a suitable method of solving it can be written down as a flowchart. In this chapter we will describe how a flowchart is constructed.

SYMBOLS USED IN A FLOWCHART

A flowchart is an arrangement of blocks joined together by arrows. Each block or symbol contains a description of one or more operations. The operations may,

for example, be adding 2 numbers together or checking whether a particular condition has been satisfied. By giving these blocks different shapes, we can see at a glance what type of operation a particular block represents. Figure 14-1 shows the standard shapes of the blocks used in a flowchart and their meaning.

1. input and output of data using punched cards
2. input and output of data using punched tape
3. input and output of data using magnetic tape
4. input and output of data using a teletype
5. input and output of data using a printer
6. input and output of data using a display
7. input and output of data using a disc
8. operation to be performed on data

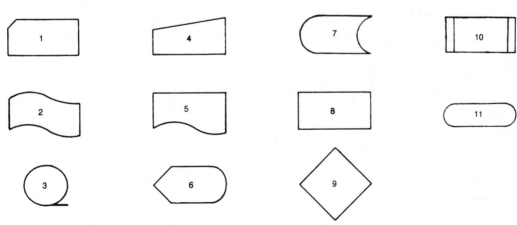

Fig. 14-1.

9. comparison of data
10. jump to a subroutine
11. start or end of a program
12. general input and output operations

The arrows in the flowchart indicate the sequence of events in the program. Figure 14-2 represents a very common combination of blocks—the program loop. In such a loop an operation is carried out first. Then a check is made to see whether a given condition has been satisfied. If it has not, the data is altered (for example, 1 is added to the data). The operation is repeated and the new result again checked. This process is repeated until the required condition has been satisfied, upon which the program continues in the 'yes' direction.

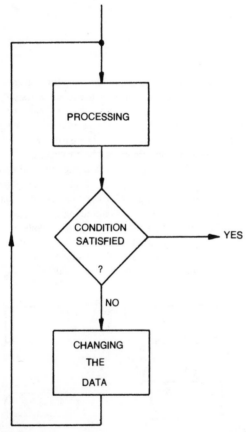

Fig. 14-2.

TYPES OF FLOWCHARTS

The purpose of problem analysis is to construct a flowchart that has a one-to-one relationship with the various steps to be taken in the program. In other words,

each block in the flowchart should be translatable into one or more instructions in the instruction set. Because it is virtually impossible to construct such a flowchart directly, we begin with a general definition of the problem. Each block, in this case, represents a number of processes or operations. We then subdivide each block until the desired one-to-one relationship with the program has been reached.

Naturally a flowchart for a program written in a higher programming language would be less detailed than one written in a machine language, such as assembly, since one instruction in a higher language represents several operations. Flowcharts can be divided into 3 categories (fig. 14-3).

System Flowcharts

In a system flowchart we indicate which devices are to be used for the input, output and storage of data. The actual method of solving the problem is represented by 1 block (fig. 14-3a).

General Flowcharts

The problem is worked out in greater detail (fig. 14-3b).

Detailed Flowcharts

The blocks in the general flowchart are so subdivided that each block represents one, and sometimes two or three, instructions (fig. 14-3c).

PROBLEM

The problem to be dealt with in the rest of this chapter is: 5 punched cards are arranged in random order, each bears a number between 1 and 99. The computer must arrange these numbers in ascending numerical sequence and print out the result.

THE SORTING PROBLEM

To represent the solution to a problem in a flow diagram one must naturally know how a computer tackles such a problem. Before trying to write a flowchart for the problem given above, we shall first generally describe how a computer arranges numbers sequentially. For simplicity we shall consider only 3 numbers. The solution to a problem is often made easier by visualizing. This we will do with our sorting problem, but using computer functions and terminology (fig. 14-4).

The numbers in their random order are fed in to sequential memory words in memory section P. The

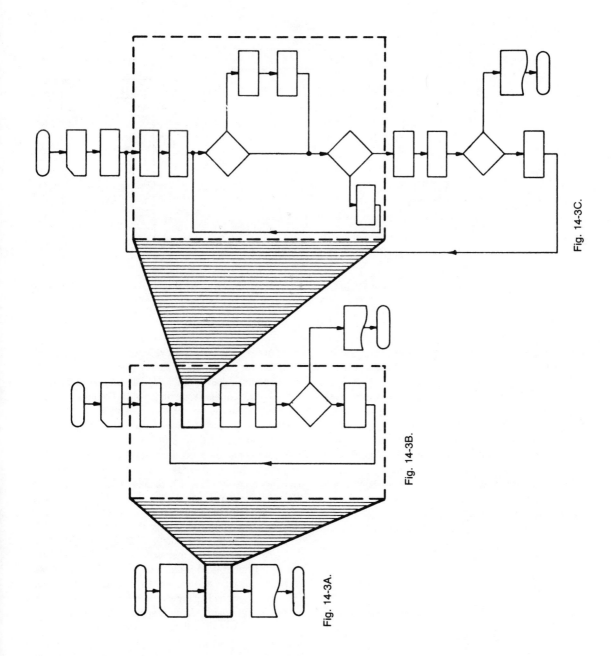

Fig. 14-3A.

Fig. 14-3B.

Fig. 14-3C.

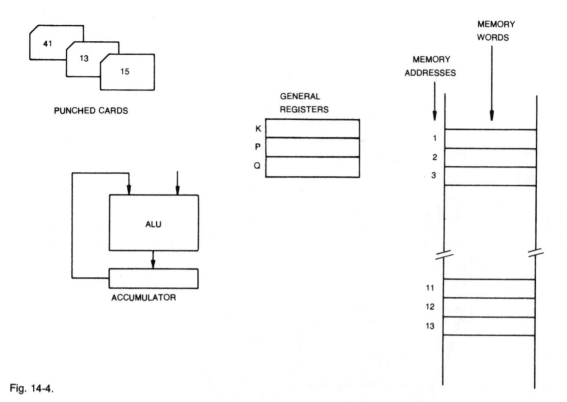

Fig. 14-4.

number on the first card to be read is entered at address 1. The following two numbers at addresses 2 and 3, respectively (fig. 14-5).

A computer can compare two numbers in a single operation. In a comparison operation the number in the accumulator is compared to the number fed in from memory. This takes place in the ALU. To enable the computer to repeatedly perform the same task, i.e. comparing a number from memory with one in the accumulator, the accumulator must be loaded with a particular value before this operation is performed for the first time. As the punched cards must be arranged in ascending sequential order, the value chosen must always be greater than the

1	41	
2	13	MEMORY SECTION P
3	15	

Fig. 14-5.

word in memory. We therefore load the accumulator with 100. We now compare the memory word in address 1 with the contents of the accumulator. The smaller of the numbers is placed in the accumulator—41. We next compare the contents of the memory word in address 2 with the contents of the accumulator. The smaller of the two numbers (41 and 13) goes to the accumulator—13. Finally, we compare the contents of the memory word in address 3 with the contents of the accumulator. Again the smaller of the two (15 or 13) goes to the accumulator, and 13 therefore remains in the accumulator.

When this operation has been performed as often as there are numbers to be arranged sequentially (3 times), the contents of the accumulator (13) are brought to the first memory word in memory section Q. The next smallest number is sorted in a second sorting operation. This can only be done successfully if the smallest number in memory section P is removed, as this would otherwise be sorted out again. We do this by loading the memory word where the smallest number was found with a value larger than the highest number to be sorted. In this case with the value 100. When the second smallest number has been found, this memory location is also loaded with the

136

value 100, etc. This implies that the computer must remember in which memory word the last number was located. The computer does this by storing the address of the value stored in the accumulator in an auxiliary register and updating this as the contents of the accumulator change. The auxiliary register then always contains the address of the smallest number found in one sorting operation.

The number of sorting operations is always equal to the number of cards entered. In this case, 3. The result of the second sort operation goes to the memory word with the address 12. The result of the third sort operation goes to the memory word with the address 13. After the sort has been completed, the numbers 41, 13 and 15 are in memory section Q in ascending sequential order (fig. 14-6).

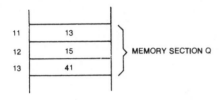

Fig. 14-6.

Our sorting exercise has emphasized the following points:

1. Before beginning the sorting we must always load the accumulator with a value higher by at least 1 than the highest number involved.

2. The number of sorting operations is equal to the number of values to be sorted.

3. The number of comparison operations is also equal to the number of numbers to be sorted.

4. We must replace the number sorted out in memory section P by a number that is at least 1 higher than the highest number to be sorted.

5. We must determine to which address the first number read in must go and to which address the first number sorted out must go.

SYSTEM FLOWCHART

The system flow diagram of the problem is shown in fig. 14-7. The main purpose of this flowchart is to show which devices are used to input and output the information. The information we enter requires 5 numbers on punched cards between 1 and 99. These values are entered using a punched card reader and are stored in the computer memory. The actual solution is represented by

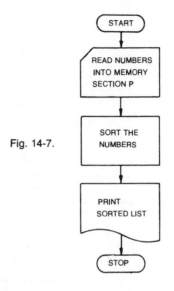

Fig. 14-7.

the block 'sort the numbers', after which the result is fed out via a printer.

GENERAL FLOWCHART

The general flowchart representing the broad solution to the problem is given in fig. 14-8. Following the start signal (block 1), the computer receives the command to read the numbers contained on the punched cards and to store these in memory words in memory section P (block 2).

Before we can start sorting we must first indicate where the smallest number must go at the end of the first sorting operation. We will chose the memory word at address 11. This memory word is located in memory section Q.

A general-purpose register can be used to store the memory address in memory section Q. We shall call it register q. The contents of this general-purpose register is q; q thus indicates where the smallest number must be stored at the end of a sorting operation. This general-purpose register is loaded with the value 11 in block 3. In this case the first memory word in memory section Q has address 11. We could just as easily have chosen the value $03FF_{16}$. Block 3 would then have contained: $q \leftarrow 03FF_{16}$. In block 4 the smallest number in memory section P is sorted out. In block 5 this smallest number is brought to the memory word at memory section Q, the address of which is in general purpose-register q. In block 6 the smallest number—sorted out from memory section Q—is replaced by the value 100 to prevent it being sorted out again during the next sorting operation.

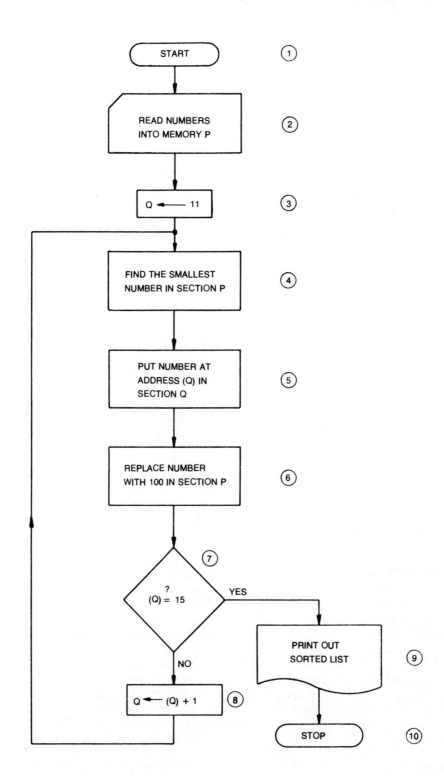

Fig. 14-8.

138

The contents of register q, which indicates the addresses in memory section Q, is incremented by 1 each time the program loop is run through. This loop is formed by blocks 4 to 8 inclusive. This register continually indicates the address to which the next number must be transferred. After the tasks set in blocks 4, 5 and 6 have been completed, the result of the comparison in block 7 (comparing the contents of general-purpose register q with the value 15) determines if all 5 numbers have been sorted. The smallest of the 5 numbers is in address 11. The largest number is thus placed in the memory word at address 15.

Before the program loop is run through for the first time, the contents of register q are 11. This is incremented by 1 each time the loop is run through. After the fourth time the contents are made equal to 15. After the program loop has been run through 5 times, the program goes through block 7 in the 'yes' direction. The sorted list is then printed out (block 9).

DETAILED FLOWCHART

In the detailed flowchart we further sub-divide those blocks in the general flowchart which cannot be carried out in one or two instructions. The level to which we will subdivide is determined by the instruction set of the microcomputer concerned. The detailed flowchart describing the problem dealt with in this chapter is in fig. 14-9. We will deal with this detailed flowchart block-for-block.

The comparison of two numbers, one of which is stored in the accumulator, takes place in the ALU. The accumulator has the symbolic name 'ACCU'. Blocks 4, 5 and 6 are replaced in fig. 14-8. The read and output (2 and 9) should also, in fact, be subdivided. However, since a computer has internal programs to do this (stored in a ROM, for example), we may leave these two blocks unchanged. Block 1 (fig. 14-9) gives the start signal. The numbers to be sorted are then read in (block 2) and stored in memory section P at addresses 1 to 5, inclusive.

Block 3 can be taken over from the general flow diagram as it is, since it can be processed in one instruction. In this block, general-purpose register q is loaded with the value 11. Q is a general-purpose register which stores the addresses to which the sorted numbers must be transferred. The smallest number of the first sorting cycle is stored at address 11.

Before starting the first sorting operation, the accumulator must be filled with a value greater than the highest number to be sorted. Thus we must load the accumulator with the value 100 (block 4).

The numbers which have been read in are stored at addresses 1 to 5 in memory section P. The address of the memory word in memory section P, the contents of which must be compared to the contents of the accumulator, is stored in general-purpose register p. The contents of p are indicated by p. In block 5 general-purpose register p is loaded with the address 1, since the first of the numbers must be compared with the contents of the accumulator. In the first comparison operation the number at address 1 is compared in the ALU, in the second the number with address 2, etc. We see that the number in general-purpose register p is also the number of comparison operations that have been carried out. Since general-purpose register p is incremented by 1 after each comparison by comparing the contents of this register with the value 5, we know precisely when 5 comparison operations have taken place. If we had, for example, stored the numbers read in at addresses 0201_{16} through 0205_{16} instead of 1 to 5, we would have had to load general-purpose register p (in block 5) with the value 0201_{16}. We would have had to compare the general-purpose register with the value 0205_{16} to see whether 5 comparisons had taken place.

Figure 14-10 shows that part of the detailed flowchart where the comparison operations take place. In block 6 the contents of the accumulator are compared to the contents of the memory word, the address of which is in register p. The brackets indicate that we are talking about the *contents* of the accumulator and the *contents* of the memory address.

Before the programmed loop formed by blocks 6, 9 and 10 in fig. 14-10 is run through for the first time, the contents of register p equals 1. This implies that this register indicates in which memory word the first number to be sorted can be found. The accumulator is loaded with the value 100 before the first comparison operation. When the task given in block 6 has been carried out for the first time, the result of the comparison will always show that the contents of the accumulator are greater than the number with which it is compared.

In block 7 the contents of the memory word which are compared to the contents of the accumulator in block 6, are put in the accumulator. The contents of the accumulator are therefore replaced. The address of this number is stored in general-purpose register k. After a comparison operation, the contents of this general-purpose register indicates the address in memory section P, where the smaller of the 2 numbers compared is located. If a yet smaller number is found in the next comparison operation, i.e. if the program continues in the

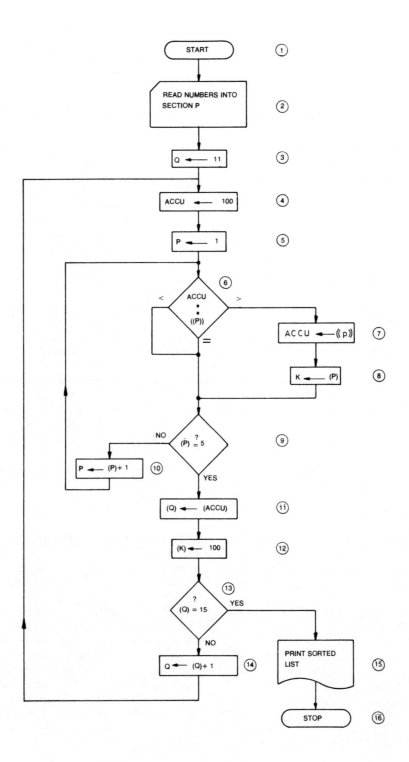

Fig. 14-9.

140

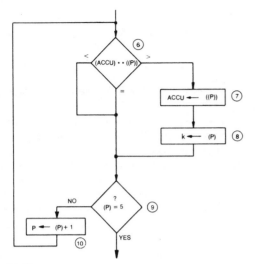

Fig. 14-10.

direction > in block 6, the contents of register k are naturally replaced by the address of the smaller number.

Earlier we reserved a general-purpose register in which to store the addresses in memory section P where the numbers to be sorted are located. In the first comparison operation, the contents of this register equal 1 since the first number—that which must be compared to the contents of the accumulator—has been placed at address 1 in memory section P. Every time the programmed loop is run through, the contents of this register are incremented by 1. It thus always contains the address of the next number to be compared. The incrementing by 1 takes place in block 10. (From now on we will use the term register when speaking of the general-purpose register. When in later chapters we speak of other types of registers, we will mention them specifically by name.)

The programmed loop—formed by blocks 6, 9 and 10—begins at block 9's 'no' exit. When this programmed loop has been run through once, the contents of register p—which indicates the addresses in memory section P—equal 2. When the programmed loop has been run through 4 times, the contents of this register is 5 and after one more compare the program continues in the 'yes' direction in block 9. Five compare operations have been performed.

The smallest number must now be placed in the memory word at address 11 in memory section Q. In block 11 the contents of the accumulator—the smallest number—are transferred to address 11.

Were we to again start sorting the same 5 numbers to find the second smallest number, the smallest number

would appear again since it is still in memory section P. We now exclude this number from further participation by entering in this memory word a content higher than the highest of the remaining numbers. In block 12 the memory word at the address indicated by register k, is given the value 100. This number can never again be the smallest.

In block 13 we can determine by comparison whether or not the contents of register q have reached the value 15; in other words, if all 5 sorting operations have been performed. If this is not the case, (q) is incremented by 1 and the sorting operation is started again. If (q) is equal to 15 (after 5 sort operations) the sorted numbers are now in address 11 to 15 in memory section Q in ascending sequential order. If q = 5, the sorted numbers are output sequentially by a printer in block 15. The stop signal is given in block 16.

SUMMARY

1. The method to be used for solving a problem can be represented in a flowchart.

2. A flowchart is an arrangement of blocks joined together by arrows. The arrows indicate the sequence of events.

3. Flowcharts can be divided into three types:

  ● system flowcharts
  ● general flowcharts
  ● detailed flowcharts.

4. The task represented by each block in the flowchart can be performed by one (or a few) instruction(s) in the instruction set.

5. The computer can compare only 2 numbers in one operation.

6. The comparison of 2 numbers takes place in the ALU. One number is present in the accumulator. The other number is fed in directly from memory.

7. In the sorting method described here, the number of sorting operations is equal to the number of numbers to be sorted. The number of comparison operations also equals the number of values to be sorted.

8. The purpose of the system flowchart is to show which input and output devices are needed to solve a problem. The problem itself is contained in one block.

9. The general flowchart only states in general terms the method of solving the problem itself.

10. The blocks in a detailed flowchart are each processed using one (sometimes two or three) instruction(s) from the instruction set.

11. The read and output blocks—made up of several operations—are processed by a built-in program in the microcomputer.

12. A flowchart always begins with the block 'START' and ends with the block 'STOP.'

REVIEW EXERCISES

1. What do we use a flowchart to describe?

2. What must a flowchart achieve?

3. How is a flowchart constructed?

4. Name three types of flowcharts and their characteristics.

5. Which words could be placed in an oval shaped block.

6. What operation does a diamond shape block represent?

7. What operation does a parallelogram represent?

8. What do the arrows in a flowchart mean?

9. How many numbers can be compared in 1 instruction? Where are these numbers located?

10. In which part of a computer does a comparison take place?

11. Which blocks make up a programmed loop?

12. How do we indicate that we refer to the *contents* of a given register?

ANSWERS

1. The flowchart is used to describe the analysis of a problem.

2. A program must be written using the flowchart as a guide.

3. A flowchart consists of blocks which are joined by arrows.

4. System flowchart: Each block represents the device used. The solution to the problem is defined in one block. General flowchart: The method of solving the problem is worked out in more detail. Detailed flowchart: The general flowchart is subdivided until each block represents 1 instruction to be processed.

5. This block specifies the start or end of a program. We could thus place the words 'START' or 'STOP' here.

6. A comparison.

7. Input or Output.

8. The arrows between blocks indicate the sequence of the program.

9. A maximum of 2 numbers can be compared at one time. One is located in the accumulator and the other is fed in directly from memory or another register.

10. In the ALU.

11. See fig. 14-2.

12. By placing the name of the register in parenthesis. For example, (b) means the contents of register b.

Chapter 15
From Task to Solution

If we are given a task to solve, we must go through several phases in a given order before we can arrive at a source program for solving this task. These phases are:

- description of the task
- analysis of the task
- drafting the system flowchart
- drafting the general flowchart
- drafting the detailed flowchart

- conversion of the detailed flowchart into a source program

In this lesson, we shall use an example illustrating how we can complete a task by running through these phases step-by-step.

In previous chapters we have superficially discussed how we can write a program which can be processed by a computer to achieve a given result from a hand-written

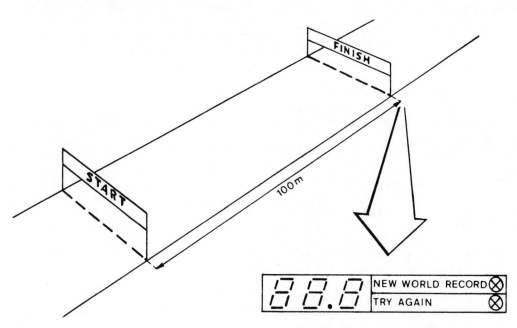

Fig. 15-1.

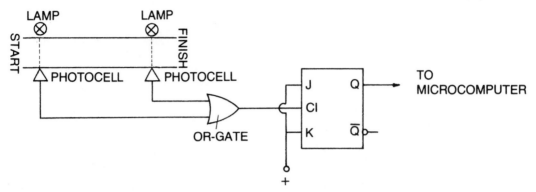

Fig. 15-2.

source program. In the next chapter we will go into this in greater detail.

DESCRIPTION OF THE TASK

The example used in this chapter is one of timing an event. We have a track 100 meters long. A runner is going to try to use this track in breaking the world record for the 100 meters (fig. 15-1). Our task is to use a microcomputer to measure his time to see if he has set a new world record. He must do this by at least 1/10 of a second.

ANALYSIS OF THE TASK

The microcomputer has been given the following assignments:

a. Measure the time elapsed between passing START and FINISH and display this time.

b. Compare this time with the old world record. Display the result of this comparison by turning on a light saying 'new world record' or 'try again'.

The input information is:

a. a signal which indicates that the starting line has been passed

b. a signal which indicates that the finish line has been passed.

These signals could be activated by a combination of photo cells and lamps. A J-K flip-flop and an OR gate can be used to combine these signals so that they can be fed into the microcomputer (fig. 15-2). The Q output of the flip-flop is '1' when the starting line has been passed and returns to '0' after the finish line has been passed. Thus, the time for which the Q output '1' is the time the runner takes to run the 100 meters. Before the start the flip-flop is reset. Q is thus 0. In this example, the time measure-

ment is the period that elapses between the moment the runner leaves the starting line and the time he crosses the finish line. This information can be represented visually with 7-segment displays.

DRAFTING THE FLOWCHARTS

The flowchart shows the methods used for solving the problem. There is often more than one possible solution for a given problem. The way in which we analyze the problem and draw up the flowchart based on this analysis determines the quality of the program finally arrived at. Flowcharts can be divided into three categories:

a. System flowcharts - where we specify the devices used for the input and output of data. The problem itself is described in 1 block.

b. General flowcharts - in which the problem is more specifically described.

Fig. 15-3.

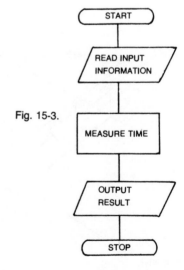

144

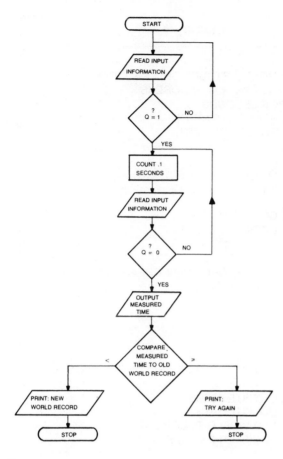

Fig. 15-4A.

c. Detailed flowcharts - in which each block represents 1 (or a very few) instruction(s) from the instruction set used in solving the task at hand.

We can formulate the system flowchart as soon as the I/O devices to be used are known (fig. 15-3). We are not going to subdivide the problem itself ('measure the time') into smaller blocks until our method for solving the problem is clearly represented in the flowchart.

This is what our general flowchart looks like (fig. 15-4a). We are not going to subdivide the block 'Add 0.1 sec' in fig. 15-4a into smaller blocks until the task given in each block can be completed using, in principle, one instruction from the instruction set.

The detailed flowchart shown in fig. 15-4b is the general flow chart in fig. 15-4a. The contents of register A are incremented by 1 every 0.1 seconds until Q = 0; in

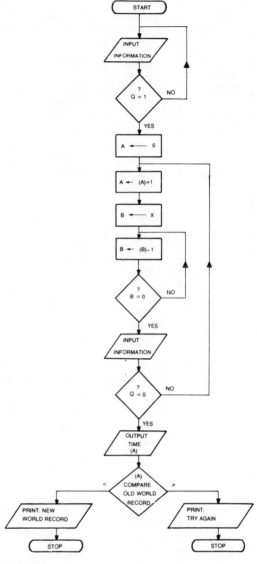

Fig. 15-4B.

other words, until the runner has crossed the finish line. The value 0.1 sec is defined by X. This must be calculated using the method described in the chapter "Sample Programs".

WRITING THE SOURCE PROGRAM

We are now at the point where we must translate the tasks described in the blocks in the detailed flowchart

LABEL	MNEMONIC	OPERAND	COMMENT
	ORG	8200H	; FIRST INSTRUCTION AT ADDRESS 8200 H
WR10:	EQU	00H	; OLD WORLD RECORD IS
WR0.1:	EQU	98H	; 9.8 SECONDS
	LXI	SP,8400	; STACK DEFINITION
BEGIN:	LXI	B, 0000H	; RESET COUNTER
START:	IN	01H	;
	ANI	01H	;
	JZ	START	; Q = 1?
COUNT:	CALL	WAIT	: 0.1 SEC WAIT LOOP
	MOV	A,C	;
	ADI	01H	; CONTENTS C + 0.1 SEC
	DAA		; DECIMAL ADJUST
	MOV	C,A	;
	MOV	A,B	;
	ACI	00H	; CONTENTS B + 1 (INCREASE 10's BY 1)
	DAA		; DECIMAL ADJUST
	MOV	B,A	;
	IN	01H	; Q = 0?
	ANI	01H	;
	JNZ	COUNT	;
	MOV	A,B	;
	OUT	02H	; OUTPUT: 10TH OF SECONDS AND UNITS
	MOV	A,C	;
	OUT	03H	; OUTPUT: 10THS
	OUT	03H	; OUTPUT: 10THS
	MVI	D,WR10	; OLD WORLD RECORD IN
	MVI	E,WR0.1	; REGISTER PAIR D,E
	MOV	A,B	;
	CMP	D	; COMPARE 10THS
	JP	AGAIN	;
	MOV	A,C	;
	CMP	E	; COMPARE UNITS AND 10THS OF SECONDS
	JP	AGAIN	;
	MVI	A,01H	;
	OUT	04H	; PRINT NEW WORLD RECORD
AGAIN:	MVI	A,02H	;
	OUT	04H	; PRINT TRY AGAIN
	JMP	BEGIN	;
WAIT	MVI	D,32H	;
LOOP2:	MVI	E,FFH	; FF17H IN REGISTER PAIR D,E
LOOP1:	DCR	E	; DECREMENT E
	JNZ	LOOP 1	;
	DCR	D	; DECREMENT D
	JNZ	LOOP 2	;
	RET		;
	END		; END OF PROGRAM

Fig. 15-5.

into a language which the computer can understand. This does not mean, however, that you, as programmer, must translate these tasks into a series of ones and zeros. The disadvantages of writing a program in this has been discussed in previous lessons. The programmer can use one of the programming languages. A translation program sees to it that this source program is finally translated into the object program.

The programming language most often used with microcomputers is assembly language. The related translation program—which translates the source program into the object program—is called the assembler or assembly translation program. From now on we shall refer to this translation program simply as the assembler.

Before we can begin with actual writing of the program, we must define our memory space. In other words we must:

(a). Determine the address of the memory word in which we shall place the first instruction in our program to be executed.

(b). Determine which part of the memory we are going to reserve for a stack, if needed.

(c). Determine which general-purpose registers or memory words we are going to use to store given variables.

When this has been done we can take the detailed flowchart and the instruction set and (finally!) begin programming. In the case of our time-measurement exam-ple, this results in the source program printed out in fig. 15-5.

FROM SOURCE PROGRAM TO SOLUTION

We now have the source program on paper. In order for the microcomputer to execute it, the following operations must be performed.

(1). Enter the source program on paper tape, coded in ASCII characters.

(2.) Translate the source program into an object program using the assembler.

(3.) Test the program using the debugger.

These operations will be discussed further in the chapter "System Software".

SUMMARY

1. In order to achieve a source program, we must first describe and analyze the problem, construct the flowcharts and convert these to the source program.

2. The Input and Output information is also included in the analysis of the problem

3. The system flowchart is written first, then the general flowchart and lastly the detailed flowchart.

4. The source program replaces each block in the detailed flowchart with the related assembly instruction.

5. A source program on paper must be put on paper tape, translated into an object program, and then tested.

Chapter 16
Sample Programs

In order to give you more confidence in drafting flow-charts and writing programs, we shall now discuss five sample programs which are often encountered in practice. We start with the assumption that you are by now very familiar with the Chapter 11. If not, please keep that chapter handy and study each instruction you come across while studying these five examples.

EXAMPLE 1

A switch is connected to b_3 of Input port 5 (fig. 16-1). If the switch is open, $b_3 = 1$. If the switch is closed, $b_3 = 0$. Write a program which examines the state of b_3 of Input port 5 and that jumps to program section A if $b_3 = 0$ and to program section B if $b_3 = 1$.

The flowchart representing the solution to this program is shown in fig. 16-2. We'll call this program TESTSW, for test switch. We use this symbolic name as a label associated with the address of the first instruction. If necessary, we can call this program during the execution of another program by using the instruction CALL TESTSW.

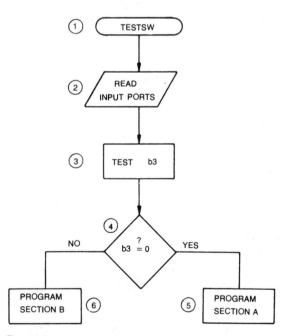

Fig. 16-2.

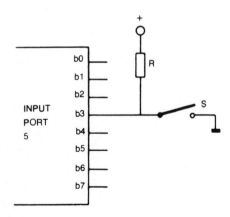

Fig. 16-1.

In block 2 the information from Input port 5 is brought to the accumulator, where the state of b_3 can be examined by masking the remaining bits (block 3). If $b_3 = 0$, the program continues further in the 'yes' direction in block 4, and a jump is made to program section A (Block 5). If $b_3 = 1$, the program continues further in the 'no' direction and jumps to program section B (block 6). The program looks like table 16-1 part A. This program is usually a part of a larger program. The ORG directive is used to indicate the address of the beginning of the program. The assembler keeps track of the addressing and thus knows the address of the first instruction of the above program. In other words, the assembly translation program calculates which address belongs to the label TESTSW.

EXAMPLE 2
Given

The switch in fig. 16-3.

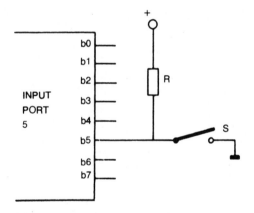

Fig. 16-3.

Problem

Write a subroutine which continually examines the condition of b_5 of Input port 5 until $b = 0$; in other words, until the switch is closed (fig. 16-3). The main program is then returned to.

Solution

The flowchart representing the solution to this problem is shown in fig. 16-4. We'll call this program WAITSW, for 'wait switch'. We use this symbolic name as a label associated with the first instruction of the subroutine. In block 2 the signal present at Input port 5 is

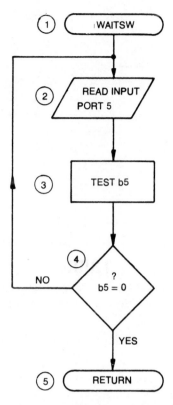

Fig. 16-4.

read in and brought to the accumulator. The state of b_5 is examined in the accumulator by masking the remaining bits. If $b_5 = 1$, the program continues further in the 'no' direction in block 4 and the procedure is repeated. This is repeated until $b_5 = 0$. The program then continues further in the 'yes' direction in block 4 and a return is made to the main program with the help of a RETurn instruction. The program looks like table 16-1 part B.

EXAMPLE 3
Given

Three switches are connected at the inputs b_0, b_1 and b_2 of Input port 2 (fig. 16-5).

If a switch is closed, a '0' is at the related Input. If a switch is open, a '1' is at the related Input. The inputs b_3 to b_7 are connected to ground and are thus '0'. We can thus offer 8 different input signals by using these three switches, i.e., $2^3 = 8$.

Problem

Write a program in which a jump must be made to one of eight different subroutines A to H, depending on

149

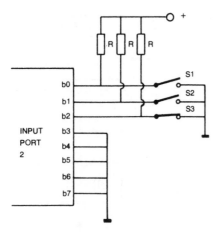

Fig. 16-5.

the signal at the Input port. Jump to subroutine A if the Input signal is 00000000_2. Jump to subroutine B if the input signal is 00000001_2, etc.

Solution

We begin with the assumption that the instructions for the eight subroutines are stored in memory as shown in fig. 16-6. The first instruction of subroutine A is at address 0300_{16}. The first instruction of subroutine B is at address 0400_{16}. We are now going to store the addresses of the first instruction in the subroutines in another part of memory as shown in fig. 16-7. We must, of course, use 2 memory words for storing a 16-bit memory word. The address of the first instruction in subroutine A is stored in the memory addresses with the addresses 0200_{16} and 0201_{16}. The address of the first instruction in subroutine B is stored in the memory addresses with the addresses 0202_{16} and 0203_{16}, etc. The input signal of Input port 2 must be multiplied by 2 and added to the value 0200_{16}. This gives us the address of the memory address in which the first byte of the address of the first instruction of the subroutine corresponding to that input signal.

If, in fig. 16-5, S_1 and S_2 are open and S_3 closed, the input signal of Input port 2 is equal to $00000011_2 = 03_{16}$. This means that a jump must be made to subroutine D. If we multiply the Input signal 03_{16} by 2 and add 0200_{16}, we have $2 \times 03_{16} + 0200_{16} = 0206_{16}$. The first byte of the address of the first instruction in subroutine D is located in the memory address with this address. By incrementing 0206_{16} by 1, we find the address of the memory word containing the second byte. It can be seen from the above that the program must be built with following steps:

● The signal connected to Input port 2 must be fed in and brought to the accumulator.

● The contents of the accumulator must be multiplied by 2 and added to the value 0200_{16}.

● The contents of the memory address with the address just found and the memory address immediately following must be put in the program counter so that the program can continue execution of the appointed subroutine.

The flowchart is shown in fig. 16-8. We'll call our program JUMPTA because we could compare the contents of the memory words in fig. 16-7 with a table in which the addresses of the instructions we have to jump to are stored.

If this is to be an independent program, we must begin with an ORG directive. This tells us that the address 0000H is associated with the label JUMPTA. See table 16-1 part C.

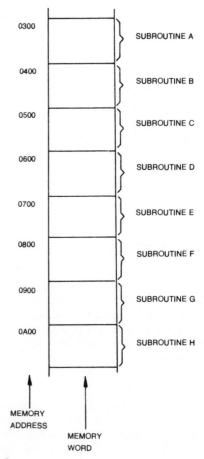

Fig. 16-6.

Note

In a RAL instruction, the contents of the accumulator shift 1 bit location to the left and b_0 is filled with the contents of the carry status flag. Because the status of the carry flag is not known after the supply voltage is turned on, we should—in the program given above—first reset the status carry flag.

EXAMPLE 4

Write a subroutine which generates a wait time of 100 μs.

A wait time can be generated by letting the microcomputer execute a number of instructions which have no function other than taking up time. An often-used method is to fill a register with a given value and then repeatedly subtract 1 from it until the contents of that register become zero. The longer the wait time we want to generate, the bigger we must make the number which we place in the register. The flowchart which describes the above-mentioned method for solving the problem is given in fig. 16-9.

We'll name this subroutine DELAY—this symbolic name being used as a label associated with the first instruction to be executed. We fill register B with the value X (block 2). The value of X depends on the length of the wait time desired. We can determine the value of X only after we know how many instructions comprise the

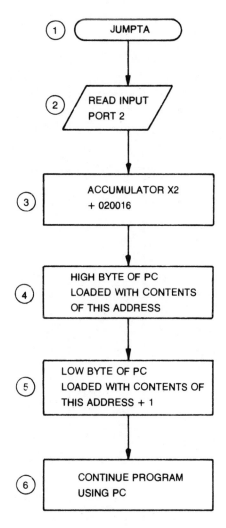

Fig. 16-8.

program, how many states each instruction contains, and how long 1 state lasts. The contents of register B are decremented by 1 (block 3). We then check (block 4) to see if this equals 0. This can be checked from the condition of the zero status flag. The zero status flag is, of course, reset when the result of a calculation zero. The program looks like table 16-1 part D. Of course, the above program does not yet work since we have not given the assembler a value of X. We do, however, know which instructions are used to make up the program so that we can calculate how long each instruction takes and thus determine how often given instructions must be repeated in order to generate the desired wait time. The MVI B,X and RET instructions are executed once. The instruc-

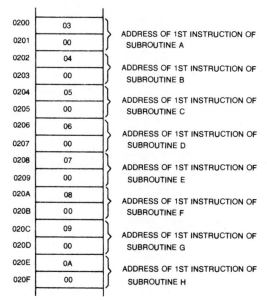

Fig. 16-7.

Table 16-1.

LABEL	MNEUMONIC	OPERAND	COMMENT
TEST SW:	IN	O5H	; INFORMATION AT INPUT PORT 5 ; TO ACCUMULATOR
	AWI	O8H	; MASK B7, B6, B5, B4, B2, ; B1 AND B0
	JZ	A	; JUMP TO SUBROUTINE A IF B3 = 0 ; IF NOT ; GO TO NEXT INSTRUCTION
B:	—		; 1ST INSTRUCTION OF PROGRAM SECTION B
	—		
	—		
A:	—		; 1ST INSTRUCTION OF PROGRAM SECTION A
	—		
	—		
WAITSW:	IN	O5H	; INFORMATION AT INPUT PORT 5 ; TO ACCUMULATOR
	ANI	20H	; MASK B7, B6, B4, B3, B2, B1 and B0
	JNZ	WAITSW	; JUMP TO WAITSW IF B5 = 1
	RET		; RETURN TO MAIN PROGRAM IF B5 = 0.
	ORG	OOOOH	; 1ST INSTRUCTION AT ADDRESS OOOOH
JUMPTA:	IN	O2H	; INPUT PORT 2 TO ACCUMULATOR,
DELAY:	MVI	B,X	; LOAD REGISTER B WITH VALUE X
FORWARD:	DCR	B	; DECREMENT CONTENT REGISTER B BY 1
	JNZ	FORWARD	; REPEAT PROCESS IF RESULT NOT 0
	RET		; IF RESULT O, RETURN TO MAIN PROGRAM
DELAY:	MVI	B,10D	; LOAD REGISTER B WITH VALUE 10D
FORWARD:	DCR	B	; DECREMENT CONTENT REGISTER B BY 1
	JNZ	FORWARD	; REPEAT PROCESS IF RESULT NOT 0
	NOP		
	NOP		; NO OPERATION
	NOP		
	NOP		
	RET		; RETURN TO MAIN PROGRAM
	ORG	0000H	; FIRST INSTRUCTION AT ADDRESS OOOOH
ALARM:	MVI	A,01H	; LOAD ACCUMULATOR WITH 01H
FLASH:	OUT	O2H	; CONTENT ACCU TO OUTPUT PORT 2
	CALL	DELAY	; WAIT
	XRI	01H	; CHANGE B0 of ACCU
	JMP	FLASH	;
a.			
ALARM:	MVI	A,01H	
FLASH:	OUT	02H	
	CALL	DELAY	
	XRI	20H	
	JMP	FLASH	
b.			
ALARM:	MVI	A,08H	
FLASH:	CALL	O5H	
	OUT	DELAY	

LABEL	MNEUMONIC	OPERAND	COMMENT
	XRI	08H	
	JMP	FLASH	
c.			
ALARM:	MVI	A,08H	
FLASH:	OUT	05H	
	CALL	DELAY	
	XRI	28H	
	JMP	FLASH	
d.			
FLASH:	MVI	A,08H	
	CALL	OUT 05H	
	XRI	DELAY	
	JMP	28H	
		FLASH	
a.			
BOTH:	IN	03H	
	ANI	COH	
	JZ	BOTH	
	XRI	ff	
	OUT	01H	
	HLT		
b.			
BOTH:	IN	03H	
	XRI	COH	
	JNZ	BOTH	
	MVI	A,ff	
	OUT	01H	
	HLT		
c.			
BOTH:	IN	O3H	
	JNZ	BOTH	
	MVI	A,ff	
	OUT	O1H	
d.	HLT		
BOTH:	IN	O3H	
	ANI	COH	
	JNZ	BOTH	
	MVI	A,ff	
	OUT	01H	
	HLT		
JUMTA	RAL		; CONTENT OF ACCUMULATOR X2
	LXI	H,O2OOH	; O2OOH IN REGISTER PAIR H,L
	ADD	L	; CONTENT L + CONTENT ACCUMULATOR
			; RESULT IN ACCUMULATOR
	MOV	L, A	; RESULT BACK TO L
			; ADDRESS FOUND NOW IN H,L
	MOV	D, M	; CONTENT MEMORY WORD WITH ADDRESS
			; IN H,L TO D
	INX	H	; INCREMENT REGISTER PAIR H,L
	MOV	E, M	; CONTENT MEMORY WORD WITH ADDRESS
			; IN H,L TO E.
			; ADDRESS 1ST INSTRUCTION OF SUB
			; ROUTINE NOW IN REGISTER PAIR D,E
	XCHG		; EXCHANGE CONTENT D,E AND H,L
			; BECAUSE PROGRAM COUNTER CAN ONLY BE
			; FILLED FROM H,L
	PCHL		; CONTENT H,L TO PROGRAM COUNTER

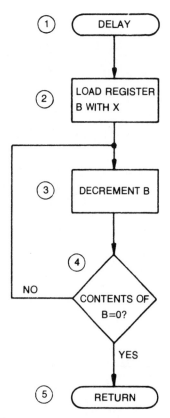

Fig. 16-9.

can never reach 83 by repeating these 2 instructions a number of times since 83 is not divisible by 7.5. We can solve this problem by executing these 2 instructions 10 times. The number X is thus equal to 10. This brings us to 75 μs, which means that we have 8 μs left over. We can "use up" these 8 μs by using 4 NOP (no operation) instructions, each of which has 4 states = 2 μs time. The final program looks like table 16-1 part E.

EXAMPLE 5

An LED is connected to b_0 of Output port 2 (fig. 16-10). The LED lights up if $b_0 = 1$. Write a program to make the light flash on and off. The frequency is not important.

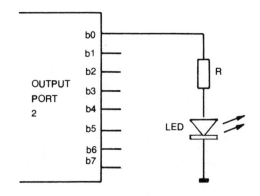

Fig. 16-10.

tions DCR B and JNZ FORWARD are executed as many times as specified by the number X. We must also, naturally, take the CALL DELAY instruction into account. The main program uses this instruction to call the subroutine DELAY.

We now refer to the instruction set to see how many states comprise each instruction. We assume that each state takes 500 ns or 0.5 μs. We now get the following figures:

CALL DELAY	= 17 states	= 8.5 μs
MVI B,X	= 7 states	= 3.5 μs
DCR B	= 5 states	= 2.5 μs
JNZ FORWARD	= 10 states	= 5.0 μs
RET	= 10 states	= 5.0 μs

The instructions, which are each executed once, together take 8.5 + 3.5 + 5.0 = 17 μs. In order to activate a wait time of 100 μs, the microcomputer must execute the instructions DCR B and JNZ FORWARD often enough so that this process takes 100 − 17 = 83 μs. Executing these 2 instructions once takes 2.5 + 5.0 = 7.5 μs. We

We can make the light blink by making b_0 of Output port 2, 1 and 0 alternately. We put the value 01H in the accumulator and give the instruction out 02H. The LED will now light up because Output port 2 relays the value 00000001_2. We now wait a given time period and make the contents of the accumulator 00H. If we again give the instruction OUT 02H, the LED goes out. After again waiting we once more make the contents of the accumulator 01H and again sent these contents to Output port 2, so that the LED goes on again. The computer can repeat this process endlessly.

We can make use of the DELAY subroutine described in example 4 for this waiting period. We would, however, have to choose a much larger value for X, since a generated wait time of 100μs is much to short to let us see if the light is on or off. The flowchart representing the above solution is given in fig. 16-11.

We'll call this program ALARM, using this symbolic name as a label associated with the address of the first instruction. We load the accumulator with the value

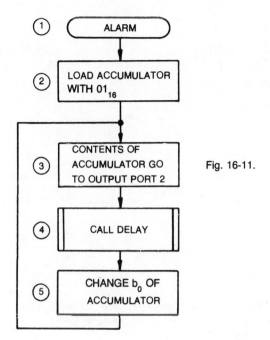

Fig. 16-11.

$00000001_2 = 01_{16}$ (block 2). We next bring this value to Output port 2 (block 3). The LED now lights up. We use the subroutine DELAY to generate a certain wait time so that the lamp continues to be lighted for a determined length of time. The subroutine DELAY is called using the instruction CALL DELAY (block 4). We then change the state of b_0 of the contents of the accumulator (block 5).

If b_0 is equal to 1, it becomes 0; if b_0 is 0, it becomes 1. We can change the state of b_0 by processing all the bits of the word with $00000001_2 = 01_{16}$, using the EXOR function.

If the contents of the accumulator are   00000001
and we process this contents with   00000001 EXOR
the result and thus new content is $\overline{00000000}$

If the contents of the accumulator are   00000000
and we process this contents with   00000001 EXOR
the result and thus new contents are $\overline{00000001}$

The program now looks like table 16-1 part F.
The last instruction is an unconditional jump. Therefore the program never gets out of the loop.

Chapter 17
Traffic Lights

There are three ways to regulate the flow of traffic.

Policeman

A policeman on point duty can take account density of traffic in each direction. However, because of the large number of junctions and the high salaries of policemen, this solution is hardly feasible nowadays.

Traffic Lights with a Fixed Duty Cycle

Using relays or conventional logic (gates and flip-flops) we can build a traffic light control system with fixed red and green intervals. However, because traffic is not taken into account this solution is not conducive to even traffic flow.

Traffic Lights Controlled by Traffic Flow

By using detectors buried in the road surface we can make a traffic light control system that operates according to traffic density. Such a system will require more logic than one that is independent of traffic flow because more functions must be performed. Since the introduction of the microprocessor it is cheaper to use a microcomputer in traffic dependent control systems.

In this chapter we will deal with the design of a traffic dependent control system using a microcomputer. We shall deal with it in the following phases:

● accurate definition of the system characteristics
● determining the solution with the aid of a flow-chart

● development of an interface between the computer and the outside world. At the same time we will make a time study.

● writing the program
● combining the above to form a system

As basis we will use the Intel 8080 microprocessor which, together with the interface and I/O units, can execute the following functions:

● signal the passing of vehicles by means of detectors

● make decisions based on the signals received
● operate the traffic lights

In this chapter we are dealing with one of the many applications of the microcomputer.

DEFINING THE SYSTEM CHARACTERISTICS

In this phase the available information and the goals are put into order. The task is as follows. Design a traffic-dependent traffic light control system for a junction between a main road and a side road. The control must be dependent on the traffic flow. Traffic will be signalled by detectors buried in the road surface. In fig. 17-1 you can find a diagram showing where the detectors are situated. The traffic lights are controlled by the signals from the detectors and by conditions incorporated in the program. From the situation at the junction, we arrive at the following requirements:

1. The traffic lights for the main road must be green when no traffic has been signalled on the side road within the last 30 seconds.

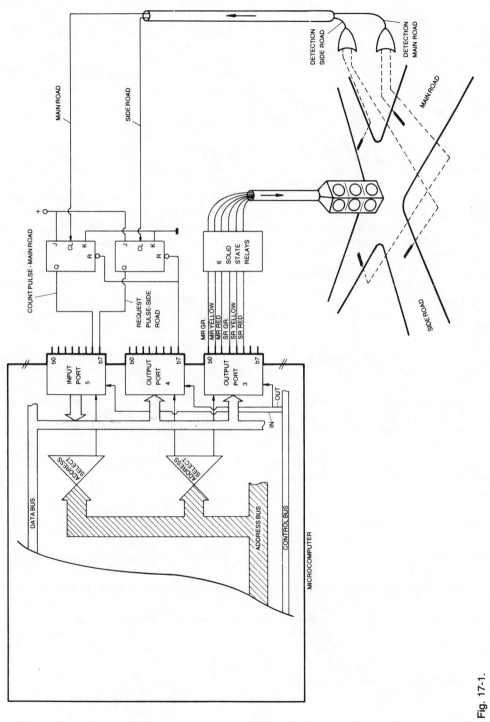

Fig. 17-1.

157

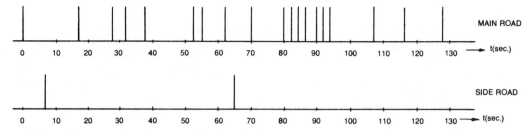

Fig. 17-2A.

2. The main road traffic lights must be green for at least 30 seconds.

3. When a vehicle is signalled on the side road, the traffic lights on the main road must immediately change unless the minimum time of 30 seconds has not elapsed, in which case the system must wait until it has elapsed.

4. The side road gets a green signal for 30 seconds unless 7 vehicles are signalled on the main road, in which case the green period of the side road is immediately interrupted. The signals from the main road are counted during its red period.

5. For both roads the amber period is 4 seconds.

6. The signals from the detectors have no influence when the lights for that road stand at green.

The above conditions will be illustrated with the aid of an example. Say that for a given time the traffic on the main and side roads is as shown in the diagram of Fig. 17-2a. Assuming that at time $T = 0$ there have been no vehicles detected on the side road within the last 30 seconds, so that at $T = 0$ the signal for the main road is at green and at red for the side road. (fig. 17-2b.). At $T = 7$ a vehicle is signalled on the side road. The signals on the main road change to amber and 4 seconds later to red. At the same moment the signal on the side road changes to green. The signals on the main road remain red until 30 seconds have elapsed or until 7 vehicles have been detected on the main road. The vehicles detected on the main road are *only* counted while the traffic signals on that road are at red. (Fig. 17-2b). The reason, therefore, that signals on the main road change to green at $T = 44$ is that the maximum period for which the side road may be green, has elapsed. At $T = 65$ a vehicle is signalled on the side road. The signal on the side road changes to green only after the minimum green period for the main road of 30 seconds, plus the 4 seconds amber time, has elapsed. At $T = 74$ the minimum green period for the main road has elapsed and the signals change to amber for 4 seconds, and then the signal changes to red. At this moment, that is at $T = 78$, the signals on the side road change to green. The signals on the side road remain green for 30 seconds or until 7 vehicles have been detected on the main road. At $T = 94$ the 7th vehicle is detected on the main road. At this moment the signals on the side road change to amber and remain so for 4 seconds. At $T = 98$ the signals on the side road change to red and those on the main road to green.

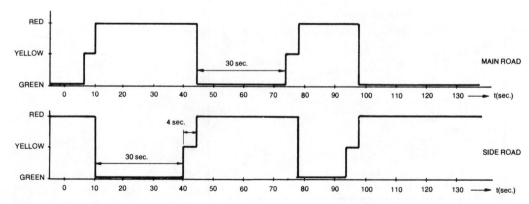

Fig. 17-2B.

SETTING UP A FLOWCHART

In this phase a *situation diagram* is set up first, according to which the system just outlined can be realized. A situation diagram is a block diagram which indicates how the system must operate on the data it receives as a function of time and external signals. It is an aid to setting up the general flowchart. The situation diagram in 17-3 shows the changes that are possible in every situation that can occur at the traffic lights. From fig. 17-3 we can see under which conditions a change is made from one state to another. In situation 1 (main road green) the program waits until 30 seconds have elapsed. Once this has occurred a check must be made as to whether there is a request for green from the side road due to a vehicle being detected there. If, in fact, a request for green has been made for the side road, then the green on the main road must terminate. If no request for green has been made, then the microcomputer waits until such a request is made. In situation 2 (main road amber) the program takes account solely of time. The amber period is always 4 seconds. The change from situation 3 (side road green) to situation 4 (side road amber) occurs when one of the following conditions is fulfilled:

● The maximum time of 30 seconds for situation 3 has elapsed.

● A green request has been received from the main road because 7 vehicles have been detected.

For situation 4 (side road amber), the same conditions are valid as for situation 2. On the basis of the above considerations we draw up a general flowchart as in fig. 17-4. Numbers 1 to 4 correspond with the related situations shown in fig. 17-3.

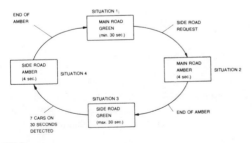

Fig. 17-3.

DEVELOPING THE INTERFACE

By interface we mean those circuits between the input equipment and the microcomputer on the one hand, and between the microcomputer and the output on the other.

In fig. 17-1 the input equipment comprises a number of detectors, the output equipment comprises lamps. The interface between the microcomputer and the I/O equipment in fig. 17-1 comprises 2 flip-flops, 2 OR-gates and 6 solid-state relays. The following points are of importance in developing the interface for the traffic light control system:

● What is the Output signal of the detector and what Input signal does the microcomputer need?

● What is the Output signal of the microcomputer and what Input signal does a lamp need?

● The signal emitted by the detector must be stored until the microcomputer, via the program, gives orders for it to be fetched. This ensures that a momentary signal is not missed when the microcomputer is executing something other than an Input signal.

THE INTERFACE BETWEEN THE MICROCOMPUTER AND OUTPUT EQUIPMENT

Six lamps are needed for each direction (front and rear). The lamps to front and rear are switched in parallel. These 12 lamps are driven by 6 bits of an output gate. The signal of an output is, of course, at TTL level, so these large lamps cannot be driven directly. Because we cannot couple the mains voltage to the microcomputer we must introduce electrical isolation between the computer and the mains. A switch that is ideally suited for this purpose is the solid-state relay. This is a semiconductor switch by which the TTL signal from the computer can drive a triac via an optic-isolator. The solid-state relays are directly driven by the Output port of the microcomputer. By means of its output instruction the computer ensures that the correct lamp lights.

THE INTERFACE BETWEEN DETECTORS AND THE MICROCOMPUTER

We will assume that the detectors are inductive loop detectors. These are loops buried in the road which form part of an oscillator. When a vehicle passes over the loop, the oscillator cuts off and an impulse is generated. There are 4 detectors, 1 for each traffic lane (fig. 17-1). The signals from the main road can be combined by means of an OR-gate, and the same is true for the signals from the side road. Thus 2 signals remain to be used by the microcomputer. The signals from the main road must be counted (7-counter) and the signals from the side road must be used to generate a green request for the side road. The question now arises as to how these signals must be passed to the computer. Must we use an external

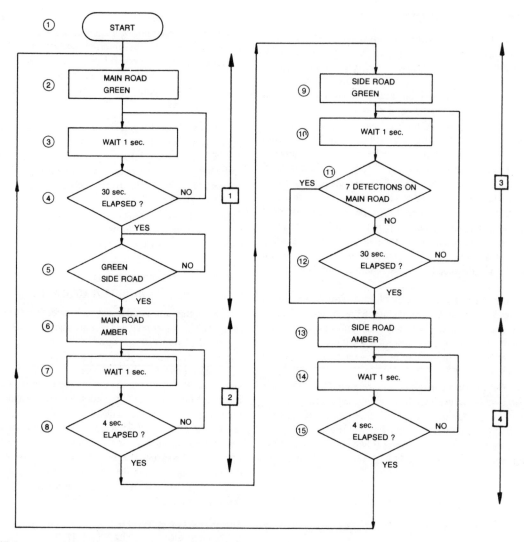

Fig. 17-4.

counter which is periodically checked by the computer as to whether a count of 7 has been reached, or can the microcomputer take care of the counting? If so, can the microcomputer handle the signals from the detectors direct, or must they be stored temporarily in a buffer (flip-flop)? The solution depends on the speed of the computer and the construction of the program. If many calculations have to be executed, little time will remain for I/O activities, which may result in a detector signal being missed. To solve the above-mentioned problems, detector impulses are stored in a flip-flop. The contents of the flip-flops can then be fetched whenever the pro-

gram requires it. Thereafter the flip-flop can be reset by means of a reset signal generated by the microcomputer. The periodic test occurs when it is necessary. Separation is thus maintained between what is happening on the road and the program.

Note

Use could also be made of the interrupt function of the microcomputer, but this would be going to far here. The buffer flip-flop check is made via an Input gate that transfers the data to the accumulator where arithmetic and logic operations can be performed on it. The Input gate only admits the signals when an input-enable signal is given. The input-enable is a signal that is generated as an Input instruction incorporated in the program, the related address being that of the appropriate input gate. The above approach requires that a decision be made in the program as to what must be done with data from the detectors. How this is done will be seen when we deal with the program.

WRITING THE PROGRAM

The software part of the traffic dependent traffic light control system is shown in figs. 17-4 and 17-5. The situation diagram is fig. 17-4, and fig. 17-5 is the resultant flowchart. Figure 17-6 is the program written in assembly language. It is a translation of the instructions appearing in the blocks of the flowchart. The comment field of an assembly instruction begins with a semi-colon and serves to explain the program. This explanation is completely ignored by the assembly translation program. Thus the statements between the dotted lines only serve to inform the reader of the logic used by the programmer in writing the program. The information given in this part can be followed in fig. 17-1.

ASSEMBLER DIRECTIVES

By means of the assembler directive ORG, we tell the assembly translation program where to enter the instruction to be executed first is stored. The assembly translation program needs this information in order to maintain a check on how the addresses are used and so to enter the correct address values for the labels.

To drive the lamps a specific combination of ones and zeros is required on the outputs of Output port 3 for each of the 4 possible conditions. So that the program need not be interrupted for complicated calculations, we allocate each of the conditions a symbolic name and calculate the related binary values in advance.

The four symbolic names are:

- MRGR = main road green; side road red
- MRAM = main road amber; side road red
- SRGR = side road green; main road red
- SRAM = side road amber; main road red

To indicate that a lamp must be lit, we set a 1 on the related Output of Output port 3. For the condition MRGR the lights must be at green for the main road and at red for the side road. This means that b_0 and b_5 of Output port 3 must be 1s. Thus, for MRGR, the outputs of Output port 3 must have the values $0010001_2 = 21_{16}$. In the same way:

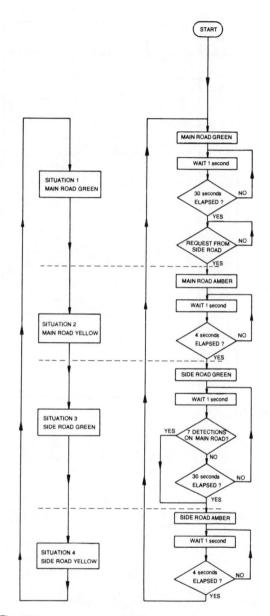

Fig. 17-5.

- MRAM = $00100010_2 = 22_{16}$
- SRGR = $00001100_2 = 0C_{16}$
- SRAM = $00010100_2 = 14_{16}$.

We inform the assembly translation program of these values by means of EQU directives. Thus, whenever the assembly translation program comes across one of these symbolic names it can immediately enter the requisite values.

161

	ORG	0000H	
MRGR	EQU	21H	signal code for main road green
MRAM	EQU	22H	signal code for main road amber
SRGR	EQU	0CH	signal code for side road green
SRAM	EQU	14H	signal code for side road amber
INIT	CALL	RESET	INITIALIZATION OF DETECTOR FLIP-FLOPS
BEGIN	MVI	MRGR	
	OUT	05H	CONTROL SIGNALS
	MVI	D.30	SECONDS COUNTER ON 30
LOOP 1	CALL	ONESEC	CALL WAITING LOOP OF 1 SECOND
	DCR	D	DECREMENT COUNTER
	JNZ	LOOP 1	NOT READY JUMP TO 1
REQUE	IN	05H	FETCH DETECTOR DATA
	RAL		SIDE ROAD DETECTORS TO CARRY FF
JNC	REQUE		WAIT FOR A SIDE ROAD REQUEST
CALL	RESET		RESET DETECTOR DATA
MV1	MR CR		
OUT	03H		CONTROL SIGNALS
	MVI	D.4	SECONDS COUNTER ON 4
LOOP 2	CALL	ONE SEC	CALL WAITING LOOP OF 1 SECOND
	DCR	D	DECREMENT COUNTER
	JNZ	LOOP 2	NOT READY JUMP TO LOOP 2
	MV1	A SRGR	
	OUT	03H	CONTROL SIGNALS
	MV1	E.00	RESET VEHICLE COUNTER
	MV1	D.30	SET SECOND COUNTER AT 30
LOOP 3	CALL	ONESEC	CALL WAITING LOOP OF 1 SECOND
	CALL	COUNTER	CALL MAIN ROAD ROUTINE
	JZ	FURTH	AT 7 VEHICLES TO FURTH
	DCR	D	DECREMENT COUNTER
	JNZ	LOOP 3	NOT READY JUMP TO LOOP 3
FURTH	MV1	SRAM	
	OUT 03	03H	CONTROL SIGNALS
LOOP 4	CALL	ONESEC	CALL WAITING LOOP OF 1 SECOND

	ORG	0000H	
Y	MV1	D.4	SECONDS COUNTER AT 4
	DCR D	D	DECREMENT COUNTER
	JNZ	LOOP 4	NOT READY JUMP TO LOOP 4
	JMP	BEGIN	RETURN TO START FOR FOLLOWING
SUBROUTINE			
RESET	MV1	A. 00H	
	OUT	04H	RESET PULSE TO FLIP-FLOPS
	MV1	A.80H	
	OUT	04H	RESET SIGNAL INACTIVE
	HE1		RETURN TO CALLING PROGRAM
SUBROUTINE			
ONESEC			
ONESEC	MV1		COUNTER EXTERNAL LOOP
LOOP 1	MV1	C.FBH	COUNTER INTERNAL LOOP
LOOP 2	NOP		NO OPERATION
	NOP		
	NOP		
	NOP		
	DCR	C	DECREMENT INTERNAL LOOP
	JNZ	LOOP 2	
	DCR	B	
	JNZ	LOOP 1	
	RET		
SUBROUTINE	COUNTER	7	DETECTIONS ON MAIN ROAD
COUNTER	TN	5	FETCH DETECTOR DATA
	RAL		
	RAL		SELECT MAIN ROAD DETECTOR
	JC	INCRM	DETECT VEHICLE JUMP TO INCRM
	RET		RETURN TO CALLING PROGRAM
INCRM	CALL	RESET	RESET DETECTOR FLIP-FLOPS
	INR	E	INCREMENT VEHICLE COUNTER
	MV1	A.7	
	CMP	E	
	JNZ	RETURN	YES JUMP TO RETURN
	MV1	E.0	SET VEHICLE COUNTER TO ZERO
RETURN	RET		RETURN TO CALLING PROGRAM

Fig. 17-6.

INITIALIZATION

The actual program begins with the initialization of the detector flip-flops, that is to say with setting them at the correct starting values. Because the initial values of the detector flip-flops must be zeros we make use of the reset subroutine for initialization. This subroutine is called up by the CALL RESET instruction. The reset subroutine is shown in fig. 17-6. The reset inputs of both detector flip-flops are connected to b_7 of Output port 4. The reset signal is active when $b_7 = 0$ and inactive when $b_7 = 1$. If we enter the value 00_{16} in the accumulator and give the OUT instruction, the flip-flops will be reset. The reset signal can be made inactive again by entering the value 80_{16} in the accumulator and again giving the OUT instruction.

WAIT 1 SECOND

The waiting time of 1 second is obtained by a subroutine named ONESEC. For this subroutine the register pair BC is filled with the value FFFH, from which 1 is successively subtracted until zero remains. The NOP instructions are used as a fine control for the waiting time so generated.

WAIT 30 SECONDS

The waiting time of 30 seconds is obtained by running through a subroutine named ONESEC 30 times. Sub-routine ONESEC is executed in 1 second. This sub-routine is also shown in fig. 17-6. Register D maintains a check on how many times the subroutine is run through. The value 30 is entered in register D and 1 is successively subtracted until zero remains. Initially this may seem a roundabout way of obtaining a waiting time of 30 seconds, because we saw in the chapter "Program Example" that it can be done in 1 step simply by entering such a value in a register pair, and that by successively subtracting 1 it takes 30 seconds before the register pair is at zero. However, by running 30 times through a 1 second subroutine, we are able to check for detection signals on the main road each time the 1 second subroutine ends.

CHECKING FOR A SIDE ROAD GREEN REQUEST

The check for a green request from the side road occurs as follows:

1. First, by means of the instruction IN 5, the data on input gate 5 is brought to the accumulator.

2. Then the RAL instruction rotates the contents of the accumulator 1 place to the left. Because detector data from the side road appears on b_7 of Input port 5, a rotation of 1 place to the left will bring data (1 or 0) into the carry status flag.

3. If the content of the status flag is zero, no request has been received from the side road and the procedure must be repeated.

4. If the content of the status flag is 1, it means that a request has been received from the side road and the program must proceed further with controlling the lights for the condition MRAM.

5. This conditional jump is realized by the instruction JNC REQ.

DETECTIONS ON THE MAIN ROAD

The step from condition 3 (SRGR) to condition 4 (SRAM) occurs when either 30 seconds has elapsed or 7 vehicles have been detected on the main road. The detections on the main road are counted by a subroutine named COUNT, shown in fig. 17-6. The detection signal is fetched by the instruction IN 05H and is entered in the accumulator. When the contents of the accumulator rotated 2 places to the left, the data that originally appeared on b_6 of Input port 5 entered in the carry status flag. By the content of the carry status flag the microcomputer can see whether or not a vehicle has been detected on the main road.

When a vehicle is signalled the carry status flag is set and, as a result of instruction JC INCRM, a jump is made to label INCRM. The detector flip-flops are reset by means of subroutine RESET and the contents of register E increased by 1. After this instruction the value 7 is entered in the accumulator and is compared with the contents of register E. If the contents of register E are not equal to 7 then, as a result of the instruction CMP E, the zero status flag is not set, and following the instruction JNC RET jumps to the instruction RET so that a return is made to the main program. If, when the detector data is fetched, it transpires that no vehicle has been detected, the carry status flag is not set and in consequence of the instruction JC INCRM no jump is made, but a return to the main program occurs.

If, after returning from the subroutine COUNT, it transpires that 7 vehicles have indeed been detected, then the zero status flag is set and, directed by the instruction JZ FURTH, a jump is made to the label FURTH.

If, after returning from the subroutine COUNT, it transpires that 7 vehicles have not been detected then the zero status flag is not set and the condition "jump on zero" is not fulfilled. The contents of register D the decremented by 1 and a return jump is made to the label LOOP 3, provided the contents of register D not zero; i.e. the 30 seconds waiting time has not elapsed.

COMBINING SOFTWARE AND HARDWARE

The last step is the combination of hardware and software. The program that has been developed is then entered into a PROM. Only to construct and test remains. For the equipment needed to program the PROM and to locate any errors one can consult the chapter "Development Equipment" and "Auxiliary Programs".

Chapter 18
System Software

If one wants a computer to execute a task, one must write a program. A program written in assembly language or in PL/M is known as a source program. The source program must be translated into an object program which must then be corrected and tested. The corrected and tested object program is known as the *work program*, because it is the one with which the computer will work. Source program, object program, and work program have the common name *user software*. To translate a source program into an object program, to test and correct the object program, and to enter the work program, the manufacturer supplies the user with a number of ready-made programs. These auxiliary programs that belong to the system have the collective name *system software*. System software is independent of application. User software and system software together form the software of the microcomputers. A survey of this is given in fig. 18-1.

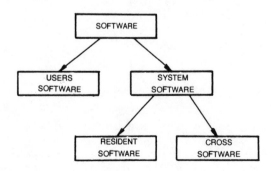

Fig. 18-1.

System software can be divided into resident software and cross software. Resident software indicates those auxiliary programs that are needed to develop a program using a computer of the same type for which the work program is intended. Cross software indicates those auxiliary programs that are needed when the work program is developed on a different type of computer. In this chapter we will deal with the programs belonging to system software.

THE MONITOR PROGRAM

The monitor program, or monitor, is an auxiliary program that is often entered in a ROM or PROM. The monitor comprises a main program and a number of subroutines. The function of the monitor is to *control the microcomputer* during the translation, testing, correcting, and entering of the user software. The monitor program is constructed as shown by the flowchart in fig. 18-2.

After the supply voltage has been switched on (START), the *bootstrap program* initializes the microcomputer. This means that the program counter, with the aid of some preparatory instructions, is filled with the address of the first instruction of the monitor. The bootstrap program cannot otherwise be called. It is, therefore, a particular sort of subroutine that only reacts to the supply voltage. The *monitor main program* ensures that the monitor enters a command loop and remains therein until the programmer, by typing one or more symbols on the TTY, requests the execution of one of the subroutines of the monitor. The subroutine is called and

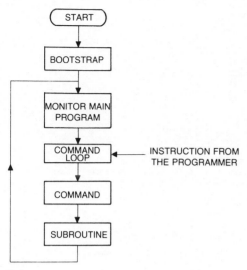

START

BOOTSTRAP

MONITOR MAIN PROGRAM

COMMAND LOOP ◄— INSTRUCTION FROM THE PROGRAMMER

COMMAND

SUBROUTINE

Fig. 18-2.

started by means of a *monitor command*. Furthermore, by means of this command the monitor hands over control of the microcomputer to the subroutine. The monitor commands a number of subroutines. We will discuss two.

The Loader

This is for control of a punched tape reader. The loader switches in the punched tape reader, ensures that the work program is set at the requisite place in the memory, and maintains a check on the start and finish addresses. After execution of the loader, a return is made to the main program of the monitor which ensures that the monitor returns to the command loop.

The Punch

This is for control of a punched tape puncher. The punch must be able to start the tape punch and have access to the start and finish addresses of the program that is to be entered on the punched tape. After the punch has been executed, a return is made to the main program of the monitor, so that the monitor returns to the command loop.

TEXT EDITOR

Having set up a flowchart that describes the method by which the problem will be solved, the tasks set out in each block of the flowchart must be translated into 1 or more assembly instructions. Then, these instructions must be entered onto punched tape using a TTY. This

means that every letter and every number or symbol will be translated by the TTY into an ASCII character. The punched tape so obtained is known as the source tape. A single mistake made in typing in the instructions ruins the punched tape and means that we must begin again. This can be avoided by the use of a text editor in making the source tape. The text editor, or editor offers the possibility of correcting and editing the users program as it is entered on the punched tape. Figure 18-3 shows how the source tape is made using the monitor and text editor. The following phases must be run through:

●After the programmer has given the instruction "read editor in" the monitor leaves the command loop.

●By means of a monitor command, the monitor calls the subroutine loader which controls the punched tape reader.

●Once the punched tape reader has read in the editor program from the punched tape, the monitor, via the monitor main program, returns to the command loop to await further instructions from the programmer.

●If the programmer now gives the instruction "start editor" a jump will be made from the monitor to the editor, via a monitor command, and typing in of the assembly instructions can commence.

The editor takes over control of the microcomputer system. When a letter is typed in it is made visible by means of a display screen or TTY and, as an ASCII coded character, entered in the memory. When a number of program lines (block) have been typed in, the programmer can check whether it is correct. Should he discover an error he can type that line in again and the procedure can be repeated.

●Once the entire program, in an error-free form, has been entered in ASCII coded characters in the memory, then *from the editor*, by means of a monitor command, the subroutine "Punch", which controls the tape punch can be called. By means of this tape punch, the program stored in the memory can be entered on the punched tape, thereby generating the source tape.

●After executing the subroutine "Punch", the monitor returns once again to the command loop to await the following instruction from the programmer.

ASSEMBLY TRANSLATION PROGRAM

The assembly translation program, or assembler, is an auxiliary program that translates the source program, written in assembly language, into an object program. The assembly translation program can also detect *formal errors* in the source program. Formal errors are errors

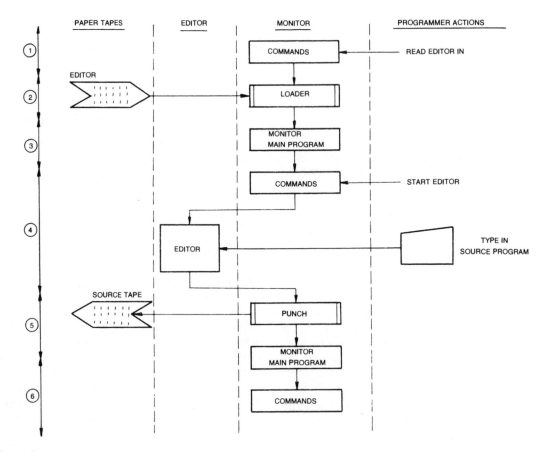

Fig. 18-3.

such as syntax errors; i.e., the indication or not of an operand, or the double use of a label, etc. When the source program is translated (assembly) into the object program, the assembly translation program runs through the source program several times. A different sort of operation is carried out each time. Examples of these operations are:

● setting up a list of used labels
● translating labels into actual address values
● exchanging mnemonics for bit patterns

During the first run through of the source program, the assembly translation program constructs a list of any formal errors. The execution of the assembly translation program cannot be interrupted to correct errors. When errors are detected the relevant instruction must be corrected via the editor and the assembly must begin again. Figure 18-4 shows how a programmer, with the aid of the monitor, the editor and the assembly translation program, can translate a source program into an object program. Figure 18-4 shows which phases must be passed through in order to translate a source program into an object program.

1. With the instruction "read editor in" the monitor leaves the command loop and issues a monitor command, whereby a jump is made to the subroutine loader. The loader controls the punched tape reader via which the editor is entered in the microcomputer memory. Once this is executed the monitor returns to the command loop.

2. Once the instruction "start editor" has been given, the typing in or assembly instructions can begin. This is done as described earlier. The source program appears eventually in the form of an error-free source tape and the monitor returns to the command loop.

3. We now set the tape with the assembly translation program in the punched tape reader and give the instruc-

166

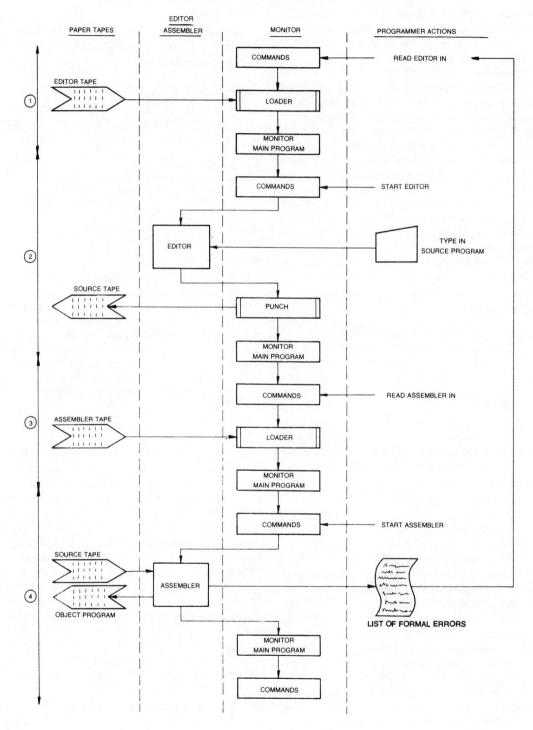

Fig. 18-4.

tion "read assembler in". This causes the monitor to call up the loader which starts and controls the punched tape reader so that the assembly translation program is stored in the memory. When this has been done the monitor returns to the command loop.

4. If we now give the instruction "start assembler" then the monitor calls the loader which controls the punched tape reader and with which the source tape is read in. Once the data on the source tape (ASCII program) is entered into memory, a start can be made with the translation. Should the assembly translation program detect a formal error during the translation, a correction must be made via the editor. If the assembly translation program has found no formal errors and the entire program has been translated, then the subroutine "Punch" can be called from the assembly translation program. The "Punch" routine controls the tape punch whereby the object program is entered on punched tape. Thereafter the monitor returns to the command loop.

Note

The assembly translation program can be stored in a ROM or PROM instead of on punched tape. In this case that part of fig. 18-4 in which the assembly program is read in become superfluous.

THE DEBUGGER

With the aid of the editor and the assembly translation program we have now obtained an object program containing no formal errors. However, this object program may still contain *logic errors* which, among other reasons, may have occurred because of:

- the use of the wrong instructions
- interchanging the sequence of instructions
- incorrect reservation of memory words
- incorrect indication of labels
- a systematic error in the flowchart
- incorrect designation of Input and Output data (for example, connection of Input data to Input port 3 and then, during the execution, giving the instruction IN 04).

If the object program were now entered into the computer then a considerable chance exists of the program being incorrectly executed or stopping somewhere, or of running endlessly round in a loop. Before we can allow the microcomputer to solve a problem, we must first test the object program. We do this with the aid of a debugging program. A debugging program is an auxiliary program offering the following possibilities:

Memory Display

By entering the requisite address with a TTY, we can cause the contents thereof to be displayed on a screen or printed-out by a printer.

Memory Change

With the aid of a TTY the contents of a memory word can be changed. The programmer enters the address and the new contents of the related memory word.

Register Display

At command of the programmer the contents of an auxiliary register, the program counter, the accumulator, the address register, the stack register, or the status flag register can be shown on a display screen.

Breakpoints

By indicating one or more memory addresses (breakpoints), the execution of the object program can be interrupted whenever the instruction is executed at such a memory address. The programmer must then check that part of the executed program by means of register and memory display. Any errors encountered can be corrected by means of memory change. Once this has been done, the programmer can allow the next part of the program to be executed by giving the instruction "continue task".

Single Step

The program is run through step-by-step, that is to say that on command of the programmer a single instruction is executed. After each instruction the programmer has the opportunity to check the execution of the instruction with the aid of memory display or register display. Should it transpire that an error has been made, it can be corrected by means of memory change. A variation of the single step is the n-step. The programmer can fill in a value for n, thus indicating the number of successive steps that may be executed. For single step n = 1. Whenever one or more instructions have been executed, depending on the value of n, the debugger enters a command loop to await a command to continue, the execution of memory or register display or of memory change. Operation with a debugger is shown schematically in fig. 18-5. With the debugging of a program we pass through the following phases:

- When the instruction "read debugger in" is given, the monitor leaves the command loop and, by means of a

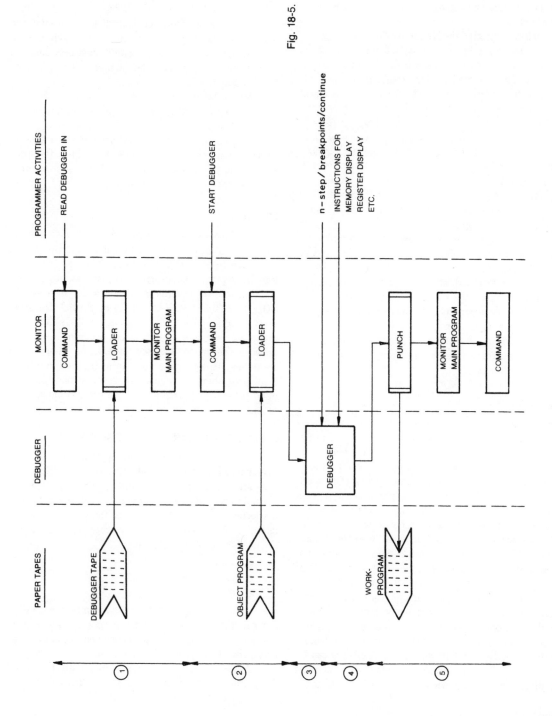

Fig. 18-5.

169

monitor command, calls up the loader. The loader starts and controls a punched tape reader whereby the debugger is entered. When the debugger has been entered in the microcomputer memory, the monitor returns to the command loop.

●If we now give the instruction "start debugger" a jump is made from the monitor to the loader which starts and controls the punched tape reader, with which the object program is read in. This object program is the result of the operation shown in fig. 18-4. Once the object program has been stored in the microcomputer memory, the debugger returns to the command loop.

●Using the TTY the programmer can now enter either a specific value for n, or the specific memory addresses (breakpoints) at which the program must be interrupted. He then gives the continue command and, depending on the value of n or on the breakpoints, 1 or more instructions are output, after which the debugger returns to the command loop.

●The programmer has now the opportunity for executing memory display, register display, or memory change. When this has been done the debugger returns to the command loop and, after receipt of the instruction "continue", outputs the following instructions.

●Once the program has been completely debugged in this way, a jump is made from the debugger to the punch, via which the final object program is entered on punched tape. This error-free object program is known as the work program.

SIMULATOR

We have seen that with the aid of such auxiliary programs as assembler, editor, monitor, and debugger we can arrive at an error-free object program; that is to say a work program. The equipment on which the development from source program to work program is done is called a development system. This developer need not have the same microprocessors, memories and peripherals as that with which the work program would be executed. It must, however, behave identically. If we work with several, different, microcomputer systems, we can develop the work programs for all of them with aid of one developer. Each time the developer must be given the characteristics of the system for which the work program is being developed. Above all, the developer must be able to simulate the peripherals in order to be able to test the Input and Output instructions. Different microcomputer systems can be simulated on the same developer. This is done using an auxiliary program known as the *simulator*. Using a simulator we can cause a microcomputer containing, for example, a 6800 microprocessor to behave exactly the same as a microcomputer with an 8080 microprocessor. The simulator offers the following:

●Simulation of the characteristics of a specific type of microprocessor. This means that the instruction set of the microprocessor to be simulated must be translated into the instruction set for the microprocessor on which the developer is based.

●Simulation of the peripherals of the microcomputer for which the work program must be developed.

●Debugging of the object program on a type of microcomputer other than that for which the program being developed is intended. A debug program is therefore included in the simulator.

COMPILER

Until now we have worked on the premise that the source program is written in assembly language and is translated into an object program using an assembly translation program. A program can also be written in one of the high-level programming languages, such as ALGOL, COBOL, FORTRAN, PL/M or BASIC. The auxiliary program that translates such a high-level programming language into an object program is called a *compiler*. The compiler does, in fact, the same as the assembler. However, because an instruction in a high-level programming language represents many instructions in the object program, the compiler is much more extensive than the assembler.

CROSS SOFTWARE AND RESIDENT SOFTWARE

A distinction is made in system software between resident software and cross software. By cross software we mean those auxiliary programs that are needed to develop a work program on a different type of microcomputer from that for which the work program is intended. The following auxiliary programs come under the heading of cross software:

●simulator
●cross assembler
●cross compiler

The cross assembler and the cross compiler are translation programs whereby a source program can be turned into a object program on a different computer than that for which the object program is intended.

Under resident software comes all the auxiliary programs of the system software that fall outside the description cross software. These are the auxiliary programs that are:

● used when the work program is developed on its own microcomputer system

● used when the development is identical to the microcomputer system for which the program is intended; i.e. when no simulation is required

● independent of whether simulation is needed or not, for example, monitor, editor, and debugger

The following auxiliary programs fall under the description resident software:

● assembler (actually, resident assembler)
● compiler (actually, resident compiler)
● monitor

5. The monitor comprises a monitor main program, the command loop and a number of subroutines.

6. During the command loop the programmer can give instructions for a subroutine to be started. The monitor then gives the command and control of the system is taken over by the subroutine.

7. The bootstrap gives the address of the monitor's first instruction after switch-on.

8. The editor is an auxiliary program whereby a source program can be entered letter-by-letter.

9. After every letter the programmer has the opportunity to make any necessary corrections.

10. All the text is stored in a memory.

11. Once the source program has been entered, the editor allows you to correct errors.

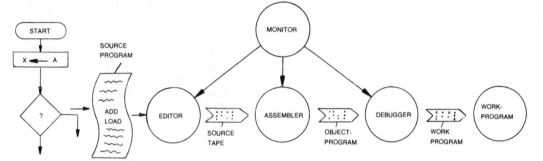

Fig. 18-6.

First, a flowchart is set up which describes the method used to solve the problem. The task set in each block of the flowchart is translated into one of two instructions written in assembly language. With the aid of the editor a source tape is created in which all letters, figures and symbols are entered in ASCII. The assembler translates the source tape into an object tape in which, the aid of the debugger, all logical errors have been located and corrected. The final result is the work program.

SUMMARY

1. The software of a computer comprises user software and system software.

2. User software is the software made by the user.

3. System software is the total software that is delivered with system and which serves to translate, correct, test, and enter.

4. The monitor controls a computer system during translation, correction, testing, and entering of the user software.

12. The assembler translates assembly language into machine language, and translates labels into actual addresses.

13. The assembler makes a list of any formal errors it detects but *cannot* be interrupted to correct them.

14. The assembler allows the translated object program to be entered on punched tape via the punch.

15. Using the debugger it is possible to execute a program in a series of parts so that any logic errors can be detected and corrected.

16. Using the n-step or breakpoints we can successively test small parts of the object program.

17. Using memory and register display the contents of memory words or of registers can be displayed on a screen.

18. Using memory change the contents of a memory word can be corrected.

19. Every step that is to be executed is started by the programmer giving a "continue" command.

20. Using the simulator the microprocessor and peripherals of a microcomputer system can be simulated on a developer.

21. The simulator also contains a debug program.

22. The compiler translates a program written in a high-level programming language into an object program.

23. A development system (developer) is an equipment specifically intended for the development of work programs.

24. Cross software comprises those auxiliary programs that are used when a microprocessor is simulated on development system during the development of a work program.

25. Cross software includes the simulator, the cross assembler and the cross compiler.

26. Resident software includes the text editor, the monitor, the debugger, the (resident) assembler, and the (resident) compiler.

27. Figure 18-6 shows how a source program is developed into a work program using the system software.

EXERCISES

1. In which two main groups can the software of a computer system be divided?
What is the difference between them?

2. How is system software subdivided?

3. Of which program parts is the monitor composed?

4. What is the function of the monitor?

5. Which functions have the bootstrap and the command loop?

6. What happens when a programmer gives a command to read in a program that is on punched tape?

7. What is the function of the text editor?

8. What is a source tape?

9. What is the function of the assembly translation program?

10. What is the purpose of the debugger?

11. What functions can be realized with the debugger?

12. How can the debugger leave the command loop?

13. What are breakpoints?

14. What is a development system?

15. What are the functions of the simulator?

16. What is a compiler?

17. What is the difference between cross software and resident software?

ANSWERS

1. User software and system software.
User software relates to the programs used for solving a problem. System software comprises all those auxiliary programs that simplify the translation, testing, correcting and entering of user software.

2. Into resident software and cross software.

3. Monitor main program, command loop, bootstrap, loader, punch.

4. The monitor controls the development system during the development of a work program.

5. The bootstrap initializes the system, that is to say, after the supply voltage is switched on it passes the address of the first instruction of the monitor main program.

6. The monitor leaves the command loop and calls the subroutine loader by means of a monitor command. The loader then takes control of the system. Once the entire program has been read in a jump is made via the monitor main program to the command loop.

7. Displaying a typed letter on the monitor screen, entering typed text in the memory, correcting errors, and allowing a source tape to be punched.

8. A punched tape containing the source code in ASCII coded characters.

9. Compiling a list of any formal errors, maintaining a list of used labels, replacing labels with actual address values, and the translation of mnemonics into bit patterns.

10. Object programs can be tested with the aid of the debugger, detecting and correcting any logic errors.

11. Register display, memory display, memory change, single step (n-step), and setting breakpoints.

12. By means of a continue command or a command to execute one of the functions described in Question 11.

13. Addresses at which the execution of the main program must be interrupted.

14. A system with all of the development software and cross software available on it.

15. The simulation of a microprocessor and peripheral and the execution of a debug program.

16. Software that produces object code from a high-level language.

17. Resident software produces work programs for the same type system as the development system. Cross software produces programs meant for a different type of system.

Chapter 19

Development Systems

Part of this chapter is derived from an article by Jean-Pierre Steger, published in *Der Elektoniker* Nov. 1976.

Once we begin practical work with microcomputers we discover very quickly that there is much more to it than a diagram and a soldering iron, as we were accustomed to in the past. Apart from getting the circuitry right we also need good software if the thing is going to work. Once a program has been entered in a ROM or PROM, there is nothing we can do to change it. In the development of a program we must therefore work very accurately. In so doing, we make use of a *M*icrocomputer *D*evelopment *S*ystem (MDS). The development system is a computer system with a microprocessor as its heart, and is provided with a quantity of system software. Because the program to be developed is based on a specific type of microprocessor, the development system must either be based on the same type of microprocessor or must be able to simulate it fully.

THE CONVENTIONAL DEVELOPMENT CYCLE

When a system is developed using conventional technology, TTL for example, one must complete the stages shown in fig. 19-1.

1. System specification:
A list must be made of the system requirements and the form in which data must be Input and Output.

2. Setting up block diagrams:
The course of the signals within the system is determined and divided into a number of separate function units.

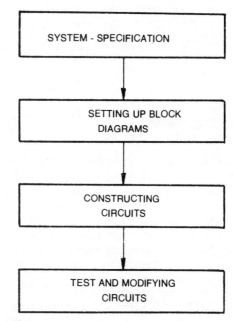

Fig. 19-1.

3. Constructing the circuits:
The function units are developed in detail, constructed and combined.

4. Testing and modifying the circuit:
The circuit is tested to see if it meets its specification. If necessary it is modified.

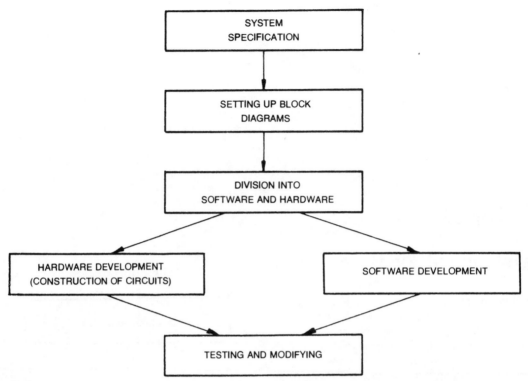

Fig. 19-2.

SYSTEM DEVELOPMENT
CYCLE WITH MICROPROCESSORS

The development of a microprocessor-based system follows pretty well the same course. However, as shown in fig. 19-2, some steps must be added.

1. Division of hardware and software:

The separate function units arrived at in the block diagram can, in general, either be executed as hardware or software. Which is chosen in a particular case depends on technical and economic considerations. For example, where a delay is needed we can either execute it in hardware using a monostable flip-flop, or in software with a waiting loop. The hardware solution has the advantage that the processor has less work to do and is free for other purposes. The software solution has the advantage that no extra components are required and that a variety of delays can be easily programmed.

2. Software development:

Setting up a flowchart, dividing it into separate routines (sub-programs), writing a program in a programming language suited to the system, and translating this into an object program (i.e. a program in machine language). In most cases adding software creates no extra problems, although problems may be shifted from hardware to software.

Connecting the microprocessor to the peripheral equipment can be looked at as a matter of routine that requires no particular effort. The real development work only starts after that point. With large computers this is left to system designers and programmers. With the somewhat simpler microprocessors, it often becomes the task of the hardware designer to do the software development, which is something that may make him feel uncomfortable! The manufacturers of microprocessors are well aware of this and do their very best to make the hardware designer feel at home with simple software. They do this by supplying extensive documentation, by offering auxiliary programs, by organizing courses and by marketing a number of very useful development aids. It is not always simple to choose from the many development systems that are on offer. It is into this area that we will try to give a certain amount of insight.

METHODS OF PROGRAM DEVELOPMENT

The purpose of program development is to produce a set on sequential instructions that control the micro-

174

processor so that the system specification is met. This work program must be produced in the form of a machine language on a medium suited to the microprocessor, such as punched tape, magnetic tape or floppy disc. For the development of the work program the manufacturer provides auxiliary programs, such as editor, assembler, simulator, etc. The problem is, however, that to make use of these programs we need a computer. There are various ways of obtaining computer capacity:

● renting a terminal connected to a commercial time-sharing computer
● by making use of a locally available computer
● purchase of a development system

DEVELOPING A PROGRAM
ON A TIME-SHARING SYSTEM

In this case the auxiliary programs offered by the manufacturer are already stored in the memory of the large computer belonging to the time-sharing organization. By renting a telephone line connection, one gains access not only to the computer but also to the auxiliary programs. The advantages are:

● No investment. One only has to provide space for a rented terminal (TTY or display terminal, for example) and a telephone connection.
● No delivery delays. A call to the time-sharing organization, and mention the name of the required auxiliary program and one can begin immediately.
● A virtually unlimited memory capacity.
● Changes in the program are simple to make.
Against this there are the following disadvantages:

●Fairly high running costs. Depending on the auxiliary program used and the required memory capacity, etc., the costs can vary from $5.00 to $25.00 per hour.
● No opportunity to test the program on the equipment for which it is intended. One must always simulate.
● No opportunity to test peripheral equipment planned for a particular application together with the developed program.

In consequence the use of time-sharing systems for program development usually occurs in the following cases:
● to evaluate different microprocessor systems
● in the event that one's own computer is overloaded
● when an experienced programmer is available
● where the user already has access to a terminal.

DEVELOPING THE WORK
PROGRAM ON AN IN-HOUSE COMPUTER

Users who already have a computer in-house will tend to put the auxiliary programs on their own computer. To do this the auxiliary programs must be adapted to the specific computer. This can take an experienced programmer anything from a half-day to a full week, and this must be kept in mind when calculating the costs. This method has the following advantages:

●Use is made of existing peripheral equipment (line-printer, magnetic tape system, display terminal, punched tape reader and punch), which can save a good deal of time.
●Use can be made of existing software.
●Considerable memory capacity is usually available.
●Additional costs are low. Depending on the supplier, a set of auxiliary programs can cost anything from $25.00 to $250.00 for a microcomputer. Naturally, all the software that goes with a microprocessor has to be paid for by the user, either in the form of expensive software or expensive hardware.
●An experienced programmer usually comes with an in-house computer, and he can assist the hardware designer with his software problems.
Here, too, there are disadvantages.

●The in-house computer must also be shared with others. The work will, therefore, be interrupted regularly.
●The testing of developed programs can only be done partly using simulation programs (which also have to be developed).
●It is barely possible or wholly impossible to connect peripheral equipment planned for an application and to test it in conjunction with the developed program.

In consequence, program development on an in-house computer only occurs in the following cases:

●with an under-occupied in-house computer
●during assembling and editing (modifying) programs in development
●in the event that so many programs must be developed that the acquisition of a minicomputer (PDP/11, for example) specially for the purpose, can be justified

DEVELOPMENT OF A WORK
PROGRAM ON A DEVELOPMENT SYSTEM

By development system we mean equipment that is specially constructed for the development of microcomputer programs. These systems are marketed by the manufacturers of microprocessors. Depending on the price, these systems can offer considerable development capability. The heart of the system is usually the same type of microprocessor as the one for which the program is intended. A program developed on such a system is thus suited to the microcomputer in question. It will be obvious, then, that every type of microprocessor requires its own specific type of development system. Acquisition of a particular sort of development system confines the purchaser to one specific type of microprocessor. *Caveat emptor!*

A development system is provided, in general, with *resident software*. This is a set of auxiliary programs specially developed for the system and ready to use. This is in contrast to *cross software* which, with a certain amount of adaptation, can be used in various types of in-house computers. The advantages of resident software are:

● independence from other computers

● low costs (usually included in the price of the development system)

● Exceptional ability to test programs in real time with all the advantage of having peripheral equipment,

such as A/D and D/A converters, traffic lights, etc. connected

The combination of development system and resident software is highly favored by the hardware designer who has to start working on software. It makes him independent of others and allows him to practice software writing at his own desk. When he makes a mistake—only he knows it! We shall now examine how such an enviable programming station is built.

THE BUILD-UP OF A DEVELOPMENT SYSTEM

Figure 19-3 shows the general arrangement of a development system. The various units (modules), depending on their size, are usually either contained on separate cards (printed circuit boards) or are all together on one board.

Microprocessor Unit

This unit comprises not only the microprocessor itself, but also the other components without which the microprocessor couldn't work. These are, for example, the clock generator, the start circuit with anti-bounce circuitry, the Direct Memory Access (DMA) circuit, for direct access to the memory, and the interrupt circuit, etc.

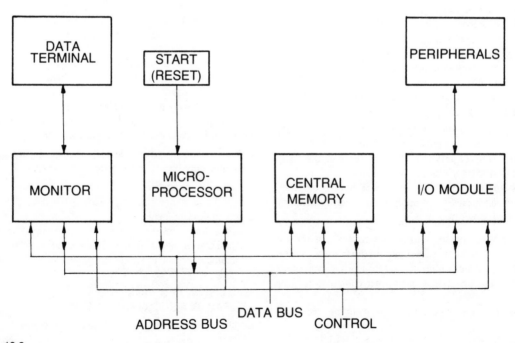

Fig. 19-3.

Monitor

The monitor forms the "intelligence" of the development system. This monitor comprises hardware and the related software and forms the line of communication between the microprocessor and terminal (e.g. TTY). Information always passes via the monitor which can intervene in the microprocessor functions. The heart of the monitor is the monitor program, usually stored in a PROM (Programmable Read Only Memory). The quality and extent of this sort of *firmware* (software in permanent form) depends on the ease with which the development system can be operated. A monitor program can occupy between a few hundred and a few thousand words.

The Central Memory

The central memory is a read-write memory, usually consisting of RAMs (Random Access Memory) and sometimes EPROMs (Erasable, Programmable, Read Only Memory), which can be erased with ultra-violet light.

All the auxiliary programs are stored in the main memory. It is also used for the temporary storage of data. Once the desired software has been developed, the auxiliary programs need not remain in the main memory. Once a program is entered in a ROM there is no further possibility of changing it! In the final microprocessor application expensive RAM is only used for the temporary storage of data. For a development system with auxiliary programs a memory capacity of 8K to 12K is not excessive (1K = 1024 words). One can work with a memory capacity as low as 1K, though in a primitive manner, such as directly in machine language.

I/O Module

A development system becomes really worthwhile if, after the initial program development, it can also be used as the prototype. All the peripheral equipment that will be used in the final application must also be capable of being connected to the development system. Only then can the system be subjected to a complete test. The peripheral equipment comprises, for example, A/D and D/A converters, machines, data displays, traffic lights, etc. Depending on the peripheral equipment, transfer of data takes place in parallel, serial synchronous, or serial asynchronous. The purpose of the I/O module is to form an interface both electrically and in speed between peripheral equipment and the structure of the microprocessor.

The I/O module is usually ICs that have been specially developed for the microprocessor in question. They contain bus-drivers and address decoders, among other things. The outputs for peripheral equipment are usually CMOS or TTL compatible and are provided with interrupt lines. A peripheral can indicate that it is ready to exchange data via an interrupt line. A peripheral can indicate that it is ready to exchange data via an interrupt line. The microprocessor then interrupts its activities and converses with the peripheral equipment. Well thought out I/O modules can save much labor in prototype development, both in hardware and software.

INPUT AND OUTPUT EQUIPMENT

Once the development of the work program is over and that program is executed by the microprocessor for which it was intended then, as far as microcomputers are concerned, we come into contact with such I/O equipment as A/D and D/A converters, solid-state relays, amps, detectors, etc. During the development of the work program, that is when operating the development system, we are concerned with totally different peripheral equipment (fig. 19-4a). With most development systems these are:

- dialogue terminal
- punched tape reader and punch
- the magnetic tape reader and recorder
- the floppy disc

In this chapter we will give a short description of these. In the chapter "Peripheral Equipment" we will describe these and other peripherals in more detail.

Dialogue Terminal

The dialogue terminal is usually a TTY or keyboard with a display monitor that is used to intervene in the program being developed. Via the dialogue terminal, which is connected to the microprocessor via the monitor, auxiliary programs such as editor, assembler and debugger can be entered and started. Should a traffic light control system, for example, not function correctly, then the programmer can use the dialogue terminal and the debugger to effect memory display or memory change. Once the program is functioning properly the dialogue terminal becomes superfluous. In the final application the dialogue terminal is not met with again. A development system is, actually, useless if a dialogue terminal is not acquired simultaneously. It is usual for the data exchange between dialogue terminal and development system to take place in ASCII code. This is a 7-bit code comprising symbols (letters and figures) plus a

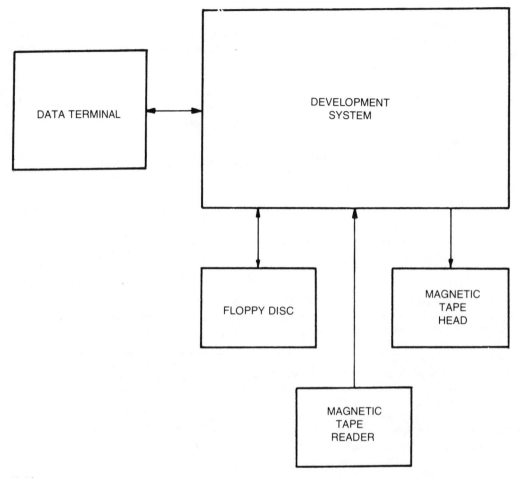

Fig. 19-4A.

number of control symbols. The ASCII coded data is fed serially (bit-by-bit) into the development system where the monitor converts it into parallel format.

Many terminals today make use of cathode ray tubes (crt). Such a display terminal has a normal keyboard, but instead of a print-out on paper the symbols entered are displayed on a picture tube. One advantage is that it is silent in operation. A disadvantage is the lack of hard copy. We have no way of checking later what we have done. This disadvantage can, of course, be negated by having a printer or paper-tape punch that is only switched in when necessary. The programming terminal begins to get somewhat expensive, but an awful lot of paper is wasted with TTYs simply because hard copy is made of every text, however insignificant.

Punched Tape Readers and Punches

Programs stored in a RAM are volatile, that is to say that with the loss of the power supply the contents of the memory are wiped out. For this reason programs are often stored on punched tape. The format in which the program is punched depends on the monitor program. There is no standard format, but just about as many formats as there are development systems. In one case the tape is full of check bits (parity bits) to gain maximum reliability, in another it is in precisely these bits that economies are made in order to keep the tape as short as possible. The simplest tape reader and punch are to be found on the ASR 33 teletype. Tape reader and punch are connected to the TTY which means that no extra connections are needed to the development system.

Magnetic Tape Reader and Recorder

Programs can also be stored on magnetic tape. The small tape cassettes from Philips are very popular at the moment. The tape must be guaranteed as suitable for computer use, quality music tapes are usually reliable. Some terminals have cassette recorders among the optional extras. They are very practical. Those who want something better can always turn to mass memories, such as the floppy disc. In every case the objection remains that the quantity of data that must be stored varies from development system to development system.

Floppy Disc System

In principle the floppy disc system is no different than the magnetic disc systems used with the larger computers. However, the floppy disc is made of Mylar™ with a magnetic layer on the surface. The disc rotates at a given speed while a radially moveable read and write head scans the various tracks.

Some development systems are designed for the attachment of a floppy disc system. Others have to be modified, and modification may not be so simple! In any case, anyone who is accustomed to working with a floppy disc system will be difficult to persuade to accept something less.

Figure 19-4 is a photograph of the various peripherals that we are likely to come across in development systems. This equipment will be dealt with in greater detail in the chapter "Peripheral Equipment." You can also see two microcomputers in the photograph. The one on the left is the one for which the program is intended. The microprocessor has been temporarily removed from it. The function of the microprocessor has been taken over by the right-hand microcomputer which is connected to the first by an adapter. All the peripheral equipment is connected to the right-hand microcomputer. This is done in order to make system testing easier.

MICROCOMPUTER TRAINING SYSTEM

Apart from the large development system, many manufacturers of microcomputers also offer a Microcomputer Training System (MTS). Although such equipment often trades on the name "Low Cost Development System," they are not suited to the development of a work program from start to finish. In many cases the memory capacity is not even sufficient for the storage of the assembler, let alone the editor or simulator (unless after extending the memory capacity one acquires at least a TTY or crt). In most MTSs the peripheral equipment comprises a hexadecimal keyboard (Input) and a number of 7-segment displays (Output). The memory capacity is usually ¼ to 1K bytes for the RAM and 1K to 4K bytes for the ROM. Programs must be entered in hexadecimal, so the programmer must function as assembler himself. Although, as has been said, an MTS is less suited to program development, they can be exceptionally useful in mastering the operation of microcomputer systems and the art of programming.

SUMMARY

1. In developing a program for a microcomputer we often make use of a development system.

2. A conventional development cycle comprises the following phrases:

- system specification
- setting up block diagrams
- constructing circuits
- testing and modifying the circuit.

3. The development cycle for a microprocessor-based system comprises the following phases:

- system specification
- setting up block diagrams
- division into hardware and software
- development of hardware and software
- testing and modifying.

4. Work programs are usually developed with the aid of auxiliary programs.

5. Auxiliary programs, or system software, can be sub-divided into resident software and cross software.

6. A work program can be developed on:

- a commercial time-sharing system
- an in-house computer
- a development system.

7. A development system comprises:

- a microprocessor
- a main memory
- an I/O module
- a monitor

8. The monitor controls the entire development system.

9. The monitor comprises software (the monitor program) and hardware (reset switches, displays, and the like).

10. The main memory temporarily stores both the auxiliary programs and the data to be handled.

11. The I/O module adapts the peripheral equipment to the remaining parts of the development system.

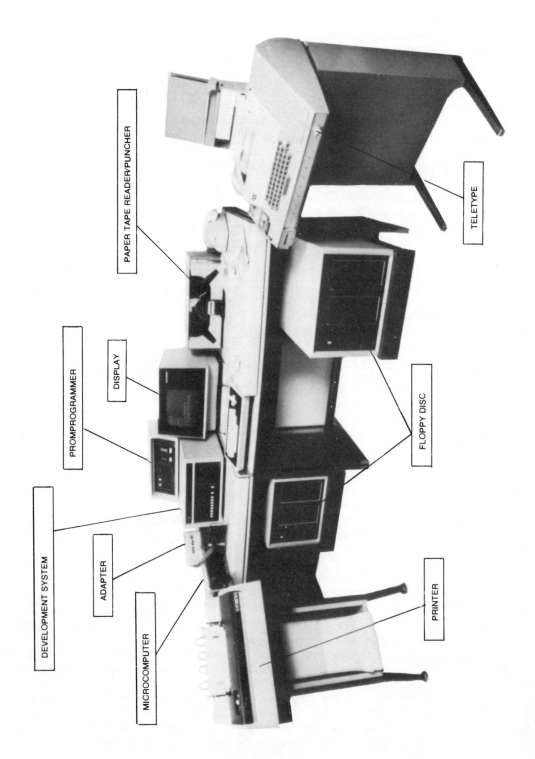

PAPER TAPE READER/PUNCHER

TELETYPE

DISPLAY

PROMPROGRAMMER

FLOPPY DISC

DEVELOPMENT SYSTEM

ADAPTER

MICROCOMPUTER

PRINTER

Fig. 19-5.

180

12. A dialogue terminal comprises a TTY or keyboard and a display screen.

13. A dialogue terminal is only used during the development of the work program.

14. A punched tape reader and punch can also be included in a dialogue terminal.

15. For the mass storage of programs and/or data, a magnetic tape or floppy disc can be used.

REVIEW EXERCISES

1. What does MDS mean?

2. What is the function of a development system?

3. What steps make a conventional development cycle?

4. At which points does a development cycle for a computer differ from this?

5. Which systems can be considered for software development?

6. What is the difference between resident software and cross software?

7. Of what is a development system built up?

8. How are the dialogue terminal and the peripherals connected up?

9. Which parts comprise the microprocessor unit?

10. What does the term firmware mean?

11. What is the function of the monitor?

12. What is the function of the I/O module?

ANSWERS

1. Microcomputer Development System.

2. The development, testing and modifying of user software.

3. See fig. 19-1.

4. Apart from constructing the circuits (hardware), software suited to the hardware must also be developed.

5. Time-sharing system, in-house computer, or development system.

6. Resident software is a number of auxiliary programs developed for a specific development system.

7. See fig. 19-3.

8. The dialogue terminal is connected direct to the monitor. The peripherals are connected to the I/O equipment.

9. Clock generator, start circuit, reset circuit, DMA circuit, interrupt circuit, etc.

10. Software stored in permanent form, for example, an auxiliary program in a PROM.

11. The monitor controls the entire development system.

12. It is via the I/O module that the microprocessor has contact with the peripherals.

Chapter 20

Peripheral Equipment

In order that a microcomputer can handle data, more is needed than the microcomputer itself. Peripheral equipment is also required.

Peripheral equipment can be divided into the following groups (fig. 20-1):

- Input equipment
- Output equipment
- control equipment
- external memories.

Figure 20-2 shows further sub-division of peripheral equipment, where the peripheral equipment that is common to microcomputer systems is mentioned. Much of the equipment shown in fig. 20-2 can be combined into a single piece of equipment. A TTY, for example, is formed by combining a keyboard, a printer, a punched tape reader and a punch, while a display comprises a monitor and keyboard. Often the TTY and the display are used not only as Input and Output equipment but also to enter control signals into the microcomputer. For this reason the TTY and the display are described under "Control Equipment".

INPUT EQUIPMENT

Input equipment converts the data to the Input into electrical signals that the computer can read. The Input devices to be dealt with in this chapter are the punched tape reader and the punched card reader. The instrumentation mentioned in fig. 20-2 includes all circuits and equipment which convert data from a process into a form that is legible to the microcomputer. Examples of these are A/D converters and the detector circuits used for the time measurement in the chapter "From Task to Solution". This instrumentation will not be dealt with further in this chapter. The keyboard, via which letters, figures and such are converted into electronic signals is dealt with under TTY.

Punched Tape Reader

A punched tape contains a number of tracks or channels. The most usual, with 7 or 8 channels, are shown in fig. 20-3. The transport holes (sprocket holes) are used to shift the tape by an equal distance each time the data is read. Figure 20-4 shows how the teeth on a sprocket wheel grip the tape in order to move it forward.

If a punched tape reader works on the *start-stop* principle, a pulse is needed to shift the tape one place after reading a character. There are also punched tape readers that run at a constant speed. Each time a sprocket hole passes the reading head a pulse is generated that causes the relevant character to be read. (The reading head is that part of the tape reader where the data on the punched tape is converted into electrical signals.) The advantage of this method is that the data transfer rate is greater than with the start-stop method. A disadvantage is that the braking distance is greater than the distance between two sprocket holes. In order to ensure that after one group of characters (BLOCK) no character is read in from the succeeding block, a space must be left between any two blocks. This is known as a gap.

Figure 20-5 shows how two transport wheels transport the punched tape past the reading station. The conversion of the data on punched tape into electronic signals

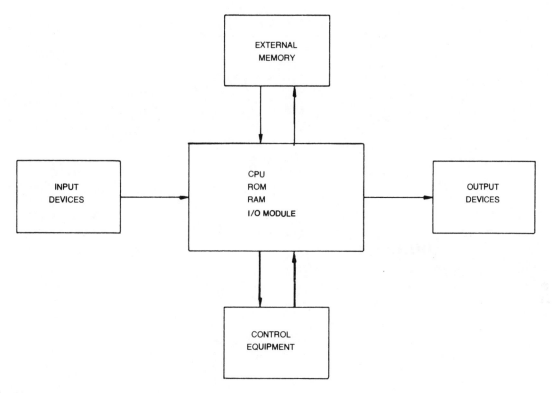

```
                    ┌──────────────────┐
                    │    EXTERNAL      │
                    │    MEMORY        │
                    └──────────────────┘
                             ↕
┌──────────────┐    ┌──────────────────┐    ┌──────────────┐
│    INPUT     │───→│  CPU             │───→│   OUTPUT     │
│    DEVICES   │    │  ROM             │    │   DEVICES    │
│              │    │  RAM             │    │              │
│              │    │  I/O MODULE      │    │              │
└──────────────┘    └──────────────────┘    └──────────────┘
                             ↕
                    ┌──────────────────┐
                    │    CONTROL       │
                    │    EQUIPMENT     │
                    └──────────────────┘
```

Fig. 20-1.

occurs via a combination of light-sensitive semiconductors and lamps. Only when a hole in punched tape passes can light reach the light-sensitive cells. The cell then generates a voltage that represents logic '1'. For 7-channel punched tape there are 8 light-sensitive cells; 7 to detect the character holes and 1 to detect the sprocket holes. By detecting the sprocket holes one can also detect the character that comprises only zeros.

Note

With 7-channel punched tape the characters can only be coded in ASCII (a 7-bit code). On 8-channel punched tape we can also use the EBCDIC code (8-bit) or ASCII with an extra parity bit. (EBCDIC = Extended Binary Coded Interchange Code).

Punched Card Reader

A punched card is a data carrying medium that we often meet with in daily life. A punched card is divided into 80 columns and 12 rows (fig. 20-6). Rows 11 and 12 form the zone, the other 10 are numeric rows. The bevelled corner simplifies the recognition of cards that have been stacked the wrong way. The advantage of punched cards is that only one card needs to be altered if one or more of the data entries need changing. The Input equipment that converts the data on punched cards into electrical signals is the punched card reader. Just like the punched tape reader, the punched car reader usually has a photoelectric reading station. One character, that is to say one column, is usually read in one pass. There are, therefore, 12 light-sensitive cells in a reading station. To increase the reliability of reading in, a punched card reader usually has two reading stations. When a character has passed both stations the readings are compared. To achieve this the reading of the first station is stored in a register until the second reading has taken place. Should the comparison show that the readings are not the same, the card will be placed in a separate bin to be corrected.

OUTPUT EQUIPMENT

Output equipment converts the electronic signals fed out from the computer into several forms:

● in legible form, e.g. letters, figures, symbols

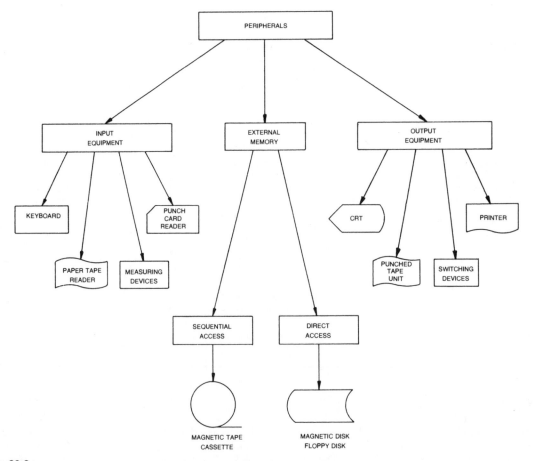

Fig. 20-2.

● in a form in which they can be later fed into a computer, e.g. punched tape

● in signals whereby, via switching equipment, a process can be directly controlled (examples of switching equipment are solid-state relays and D/A converters).

The Output equipment that we will deal with here are the

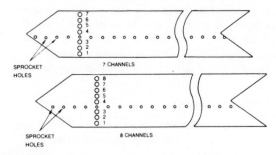

Fig. 20-3.

punched tape punch and the printer. The monitor will be dealt with under control equipment.

Punched Tape Punch

A punched tape converts electronic signals into holes in a punched tape. The tape must be stationary while the holes are being punched. For this reason every punch works on the stop-start principle. The tape punch is seldom met with as an isolated piece of equipment. It is, in fact, mostly part of the TTY. The advantage of this is that, as well as being operated by the computer, it can also be operated via the keyboard. Each letter, figure or symbol that we type results in a combination of holes on the tape coded according to the ASCII code.

Printer

A printer (or line printer) is a piece of Output equipment that converts the Output data of a computer into

184

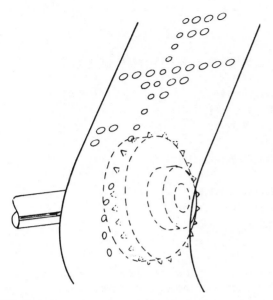

Fig. 20-4.

letters, figures or symbols, and prints them. Figure 20-7 is a photograph of a printer. A printer produces hard copy, usually on a folded paper sheet that is a long strip of paper with transport holes along both edges. At regular intervals along the strip there are perforations across the entire breadth.

In fig. 20-8 one can see how the paper is folded in concertina fashion both before and after printing. The paper tractors are toothed wheels. The teeth fit in the transport holes in the paper. The paper tractors shift the paper after each line printout. The number of characters that can be printed on each line depends on the printer. Common line widths, at the moment, are 32, 64, 80, 120 and 132 characters. It is obvious that the paper width must be adapted to the number of characters per line. Use is sometimes made of several thicknesses of paper inter-

leaved with carbon paper. This allows the production of several copies simultaneously.

CONTROL EQUIPMENT

It is via the control equipment that the interchange of data takes place between the operator and the computer. Depending on the capacity of the control equipment such operations as the following can be executed:

● entering data, programs, or parts of programs into the main or external memory

● checking or changing the contents of memory locations

● passing commands to the monitor program (e.g. 'start assembler').

The contol devices to be dealt with in this chapter are the console, the TTY, and the display.

Console

The console is a control apparatus whereby we can use switches and lamps (LEDs) in order to communicate with the computer. Figure 20-9 shows an example of a console. Sixteen switches are used to set up a binary address. By depressing the 'load address' button we can select an address in memory. The 8 data lamp shows the binary contents of the memory word we have selected. Using the 8 data switches we can set up new contents for this memory word and by pressing the 'load data' button we can enter it into the memory word. To start the execution of a program we use the 16 address switches to set up the address of the first instruction. By pressing first the 'load address' button and then the 'start' button the program is started. Usually there is also a 'reset' button on the console. With the 'reset' button we can enter 0000_{16} in the program counter. If there is no reset button we must set all 16 address switches to 0 and depress the 'address load' button, and then 'start'.

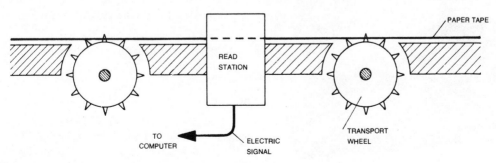

Fig. 20-5.

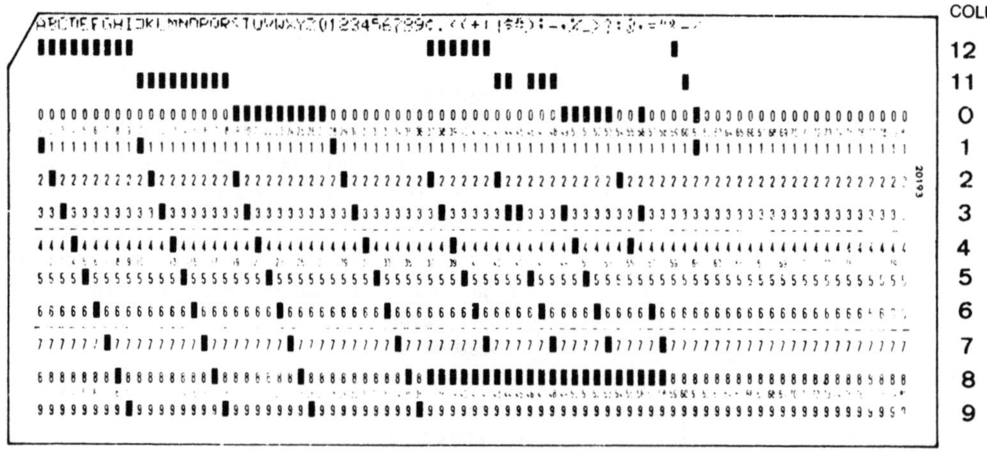

Fig. 20-6.

Teletype

The teletype, originally developed for Telex purposes, is very similar to a typewriter. It comprises a keyboard and printing mechanism, to which a paper tape reader/punch are usually added. With a TTY the paper is roll-fed and not in single sheets as with a typewriter. When we press one of the keys the appropriate symbol is printed out. Figure 20-10 shows a TTY in combination with a tape reader/punch. A TTY prints only capitals, no lower-case letters.

Figure 20-11 shows the signals that a modern TTY sends to the computer. Each character begins with a start-bit. This is a 0 (no current). Thereafter come the 8 bits that represent the character, coded in ASCII. (For ASCII only 7 bits are needed but there is usually a parity bit added.) The tenth bit is the stop-bit which indicates the end of the character. The stop-bit is always a 1 (current flows). The start bit is the same length as the character bits. The stop-bit, depending on the type of TTY, may be the same length, 1.5 times as long or twice as long as the other bits. The bits are transmitted sequentially (serial I /O). This means that there must be an interface circuit between the TTY and the microcomputer which has the following tasks:

● Adaptation of the speed of the TTY to that of the microcomputer.

● During Input, convert the TTY signals to parallel format and during Output, convert the parallel signals from the microcomputer to serial format signals for the TTY. One can write a program for this, so that the task is assumed by the microcomputer itself.

● Generate drive signals for the TTY (for example, line feed and carriage return).

The number of bits that a TTY can transmit and receive per second is known as the *baud rate*. A baud rate of 110 means that the maximum transmission rate of the TTY is 110 bits per second. Each bit then has a length of $\frac{1}{110}$ second = 9.1 ms. If the stop-bit is twice as long as the other bits, a complete character $(9 \times 9.1) + (2 \times 9.1)$ ms = 100 ms. Thus at maximum 10 characters per second can be transmitted.

Display

A display, strictly speaking, is simply a picture tube or monitor device on which the output data from the computer is displayed in the form of words, figures, or graphics. In most cases, however, the monitor is coupled

Fig. 20-7.

186

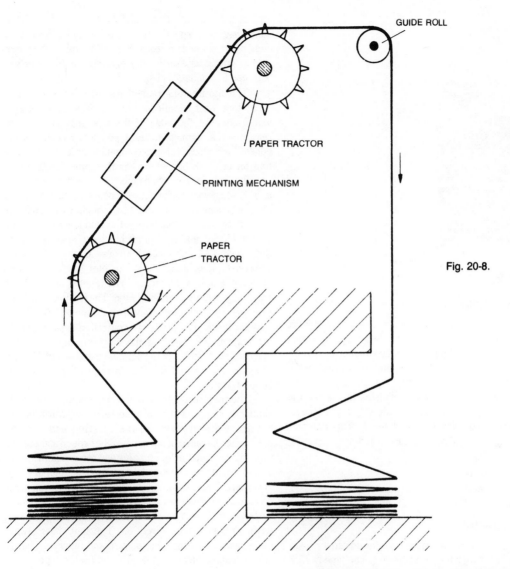

GUIDE ROLL

PAPER TRACTOR

PRINTING MECHANISM

PAPER
TRACTOR

Fig. 20-8.

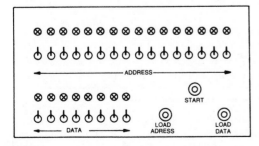

ADDRESS

START

DATA

LOAD
ADRESS

LOAD
DATA

Fig. 20-9.

to a keyboard which functions as Input apparatus. Because the combination of monitor and keyboard is usually spoken of as a display, we will adhere to that usage here. Just like the TTY, a display is used as:

● Input equipment
● Output equipment
● Control equipment for changing register contents or giving instructions to the monitor program, for example.

The keyboard of the display is virtually identical to the keyboard of the TTY (fig. 20-12). The disadvantage of the display is that it provides no hard copy of what is typed in.

187

Fig. 20-10.

EXTERNAL MEMORY

External memories are used for the storage of large quantities of data or programs for later use. External memories are divided into sequential memories and direct access memories. With sequential memories all the characters from the start to required place must pass the read head. With direct access memories this is not the case. Either the required place is directly accessible or only a few need pass the read head. The external memories to be dealt with in this lesson are:

- the magnetic tape unit
- the cassette unit
- the magnetic disc unit
- the floppy disc.

Magnetic Tape Unit

A magnetic tape comprises a synthetic carrier (usually Mylar™) baring a magnetic coating. The tape is 12.7 mm broad (0.5 in). There are 7-channel and 8-channel tapes having, respectively, 7 and 8 data-carrying channels or tracks next to each other. Few microcomputers use magnetic tape of this variety, but those that do usually use 8-channel, coded in ASCII.

The bits are not arranged in sequence but in such an order that least significant bits (those with the lowest value) come at the edge of the tape (fig. 20-13). The reason is that damage to the tape usually occurs at the edges. Each character is accompanied by a synchronization bit or clock bit, which has the same function as a sprocket hole on a punched tape. The synchronization bit is a 1 whenever a character appears at that location. Because magnetic tape cannot be brought to a stop in the space between two characters, the data is written on the tape in blocks, and is read off block-by-block. Between each block is a blank space, known as an inter-block gap. This can be seen in fig. 20-14. The inter-block gaps have a standard length of 0.6 inches. The lengths of the blocks may vary within certain limits. These limits are, for example, a minimum of 10 and a maximum of 2500 characters per block. The limits are controlled by software. At the beginning and end of the magnetic tape there are markers which indicate the beginning and end of the tape. They are known as BOT (Beginning of Tape) and EOT (End of Tape).

The transport mechanism of a magnetic tape unit is similar to that of a normal tape recorder. Much higher requirements are set on the starting and braking mechanism because of the much higher speed and shorter time that is available for stopping and reaching full speed. The read and write section is also much like that of a tape recorder. This is shown in fig. 20-15. Magnetic tapes can be read in the reverse as well as in the forward direction. Because there is only one erase head the unit can only write in the forward direction. The unit must always erase before writing. The forward and reverse cleaners are to remove any dust that may be on the tape.

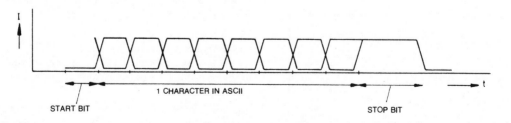

Fig. 20-11.

Fig. 20-12.

Figure 20-16 shows a magnetic tape unit. Depending on the memory capacity required, several magnetic tape units, or tape stations as they are called, can be connected to one computer. Just as with a tape recorder the tapes can be changed, which means that the memory capacity is virtually unlimited.

Figure 20-17 shows a reel with magnetic tape. Standardized measurements are:

tape length: 730 m
reel diameter: 26.7 cm

The magnetic tape unit is a sequentially accessible memory, that is to say the whole tape must be scanned until the required data block is found. The access time of a tape can, therefore, be very long (e.g. 3 min). On the other hand, a considerable amount of data is stored in a fairly small area. The following are some of the terms met with in connection with magnetic tape units.

Tape Speed. This is the speed with which the tape is transported past the read/write heads. (Common values are: 37.5, 75, 112.5, and 150 inches per second.)

Data Density. This is the number of characters or bytes that can be written into a unit length. Data density

is usually given as BPI (Bytes Per Inch). Common values are: 200, 556, 800, 1600, and 3200 BPI.

Example. A magnetic tape unit has a tape speed of 150 inches per second. The data density of the tape is 1600 BPI. What is the read rate of the magnetic tape?

The read rate is the maximum number of characters per second that can be read. On the magnetic tape there are 1600 bytes per inch, while the tape passes the read head at 150 inches per second. The number of characters that can be read per second is, therefore, $150 \times 600 = 240000$.

Example. A magnetic tape unit has a tape speed of 150 inches per second (1 inch = 2.5 cm). The tape is 720 m long. What is the average access time?

150 inches per second is about 3.7 meters per second. To arrive at data at the end of the tape will take $\frac{720}{3.7}$ seconds = 195 seconds. Data at the beginning of the tape is directly accessible, so that the average access time is 98 seconds = 1.6 minutes approximately.

Cassette Unit

A cassette unit is very similar to an ordinary audio cassette recorder. The tape is in an easy to change cassette. By means of an interface circuit (MODEM = MOdulator-DEModulator) an ordinary cassette recorder can be connected to a computer. The disadvantage of this is that recorders cannot be reversed by the microcomputer, so access to data already past can only be achieved by manual rewind. With a cassette unit the characters are not written simultaneously next to each other, but consecutively, one after another. The tape speed, data density and read /write rate of cassette units are much lower than those of magnetic tape units. However, a cassette unit is much cheaper.

Magnetic Disc Unit

A magnetic disc is a plastic disc with a thin magnetic coating on one or both sides. The disc is 14 inches or

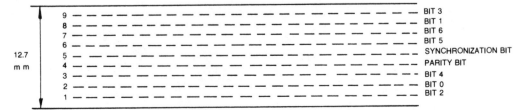

Fig. 20-13.

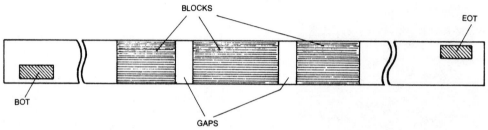

Fig. 20-14.

about 35 cm in diameter. The disc is often compared to a stereo record. There are, however, 2 major differences.

- A stereo record can only be played (read) while a disc can be written as well as read.
- A stereo record has a single spiral groove (track) running from the outside to the center. A disc has 203 concentric tracks.

Data is written on a magnetic disc in series just as with the cassette. Tracks are also sub-divided into blocks. Each block has its own address. Because the disc rotates at a constant speed and is not required to stop, no block gaps are needed. Discs usually come in the form of disc packs that, depending on the number of discs, have, 1, 2, 10, or 20 writable surfaces. Figure 20-18 shows a disc pack with 10 writable surfaces. Thus 10 read/write heads are needed. The heads are mounted on an arm which is mounted on a carriage. The carriage places the heads over the required track. The tracks on the disc are concentric and are numbered from circumference to center, 000 to 202. Of these 203 tracks only 200 are used, the other 3 are held in reserve.

To address a specific block the following three facts are needed:

- the track number (between 000 and 199)
- the head number (each writable surface has its own read/write head)
- the sector number (each track is divided into sectors (blocks).

The total access time is therefore equal to the sum of the following three waiting times.

- The time needed to place a head on the right track (this is about 60 ms).
- The time needed to select the right head. This is an electronic address selection and the time can be neglected compared with the time in point 1.
- The time that passes before the requisite block passes the read/write heads. The discs run at 2400 rpm. One revolution takes 25 ms. The average delay is, therefore, 12 ms.

The total access time of a magnetic disc unit is fairly short, which is why the magnetic disc unit is often counted among the direct-access memories.

Figure 20-19. shows a number of magnetic discs housed in plastic container. These magnetic disc packets are easy to change so that the capacity of a disc memory can be extended as desired. Each track contains

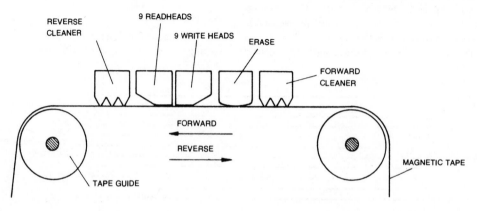

Fig. 20-15.

Fig. 20-16.

about 32000 bits, which is 4000 bytes. 375 of these are usually used for addressing the blocks, which means that each track can store 3625 bytes. In the disc packs discussed there are 200 tracks on each of 10 discs, so that the total capacity of the disc pack is $200 \times 10 \times 3625 = 7250000$ bytes. A pack with 20 writable surfaces would thus have a capacity of 14500000 bytes, or 14.5 Megabytes.

Floppy Disc System

A floppy disc is a flexible plastic disc with a magnetic coating. There can be one or two writable surfaces that, just like the magnetic disc, are divided into concentric tracks. Reading and writing are done in almost the same way as with magnetic discs. Because a floppy disc unit contains only one disc, only a single read/write head is required. Unlike the magnetic disc, the head actually touches the floppy disc. To cut down wear, the disc only spins when the unit is accessed. To address a specific block only a track number and a block number are required (sector number).

Note

The values mentioned in this chapter are only intended to give an impression of the order of speed or capacity of a given system. There are no standard values.

SUMMARY

1. Input equipment converts data to be Input into electronic signals that are readable by the computer.

2. The most common types of Input equipment met with in connection with microprocessors are:

- the punched tape reader
- the punched card reader

3. In the reading station of a punched tape reader the data, which is represented on the tape by punched holes, is converted into electronic signals. This is usually done by a combination of light-sensitive cells and lamps.

4. On the punched card, too, data is represented by punched holes. Each punched card is divided into 80 columns of 12 rows.

5. On punched tape the data to be input is coded as punched holes.

6. Output equipment converts the Output data from the computer into non-electrical signals, for example, letters, figures, punched holes, or signals to control a process.

7. With microcomputers the most common Output devices are:

- the tape punch
- the printer

8. A paper tape punch converts the Output data from the computer into punched holes on paper tape.

Fig. 20-17.

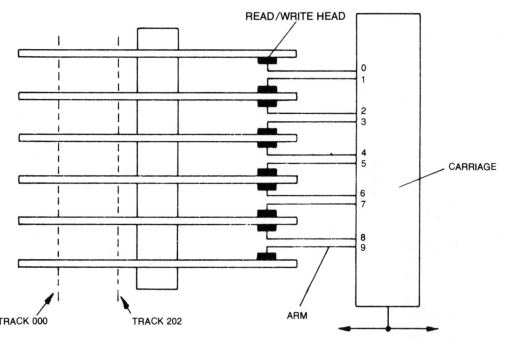

READ/WRITE HEAD

CARRIAGE

ARM

TRACK 000

TRACK 202

0
1
2
3
4
5
6
7
8
9

Fig. 20-18.

9. A printer converts the output data from the computer into letters, figures, or symbols on continuous stationery.

10. An external memory stores large quantities of data for later use.

11. The external memories most often used with microprocessors are:

- the magnetic tape unit
- the cassette unit
- the magnetic disc unit
- the floppy disc

12. With magnetic tape, data is usually entered in blocks. Between blocks there is a block gap within which the tape can be brought to a stop or can come up to full speed.

13. The cassette unit is similar to ordinary audio cassette recorders. The tape is in an easily changeable cassette. Bits are written on the tape in series.

14. With magnetic discs, data is written onto plastic discs. Tracks on the discs are concentric. Tracks are divided into blocks, each of which has its own address. Because the disc rotates at a constant speed and is not required to stop, block gaps are unnecessary.

15. Contrary to a magnetic disc unit, a floppy disc contains only one disc. This disc is of flexible (floppy) material.

REVIEW EXERCISES

1. Name 4 groups of peripheral equipment.

2. Name 3 Input devices, 3 Output devices and 4 external memories.

3. What is the function of an Input device?

4. What is a sprocket hole?

5. What is understood by the start-stop principle?

6. What is a gap?

7. How are punched holes converted into electrical signals?

8. According to which code is data registered on 7 and 8 channel punched tape?

Fig. 20-19.

9. How is a punched card sub-divided?

10. How many characters can be entered on a punched card?

11. What advantage has punched card over punched tape?

12. How many light-sensitive cells are there in the reading station of a punched card reader?

13. What is done to increase the reliability of a punched card reader?

14. What is the function of an Output device?

15. What is understood by switching equipment?

16. What is continuous stationery?

17. What is control device?

18. What operations can we perform with a control device?

19. What is a console?

20. How is a TTY built up?

21. How many bits are needed to transmit one character to and from a TTY?

22. What is baud rate?

23. What comprises a display?

24. What is a function of an external memory?

25. What do BOT and EOT mean?

26. What is understood by tape speed, data density, and read/write speed?

27. What facts are needed in order to address a block on a magnetic disc?

ANSWERS

1. Input, Output, and control equipment, and external memories.

2. Input equipment: keyboard, punched tape reader, and punched card readers.

   Output equipment: monitor screen tape punch, and printer.

   External memories: magnetic tape unit, cassette unit, magnetic disc unit, and floppy disc.

3. To convert Input data into electrical signals.

4. The sprocket holes are holes in the punched tape placed at regular intervals from each other. They are used to step the punched tape forward exactly the same distance every time.

5. With the start-stop principle a punched tape reader stops each time a character is read. A control pulse ensures that the punched tape keeps stepping one place forward.

6. A gap is the block space on a punched tape. It is a piece of the tape in which no holes are punched.

7. By a combination of light-sensitive cells and lamps.

8. With a 7-channel tape the characters are entered in ASCII. With an 8-channel tape the characters are entered either in EBCDIC or in ASCII with parity.

9. In 80 columns and 12 rows.

10. Each character takes 1 column, therefore 80 characters can be registered.

11. To modify 1 or more characters only one punched card need be altered.

12. A punched card is read column-by-column. Each column can contain 12 holes, so 12 light-sensitive cells are needed.

13. Two reading stations are provided and their results are compared. If there is any discrepancy the card is put into a separate bin.

14. An Output device converts the data to be Output by the computer into non-electronic signals.

15. Switching equipment is used to convert the data Output by the computer into signals whereby a process can be directly controlled.

16. Continuous stationery is a long sheet of paper having transport holes along both edges. At regular intervals over the breadth of the paper there are perforations. This paper, which is used by the printer, folds up concertina fashion.

17. It is via the control equipment that data is exchanged between programmer and computer.

18. Input data and programs. Check and alter the contents of memory locations. Convey commands to the monitor program.

19. A control panel with which we can converse with the computer using switches and lamps.

20. From a keyboard and a printing mechanism. A punched tape reader and punch is usually also included.

21. In total 10 toll bits are needed: One start bit, one to two stop bits, and eight character bits.

22. The number of bits that can be transmitted per second.

23. A keyboard and a monitor screen.

24. To store large quantities of data and programs for later use.

25. Beginning Of Tape and End Of Tape.

26. The tape speed is the speed with which the tape passes the read/write heads. The data density is the number of bytes that can be stored on one inch of magnetic tape. The read/write speed is the maximum number of characters that can be read or written per second.

27. The track number. The head number. The sector number.

Chapter 21

I/O Interfacing

If we want a computer to execute a certain task we must write a program for it. The data that passes between I/O equipment and the computer comprises the following signals (fig. 21-1).

●Status signals which indicate to the computer the state of the I/O equipment (power on, data ready, etc.).

●Control signals, that is the commands that are sent from the computer to the I/O equipment.

●Data signals, which are the actual data transferred between computer and I/O equipment.

The transfer of status and control signals allows a device to be controlled correctly. The tape reader, for example, offers to the computer at Input port, parallel data that it has read. The tape reader sends a status signal via one line, to another Input port to indicate that the data is valid. The computer then sends a read command to the punched tape reader on a different line, through an Output port.

The communication runs as follows. To begin with the status line and the command line are quiescent. An answer must be given to every action from either side, so that both sides are aware of the current status. When the computer needs data a command line from the computer is activated. The tape reader receives this command and begins the read action. As soon as the read action is finished the tape reader enters the data that has been read on one Input port and then, by activating the status line, indicates that the data is valid. While the reader is carrying out these activities, the computer samples the status of the tape reader. As long as there is no change in the status the computer keeps taking samples. Once a change has occurred and the computer has become aware of the change via a test, it samples the data offered by means of an Input instruction. The computer then removes the control signal from the tape reader as an indication that the data has been accepted. In answer, the tape reader removes the status signal. In this way a device can be controlled using a program. When both sides send signals it is called *synchronous transmission*, or *handshaking*.

PROGRAMMED INPUT/OUTPUT

Whenever the exchange of data occurs on the basis of a programmed I/O the control of the computer system is in the hands of the program. A problem with programmed I /O is the difference in speeds between the microcomputer and the peripheral equipment. With certain Output operations it can happen that the microcom-

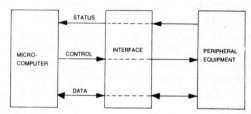

Fig. 21-1.

194

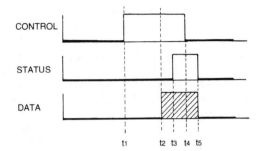

Fig. 21-2.

puter transmits data while the Output equipment is still busy handling the previous data. With an Input operation the microcomputer can read the same data in several times in succession, simply because the peripheral is not yet able to produce the succeeding data. When the I /O drivers are written with delays or checks to account for time differences, it is called *asynchronous communication*. This requires little extra hardware, but is harder to program. For this reason, the handshaking signals are usually employed, even though extra hardware is needed.

PROGRAMMED INPUT WITH HANDSHAKE

To perfectly synchronize Input equipment the microcomputer during an Input operation we can make a test. For this purpose the Input equipment sends a signal to the microcomputer that indicates that new data is available. The signal is called *data in available*, or *DAVIN* for short. Before the microcomputer executes an Input operation, it must test as to whether or not this signal is available. In its turn, the microcomputer must indicate when it has finished handling one piece of data and is ready for the next. With some Input devices the data sent out is only briefly available. If the microcomputer is still busy with the previous data, it misses the succeeding data.

Most peripherals work on a question-and-answer basis as described below. By making a *data request signal* 0, the microcomputer indicates that it is ready to receive the succeeding data. Therefore, before a peripheral transmits the next piece of data, it must first test whether the data request signal is 0 or 1. The exchange of the test signals (DAVIN and data request) is known as handshake.

Figure 21-3 shows the test signals as a function of time. The arrows indicate the relationship of the signals to each other. When the data request signal is 0 it indicates to the Input equipment that the microcomputer has finished handling the data and is ready for succeeding data. The Input equipment then transmits the new data to

the microcomputer and simultaneously makes the DAVIN signal 1. On receiving this signal the microcomputer accepts the data and makes the data request signal 1. This means that the microcomputer has accepted the data and is processing it.

Once the Input equipment sees this, it can remove the data and the DAVIN signal because the data is now safely in the computer. When the microcomputer has finished processing the data it makes the data request signal 0 and the following cycle is begun.

Figure 21-4 shows a flowchart of how a microcomputer realizes this method of data Input with handshake. We write the program in the form of a subroutine called DATAIN. The subroutine is called to enter one word. In block 1 the microcomputer makes the data request signal 0, thereby requesting data. Blocks 2 and 3 form a program loop which is run through until the DAVIN signal becomes 1. When the DAVIN signal becomes 1 it means that new data is present and in block 4 it is taken over by the computer. In block 5 the computer makes the data request signal 1, after which it waits in blocks 6 and 7 until the DAVIN signal becomes 0. When the DAVIN signal becomes 0 the computer stores the data entered in block 4 in the memory and returns to the main program.

Note

In some cases one test signal is sufficient for an Input operation. This *strobe signal* is generated in the Input equipment and indicates whether the data to be entered is valid or not. When the strobe signal is active, that is say, when the data is valid, the computer must accept the data within a predetermined period (say, 10 ms). The microcomputer may only accept the succeeding data when the strobe pulse has been briefly 0 and becomes again active.

PROGRAMMED OUTPUT WITH HANDSHAKE

With the Output of data problems also arise because of the difference in speed between the microcomputer

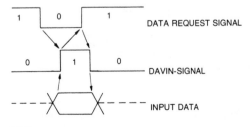

Fig. 21-3.

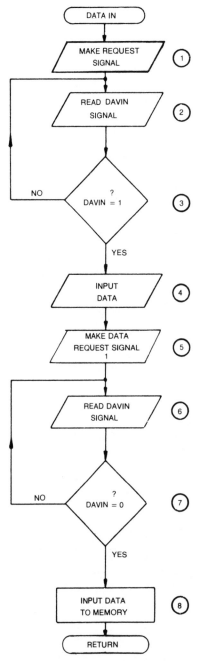

Fig. 21-4.

takes some time before the computer can output new data, so that the Output equipment reads the same data several times or misses it completely.

With an Output operation, the output equipment must transmit a signal to the microcomputer indicating when it is ready to receive new data. This signal is known as the *device busy signal.* Before the microcomputer outputs data it must test for the presence of this signal. In its turn, the microcomputer must indicate when new data is available for the Output equipment. The signal with which it does this is called the *data out available* signal, or DAVOUT for short. The output equipment must, therefore, test as to whether the DAVOUT signal is present or not before it accepts specific data.

Figure 21-5 shows the test signals and the data to be output. The arrows show their relationship to each other. Whenever the Output equipment makes the device busy signal 0 it means that it is ready to accept new data. The microcomputer then makes the DAVOUT signal 1 and transmits the output data. The Output equipment begins processing this data and makes the device busy signal 1. This means that the data is safely in the Output equipment so that the microcomputer can remove both the DAVOUT signal and the data. Once the Output equipment has finished processing the data, it makes the device busy signal 0 and the next cycle can begin.

Figure 21-6 shows by means of a flowchart how a microcomputer can realize all this with the aid of an *output routine.* Once the start signal is given in block 1, the data to be Output is prepared in block 2. This means that the data from the memory is already in the accumulator. Blocks 3 and 4 form a program loop which is run through until the device busy signal becomes 0. Once this has happened, the data is output in block 5 by means of an OUT instruction and the DAVOUT signal is made 1. Blocks 7 and 8 form another program loop which is run through until the Output equipment makes the device busy signal 1, that is to say, until it has accepted the data. When this happens the microcomputer makes the DAVOUT signal 0 and returns to the main program.

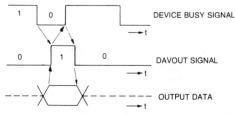

Fig. 21-5.

and the peripheral. It can occur that the microcomputer outputs certain data while the Output equipment is still busy handling the previous data. It can also occur that it

196

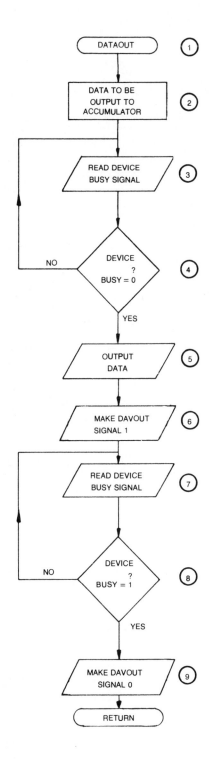

Fig. 21-6.

THE DISADVANTAGE OF PROGRAMMED I/O

In the previous section we saw how correct synchronization between peripherals and microcomputer can be obtained by the use of test signals. This means that the computer can do nothing else except Input and Output data. Between times it is somewhere in a program loop waiting for test signals to become active or not. The system is extremely inefficient because no work can be performed other than Input or Output of data. The solution to this problem is the interrupt I/O, which will be dealt with next.

INTERRUPT I/O

When a microcomputer is capable of handling *interrupt requests* from peripherals, programs and I/O routines can be interleaved.

Whenever an Input device wishes to Input data to the computer it forces an interrupt (fig. 21-7). That is to say, the Input equipment transmits a signal to the interrupt Input of the microprocessor. Immediately the microprocessor detects an interrupt signal, it stops execution of the main program and jumps to a sub-program that handles data Input. Such a sub-program is called an *interrupt service routine.* Once the interrupt service routine has been executed, a return is made to the main program. The Input and Output of a data series is as shown in fig. 21-8.

OUTPUT ON AN INTERRUPT BASIS

When an Output operation on the basis of an interrupt is to be expected, it is advantageous to have the interrupt service routine preceded by a sub-program that prepares the data to be Output, that is to say, remove it from memory and enter it in a predetermined memory location. This sub-program can be, for example, at the beginning of the main program. Now, when an Output device indicates an interrupt request, the OUT instruction can be given directly after the data has been fetched from memory. Figure 21-9 shows an interrupt service routine for an Output operation.

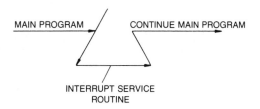

Fig. 21-7.

197

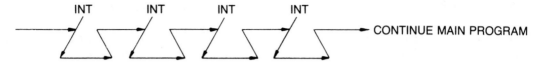

CONTINUE MAIN PROGRAM

Fig. 21-8.

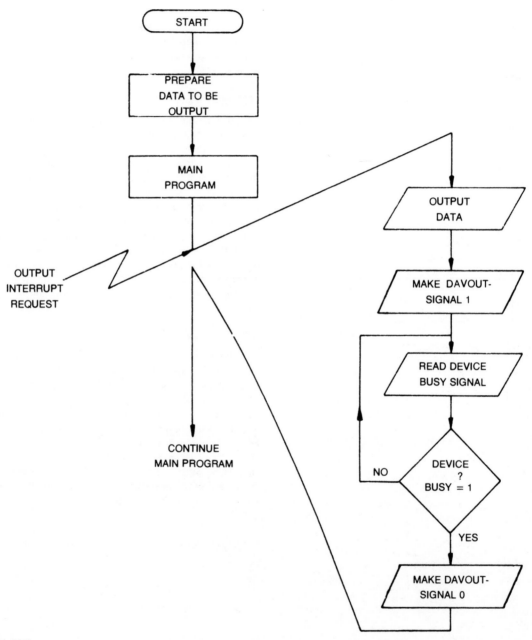

Fig. 21-9.

INPUT ON AN INTERRUPT BASIS

Figure 21-10 shows an interrupt service routine for an Input operation. At the beginning of the main program the computer makes the data request signal 0, so that the peripheral can interrupt at any desired time.

Note

An interrupt service routine need not, be only for the Input or Output of data. It can also, be a program of any length or function.

THE INTERRUPT VECTOR

A microcomputer usually has more than one I/O device. This means that there must be more than one interrupt request line, and that when an interrupt request is made, the jump is made to the right interrupt service routine. Therefore, with most microprocessors, a number of extra bits (usually 3) are offered, with the interrupt request, which the microprocessor can use to form a memory address. In this case we speak of an *interrupt vector*. The contents of the memory word with this address and the contents of the two following memory words form a jump instruction to the first instruction of the relevant interrupt service routine.

Figure 21-11 shows how this all works in an 8080 CPU. At a certain moment, an I/O device transmits an interrupt request via the interrupt controller to the INT input of the microprocessor. Once this interrupt request has been accepted, the microprocessor transmits a signal back to the interrupt controller via the INTA output (INTA = interrupt acknowledge) and goes into the HOLD mode. When INTA and DBIN are ready the Interrupt controller transmits a code to the data bus that indicates from which peripheral the interrupt request originates. For each I/O device there is a different code. For a TTY it may be $CF_{16} = 11001111_2$, for a punched card punch, $EF_{16} = 11101111_2$, etc. The general form of the code is 11AAA111. Where AAA represents the device. Depending on which peripheral the interrupt request originates from, the interrupt controller enters a given combination for AAA. This instruction that is placed on the date lines is called a *restart instruction,* because it restarts the program counter from 00_{16} plus a displacement. The restart instruction causes the following processes:

●The contents of the program counter are stored in the stack and the stack pointer is updated, so that after execution of the interrupt service routine the jump back to the main program can be correctly performed.

●The value 0000000000 AAA 000_2 is entered into the program counter.

After the restart instruction has been executed, the program proceeds from the address 0000000000 AA 000_2.

When a TTY offers the interrupt controller the value 001_2 for AAA then the value 11 001 111_2 will be entered in the instruction register. This is the RST 01 instruction because $001_2 = 1_{10}$. After execution of this restart instruction the program proceeds with address 0000000000 001 $000_2 = 0008_{16}$. The content of this memory word and of the succeeding memory words is usually, as has been said, a jump instruction. If this jump instruction is, for example, JMP 2000H then the first instruction of the interrupt service routine is at address 2000_{16}.

Should an I/O device offer, via the interrupt controller the value 000_2 for AAA, then the value 11 000 111_2 will be entered in the instruction register. This is the RST 00 instruction, because $000_2 = 0_{10}$. After executing the start instruction the program proceeds with address 00000000 00 000 $000_2 = 0000_{16}$, which contains the first byte of the jump instruction. Because AAA is a combination of 3 bits there are $2^3 = 8$ different restart instructions.

Figure 21-12 shows the memory locations of two jump instructions and the relevant interrupt service routines. In consequence of the RST 01 instruction, for example, the value 00000000 00001000$_2 = 0008_{16}$ is entered in the program counter. The content of the memory word at this address and of the following memory words form a jump instruction to the first instruction of the interrupt service routine relevant to the RST 01 instruction.

Just as with a subroutine the last instruction of an interrupt service routine is a return instruction. This ensures that the program counter is filled with the value that was stored in the stack by the restart instruction. After execution of the interrupt service routine a return is made to the main program at the point where it was interrupted by the interrupt request.

Note 1

Just as with subroutines it is possible to nest interrupt service routines. The execution of an interrupt service routine is then interrupted by an interrupt request from another I/O device. It is also possible to allocate priorities to interrupt requests from I/O equipment, however, the interrupt controller must ensure that two interrupt requests arriving simultaneously are processed in order of priority.

Note 2

It is possible that during the execution of an interrupt service routine the contents of status flags or the contents of certain registers are altered. It is recom-

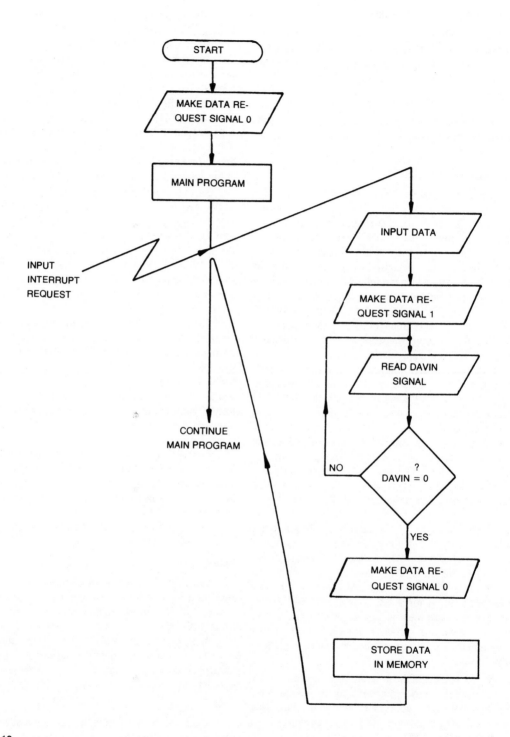

Fig. 21-10.

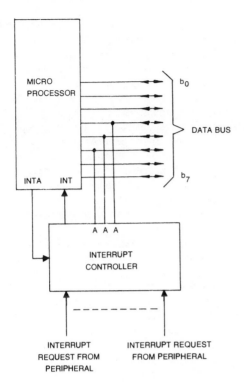

Fig. 21-11.

mended, therefore, that these contents be made safe before the interrupt service routine is begun. This can be done by storing them in a stack, for example.

SUMMARY

1. The exchange of data between peripherals and the microcomputer can occur on the basis of programmed I/O or of interrupt I/O.

2. The problem with programmed I/O is the difference in speeds between the microcomputer and the peripherals.

3. The handshake principle is used to obtain correct synchronization between peripheral and microcomputer.

4. With a programmed Input with handshake, the microcomputer transmits a data request signal to the Input equipment, that indicates when the microcomputer is ready to receive new data.

5. The peripheral transmits a DAVIN signal to the microcomputer that indicates whether the data to be entered is valid or not.

6. With programmed Output with handshake, the output equipment transmits a device busy signal to the microcomputer that indicates that the Output equipment is ready to receive new data.

7. The microcomputer transmits a DAVOUT signal to the peripheral that indicates when the data to be Output is valid.

8. The disadvantage of programmed I/O is that, the computer is not able to do anything else except Input and Output data.

9. By data exchange on the basis of an interrupt I/O, main program and I/O routines can be interleaved.

10. An interrupt service routine is a program which takes care of the exchange of data between microcomputer and peripherals, once the peripheral has made an interrupt request.

11. An interrupt vector is a memory address that the CPU forms after receipt of a restart instruction.

12. The content of the memory word with this address and of the two succeeding words are usually a jump instruction to the first instruction of the interrupt service routine requested.

13. A restart instruction is offered to the CPU by the interrupt controller as a sort of CALL instruction of 1 byte which contains an abbreviated form of the memory address.

REVIEW EXERCISES

1. Name two methods by which data can be exchanged between a peripheral and the microcomputer.

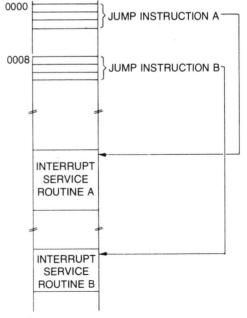

Fig. 21-12.

2. What is the problem with programmed I/O? How is it avoided?

3. What is the function of the DAVIN signal?

4. From which device does the DAVOUT signal come?

5. Draw the test signals for programmed Input with handshake and show how these signals are related to each other.

6. From which device does the strobe signal come?

7. What is the disadvantage of programmed I/O?

8. What is an interrupt request?

9. What is an interrupt service routine?

10. What is an interrupt vector?

11. What is the restart instruction for?

12. How is a restart instruction formed?

13. How many different restart instructions are there?

14. What is the last instruction of an interrupt service routine?

ANSWERS

1. Programmed I/O and interrupt I/O.

2. The difference in speeds between the peripheral equipment and the microprocessor, which is avoided by applying the handshake principle.

3. With a DAVIN signal the peripherals indicate when the data to be entered is valid.

4. From the microcomputer.

5. See figs. 21-3 and 21-5 in this chapter.

6. From the peripheral.

7. The disadvantage is that the microcomputer is not able to do anything else except Input and Output data. The rest of the time is spent in a waiting loop.

8. A request from a peripheral to interrupt the main program and execute an interrupt service routine.

9. A program that, after an interrupt request, cares for the exchange of data between the microcomputer and the peripheral.

10. An interrupt vector is the address where the interrupt routine starts.

11. To push the program counter and direct the CPU to the interrupt vector when a main program has been interrupted.

12. When an interrupt request has been accepted, the interrupt controller transmits this instruction to the data bus. The microprocessor enters the data from the data bus into the instruction register.

13. $2^3 = 8$.

14. A return, which that ensures that the return address, which was stored by the RST instruction on receipt of the interrupt is entered into the program counter.

Appendix A

8080 Instruction Set

A computer, no matter how sophisticated, can only do what it is "told" to do. One "tells" the computer what to do via a series of coded instructions referred to as a **Program**. The realm of the programmer is referred to as **Software**, in contrast to the **Hardware** that comprises the actual computer equipment. A computer's software refers to all of the programs that have been written for that computer.

When a computer is designed, the engineers provide the Central Processing Unit (CPU) with the ability to perform a particular set of operations. The CPU is designed such that a specific operation is performed when the CPU control logic decodes a particular instruction. Consequently, the operations that can be performed by a CPU define the computer's **Instruction Set.**

Each computer instruction allows the programmer to initiate the performance of a specific operation. All computers implement certain arithmetic operations in their instruction set, such as an instruction to add the contents of two registers. Often logical operations (e.g., OR the contents of two registers) and register operate instructions (e.g., increment a register) are included in the instruction set. A computer's instruction set will also have instructions that move data between registers, between a register and memory, and between a register and an I/O device. Most instruction sets also provide **Conditional Instructions.** A conditional instruction specifies an operation to be performed only if certain conditions have been met; for example, jump to a particular instruction if the result of the last operation was zero. Conditional instructions provide a program

with a decision-making capability.

By logically organizing a sequence of instructions into a coherent program, the programmer can "tell" the computer to perform a very specific and useful function.

The computer, however, can only execute programs whose instructions are in a binary coded form (i.e., a series of 1's and 0's), that is called **Machine Code.** Because it would be extremely cumbersome to program in machine code, programming languages have been developed. There are programs available which convert the programming language instructions into machine code that can be interpreted by the processor.

One type of programming language is **Assembly Language.** A unique assembly language mnemonic is assigned to each of the computer's instructions. The programmer can write a program (called the **Source Program**) using these mnemonics and certain operands; the source program is then converted into machine instructions (called the **Object Code**). Each assembly language instruction is converted into one machine code instruction (1 or more bytes) by an **Assembler** program. Assembly languages are usually machine dependent (i.e., they are usually able to run on only one type of computer).

THE 8080 INSTRUCTION SET

The 8080 instruction set includes five different types of instructions:

- **Data Transfer Group**—move data between registers or between memory and registers

- **Arithmetic Group**—add, subtract, increment or decrement data in registers or in memory
- **Logical Group**—AND, OR, EXCLUSIVE-OR, compare, rotate or complement data in registers or in memory
- **Branch Group**—conditional and unconditional jump instructions, subroutine call instructions and return instructions
- **Stack, I/O and Machine Control Group**— includes I/O instructions, as well as instructions for maintaining the stack and internal control flags.

Instruction and Data Formats:

Memory for the 8080 is organized into 8-bit quantities, called Bytes. Each byte has a unique 16-bit binary address corresponding to its sequential position in memory. The 8080 can directly address up to 65,536 bytes of memory, which may consist of both ready-only memory (ROM) elements and random-access memory (RAM) elements (read/write memory).

Data in the 8080 is stored in the form of 8-bit binary integers:

DATA WORD

D_7	D_6	D_5	D_4	D_3	D_2	D_1	D_0

MSB   LSB

When a register or data word contains a binary number, it is necessary to establish the order in which the bits of the number are written. In the Intel 8080, BIT 0 is referred to as the **Least Significant Bit (LSB)**, and BIT 7 (of an 8 bit number) is referred to as the **Most Significant Bit (MSB).**

The 8080 program instructions may be one, two or three bytes in length. Multiple byte instructions must be stored in successive memory locations; the address of the first byte is always used as the address of the instructions. The exact instruction format will depend on the particular operation to be executed.

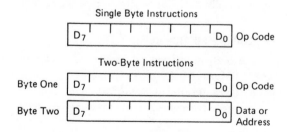

Addressing Modes:

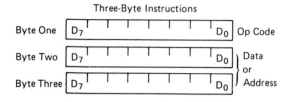

Often the data that is to be operated on is stored in memory. When multi-byte numeric data is used, the data, like instructions, is stored in successive memory locations, with the least significant byte first, followed by increasingly significant bytes. The 8080 has four different modes for addressing data stored in memory or in registers:

- Direct—Bytes 2 and 3 of the instruction contain the exact memory address of the data item (the low-order bits of the address are in byte 2, the high-order bits in byte 3).
- Register—The instruction specifies the register or register-pair in which the data is located.
- Register Indirect—The instruction specifies a register-pair which contains the memory address where the data is located (the high-order bits of the address are in the first register of the pair, the low-order bits in the second).
- Immediate—The instruction contains the data itself. This is either an 8-bit quantity or a 16-bit quantity (least significant byte first, most significant byte second).

Unless directed by an interrupt or branch instruction, the execution of instructions proceeds through consecutively increasing memory locations. A branch instruction can specify the address of the next instruction to be executed in one of two ways:

- Direct—The branch instruction contains the address of the next instruction to be executed. (Except for the 'RST' instruction, byte 2 contains the low-order address and byte 3 the high-order address.)
- Register indirect—The branch instruction indicates a register-pair which contains the address of the next instruction to

be executed. (The high-order bits of the address are in the first register of the pair, the low-order bits in the second.)

The RST instruction is a special one-byte call instruction (usually used during interrupt sequences). RST includes a three-bit field; program control is transferred to the instruction whose address is eight times the contents of this three-bit field.

Condition Flags:

There are five condition flags associated with the execution of instructions on the 8080. They are Zero, Sign, Parity, Carry, and Auxiliary Carry, and are each represented by a 1-bit register in the CPU. A flag is "set" by forcing the bit to 1; "reset" by forcing the bit to 0.

Unless indicated otherwise, when an instruction affects a flag, it affects it in the following manner:

Zero: If the result of an instruction has the value 0, this flag is set; otherwise it is reset.

Sign: If the most significant bit of the result of the operation has the value 1, this flag is set; otherwise it is reset.

Parity: If the modulo 2 sum of the bits of the result of the operation is 0, (i.e., if the result has even parity), this flag is set; otherwise it is reset (i.e., if the result has odd parity).

Carry: If the instruction resulted in a carry (from addition), or a borrow (from subtraction or a comparison) out of the high-order bit, this flag is set; otherwise it is reset.

Auxiliary Carry: If the instruction caused a carry out of bit 3 and into bit 4 of the resulting value, the auxiliary carry is set; otherwise it is reset. This flag is affected by single precision additions, subtractions, increments, decrements, comparisons, and logical operations and increments preceding a DAA (Decimal Adjust Accumulator) instruction.

Symbols and Abbreviations:

The following symbols and abbreviations are used in the subsequent description of the 8080 instructions:

SYMBOLS	MEANING
accumulator	Register A
addr	16-bit address quantity
data	8-bit data quantity
data 16	16-bit data quantity
byte 2	The second byte of the instruction
byte 3	The third byte of the instruction
port	8-bit address of an I/O device
r,r1,r2	One of the registers A,B,C,D,E,H,L
DDD,SSS	The bit pattern designating one of the registers A,B,C,D,E,H,L (DDD=destination, SSS = source):

DDD or SSS	REGISTER NAME
111	A
000	B
001	C
010	D
011	E
100	H
101	L

rp — One of the register pairs:
B represents the B,C pair with B as the high-order register and C as the low-order register;
D represents the D,E pair with D as the high-order register and E as the low-order register;
H represents the H,L pair with H as the high-order register and L as the low-order register;
SP represents the 16-bit stack pointer register.

RP — The bit pattern designating one of the register pairs B,D,H,SP:

RP	REGISTER PAIR
00	B-C
01	D-E
10	H-L
11	SP

rh — The first (high-order) register of a designated register pair.

rl — The second (low-order register of a designated register pair.

SYMBOL   MEANING

PC   16-bit program counter register (PCH and PCL are used to refer to the high-order and low-order 8 bits respectively).

SP   16-bit stack pointer register (SPH and SPL are used to refer to the high-order and low-order 8 bits respectively).

r_m Bit m of the register r (bits are number 7 through 0 from left to right).

Z,S,P,CY,AC   The condition flags:
         Zero,
         Sign,
         Parity,
         Carry,
         and Auxiliary Carry, respectively.

( )   The contents of the memory location or registers enclosed in the parentheses.

←   "Is transferred to"

∧   Logical AND

∀   Exclusive OR

∨   Inclusive OR

+   Addition

−   Two's complement subtraction

*   Multiplication

↔   "Is exchanged with"

$\overline{n}$ The one's complement (e.g., $(\overline{A})$)

      The restart number 0 through 7

NNN   The binary representation 000 through 111 for restart number 0 through 7 respectively.

Description Format:

The following pages provide a detailed description of the instruction set of the 8080. Each instruction is described in the following manner:

1. The MAC 80 assembler format, consisting of the instruction mnemonic and operand fields, is printed in **BOLDFACE** on the left side of the first line.
2. The name of the instruction is enclosed in parenthesis on the right side of the first line.
3. The next line(s) contain a symbolic description of the operation of the instruction.
4. This is followed by a narrative description of the operation of the instruction.
5. The following line(s) contain the binary fields and patterns that comprise the machine instruction.
6. The last four lines contain incidental information about the execution of the instruction. The number of machine cycles and states required to execute the instruction are listed first. If the instruction has two possible execution times, as in a Conditional Jump, both times will be listed, separated by a slash. Next, any significant data addressing modes (see Pages 204-206) are listed. The last line lists any of the five Flags that are affected by the execution of the instruction.

Data Transfer Group:

This group of instructions transfers data to and from registers and memory. **Condition flags are not affected** by any instruction in this group.

MOV r1, r2   (Move Register)

  (r1) ← (r2)

The content of register r2 is moved to register r1.

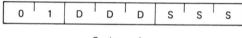

            Cycles: 1
            States: 5
       Addressing: register
             Flags: none

MOV r, M   (Move from memory)

  (r) ← ((H) (L))

The content of the memory location, whose address is in registers H and L, is moved to register r.

            Cycles: 2
            States: 7
       Addressing: reg. indirect
             Flags: none

MOV M, r   (Move to memory)

  ((H) (L)) ← (r)

The content of register r is moved to the memory location whose address is in registers H and L.

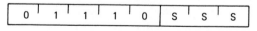

            Cycles: 2
            States: 7
       Addressing: reg. indirect
             Flags: none

MVI r, data   (Move Immediate)

(r) ← (byte 2)

The content of byte 2 of the instruction is moved to register r.

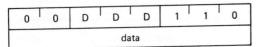

Cycles: 2
States: 7
Addressing: immediate
Flags: none

MVI M, data   (Move to memory immediate)

((H) (L)) ← (byte 2)

The content of byte 2 of the instruction is moved to the memory location whose address is in registers H and L.

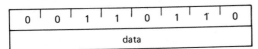

Cycles: 3
States: 10
Addressing: immed./reg. indirect
Flags: none

LXI rp, data 16   (Load register pair immediate)

(rh) ← (byte 3),

(rl) ← (byte 2)

Byte 3 of the instruction is moved into the high-order register (rh) of the register pair rp. Byte 2 of the instruction is moved into the low-order register (rl) of the register pair rp.

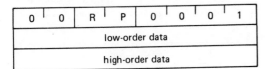

Cycles: 3
States: 10
Addressing: immediate
Flags: none

LDA addr   (Load Accumulator direct)

(A) ← ((byte 3)(byte 2))

The content of the memory location, whose address is specified in byte 2 and byte 3 of the instruction, is moved to register A.

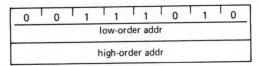

Cycles: 4
States: 13
Addressing: direct
Flags: none

STA addr   (Store Accumulator direct)

((byte 3)(byte 2)) ← (A)

The content of the accumulator is moved to the memory location whose address is specified in byte 2 and byte 3 of the instruction.

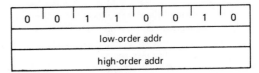

Cycles: 4
States: 13
Addressing: direct
Flags: none

LHLD addr   (Load H and L direct)

(L) ← ((byte 3)(byte 2))

(H) ← ((byte 3)(byte 2) + 1)

The content of the memory location, whose address is specified in byte 2 and byte 3 of the instruction, is moved to register L. The content of the memory location at the succeeding address is moved to register H.

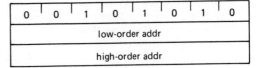

Cycles: 5
States: 16
Addressing: direct
Flags: none

SHLD addr   (Store H and L direct)

((byte 3)(byte 2)) ← (L)

((byte 3)(byte 2) + 1) ← (H)

The content of register L is moved to the memory location whose address is specified in byte 2 and byte 3. The content of register H is moved to the succeeding memory location.

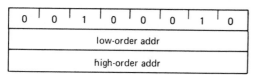

0	0	1	0	0	0	1	0
low-order addr							
high-order addr							

Cycles: 5
States: 16
Addressing: direct
Flags: none

LDAX rp   (Load accumulator indirect)

(A) ← ((rp))

The content of the memory location, whose address is in the register pair rp, is moved to register A. Note: only register pairs rp=B (registers B and C) or rp=D (registers D and E) may be specified.

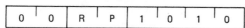

0	0	R	P	1	0	1	0

Cycles: 2
States: 7
Addressing: reg. indirect
Flags: none

STAX rp   (Store accumulator indirect)

((rp)) ← (A)

The content of register A is moved to the memory location whose address is in the register pair rp. Note: only register pairs rp=B (registers B and C) or rp=D (registers D and E) may be specified.

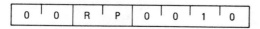

0	0	R	P	0	0	1	0

Cycles: 2
States: 7
Addressing: reg. indirect
Flags: none

XCHG   (Exchange H and L with D and E)

(H) ←→ (D)

(L) ←→ (E)

The contents of registers H and L are exchanged with the contents of registers D and E.

1	1	1	0	1	0	1	1

Cycles: 1
States: 4
Addressing: register
Flags: none

Arithmetic Group:

This group of instructions performs arithmetic operations on data in registers and memory.

Unless indicated otherwise, all instructions in this group affect the Zero, Sign, Parity, Carry, and Auxiliary Carry flags according to the standard rules.

All subtraction operations are performed via two's complement arithmetic and set the carry flag to one to indicate a borrow and clear it to indicate no borrow.

ADD r   (Add Register)

(A) ← (A) + (r)

The content of register r is added to the content of the accumulator. The result is placed in the accumulator.

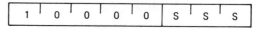

1	0	0	0	0	S	S	S

Cycles: 1
States: 4
Addressing: register
Flags: Z,S,P,CY,AC

ADD M   (Add memory)

(A) ← (A) + ((H) (L))

The content of the memory location whose address is contained in the H and L registers is added to the content of the accumulator. The result is placed in the accumulator.

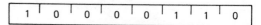

1	0	0	0	0	1	1	0

Cycles: 2
States: 7
Addressing: reg. indirect
Flags: Z,S,P,CY,AC

ADI data   (Add immediate)

(A) ◄— (A) + (byte 2)

The content of the second byte of the instruction is added to the content of the accumulator. The result is placed in the accumulator.

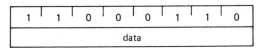

Cycles: 2
States: 7
Addressing: immediate
Flags: Z,S,P,CY,AC

ADC r   (Add Register with carry)

(A) ◄— (A) + (r) + (CY)

The content of register r and the content of the carry bit are added to the content of the accumulator. The result is placed in the accumulator.

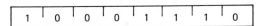

Cycles: 1
States: 4
Addressing: register
Flags: Z,S,P,CY,AC

ADC M   (Add memory with carry)

(A) ◄— (A) + ((H) (L)) + (CY)

The content of the memory location whose address is contained in the H and L registers and the content of the CY flag are added to the accumulator. The result is placed in the accumulator.

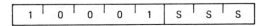

Cycles: 2
States: 7
Addressing: reg. indirect
Flags: Z,S,P,CY,AC

ACI data   (Add immediate with carry)

(A) ◄— (A) + (byte 2) + (CY)

The content of the second byte of the instruction and the content of the CY flag are added to the contents of the accumulator. The result is placed in the accumulator.

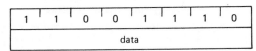

Cycles: 2
States: 7
Addressing: immediate
Flags: Z,S,P,CY,AC

SUB r   (Subtract Register)

(A) ◄— (A) − (r)

The content of register r is subtracted from the content of the accumulator. The result is placed in the accumulator.

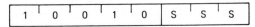

Cycles: 1
States: 4
Addressing: register
Flags: Z,S,P,CY,AC

SUB M   (Subtract memory)

(A) ◄— (A) − ((H) (L))

The content of the memory location whose address is contained in the H and L registers is subtracted from the content of the accumulator. The result is placed in the accumulator.

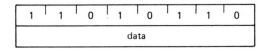

Cycles: 2
States: 7
Addressing: reg. indirect
Flags: Z,S,P,CY,AC

SUI data   (Subtract immediate)

(A) ◄— (A) − (byte 2)

The content of the second byte of the instruction is subtracted from the content of the accumulator. The result is placed in the accumulator.

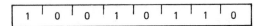

Cycles: 2
States: 7
Addressing: immediate
Flags: Z,S,P,CY,AC

SBB r   (Subtract Register with borrow)

(A) ◄— (A) − (r) − (CY)

The content of register r and the content of the CY flag are both subtracted from the accumulator. The result is placed in the accumulator.

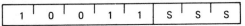

Cycles: 1
States: 4
Addressing: register
Flags: Z,S,P,CY,AC

SBB M (Subtract memory with borrow)

(A) ← (A) − ((H) (L)) − (CY)

The content of the memory location whose address is contained in the H and L registers and the content of the CY flag are both subtracted from the accumulator. The result is placed in the accumulator.

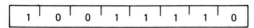

1	0	0	1	1	1	1	0

Cycles: 2
States: 7
Addressing: reg. indirect
Flags: Z,S,P,CY,AC

SBI data (Subtract immediate with borrow)

(A) ← (A) − (byte 2) − (CY)

The contents of the second byte of the instruction and the contents of the CY flag are both subtracted from the accumulator. The result is placed in the accumulator.

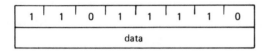

1	1	0	1	1	1	1	0

data

Cycles: 2
States: 7
Addressing: immediate
Flags: Z,S,P,CY,AC

INR r (Increment Register)

(r) ← (r) + 1

The content of register r is incremented by one. Note: All condition flags **except CY** are affected.

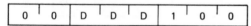

0	0	D	D	D	1	0	0

Cycles: 1
States: 5
Addressing: register
Flags: Z,S,P,AC

INR M (Increment memory)

((H) (L)) ← ((H) (L)) + 1

The content of the memory location whose address is contained in the H and L registers is incremented by one. Note: All condition flags **except CY** are affected.

0	0	1	1	0	1	0	0

Cycles: 3
States: 10
Addressing: reg. indirect
Flags: Z,S,P,AC

DCR r (Decrement Register)

(r) ← (r) − 1

The content of register r is decremented by one. Note: All condition flags **except CY** are affected.

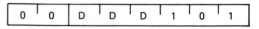

0	0	D	D	D	1	0	1

Cycles: 1
States: 5
Addressing: register
Flags: Z,S,P,AC

DCR M (Decrement memory)

((H) (L)) ← ((H) (L)) − 1

The content of the memory location whose address is contained in the H and L registers is decremented by one. Note: All condition flags **except CY** are affected.

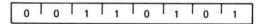

0	0	1	1	0	1	0	1

Cycles: 3
States: 10
Addressing: reg. indirect
Flags: Z,S,P,AC

INX rp (Increment register pair)

(rh) (rl) ← (rh) (rl) + 1

The content of the register pair rp is incremented by one. Note: **No condition flags are affected.**

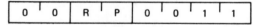

0	0	R	P	0	0	1	1

Cycles: 1
States: 5
Addressing: register
Flags: none

DCX rp (Decrement register pair)

(rh) (rl) ← (rh) (rl) − 1

The content of the register pair rp is decremented by one. Note: **No condition flags are affected.**

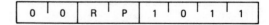

0	0	R	P	1	0	1	1

Cycles: 1
States: 5
Addressing: register
Flags: none

DAD rp   (Add register pair to H and L)

(H) (L) ◄── (H) (L) + (rh) (rl)

The content of the register pair rp is added to the content of the register pair H and L. The result is placed in the register pair H and L. Note: **Only the CY flag is affected.** It is set if there is a carry out of the double precision add; otherwise it is reset.

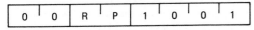

0	0	R	P	1	0	0	1

Cycles: 3
States: 10
Addressing: register
Flags: CY

DAA   (Decimal Adjust Accumulator)

The eight-bit number in the accumulator is adjusted to form two four-bit Binary-Coded-Decimal digits by the following process:

1. If the value of the least significant 4 bits of the accumulator is greater than 9 **or** if the AC flag is set, 6 is added to the accumulator.

2. If the value of the most significant 4 bits of the accumulator is now greater than 9, **or** if the CY flag is set, 6 is added to the most significant 4 bits of the accumulator.

NOTE: All flags are affected.

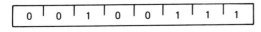

0	0	1	0	0	1	1	1

Cycles: 1
States: 4
Flags: Z,S,P,CY,AC

Logical Group:

This group of instructions performs logical (Boolean) operations on data in registers and memory and on condition flags.

Unless indicated otherwise, all instructions in this group affect the Zero, Sign, Parity, Auxiliary Carry, and Carry flags according to the standard rules.

ANA r   (AND Register)

(A) ◄── (A) ∧ (r)

The content of register r is logically anded with the content of the accumulator. The result is placed in the accumulator. **The CY flag is cleared.**

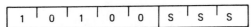

1	0	1	0	0	S	S	S

Cycles: 1
States: 4
Addressing: register
Flags: Z,S,P,CY,AC

ANA M   (AND memory)

(A) ◄── (A) ∧ ((H) (L))

The contents of the memory location whose address is contained in the H and L registers is logically anded with the content of the accumulator. The result is placed in the accumulator. **The CY flag is cleared.**

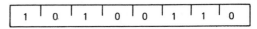

1	0	1	0	0	1	1	0

Cycles: 2
States: 7
Addressing: reg. indirect
Flags: Z,S,P,CY,AC

ANI data   (AND immediate)

(A) ◄── (A) ∧ (byte 2)

The content of the second byte of the instruction is logically anded with the contents of the accumulator. The result is placed in the accumulator. **The CY and AC flags are cleared.**

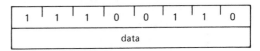

1	1	1	0	0	1	1	0
			data				

Cycles: 2
States: 7
Addressing: immediate
Flags: Z,S,P,CY,AC

XRA r   (Exclusive OR Register)

(A) ◄── (A) ∀ (r)

The content of register r is exclusive-or'd with the content of the accumulator. The result is placed in the accumulator. **The CY and AC flags are cleared.**

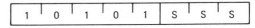

1	0	1	0	1	S	S	S

Cycles: 1
States: 4
Addressing: register
Flags: Z,S,P,CY,AC

XRA M (Exclusive OR Memory)

(A) ← (A) ∀ ((H) (L))

The content of the memory location whose address is contained in the H and L registers is exclusive-OR'd with the content of the accumulator. The result is placed in the accumulator. **The CY and AC flags are cleared.**

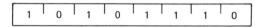

1	0	1	0	1	1	1	0

Cycles: 2
States: 7
Addressing: reg. indirect
Flags: Z,S,P,CY,AC

XRI data (Exclusive OR immediate)

(A) ← (A) ∀ (byte 2)

The content of the second byte of the instruction is exclusive-OR'd with the content of the accumulator. The result is placed in the accumulator. **The CY and AC flags are cleared.**

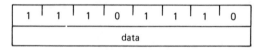

1	1	1	0	1	1	1	0

data

Cycles: 2
States: 7
Addressing: immediate
Flags: Z,S,P,CY,AC

ORA r (OR Register)

(A) ← (A) V (r)

The content of register r is inclusive-OR'd with the content of the accumulator. The result is placed in the accumulator. **The CY and AC flags are cleared.**

1	0	1	1	0	S	S	S

Cycles: 1
States: 4
Addressing: register
Flags: Z,S,P,CY,AC

ORA M (OR memory)

(A) ← (A) V ((H) (L))

The content of the memory location whose address is contained in the H and L registers is inclusive-OR'd with the content of the accumulator. The result is placed in the accumulator. **The CY and AC flags are cleared.**

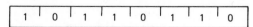

1	0	1	1	0	1	1	0

Cycles: 2
States: 7
Addressing: reg. indirect
Flags: Z,S,P,CY,AC

ORI data (OR Immediate)

(A) ← (A) V (byte 2)

The content of the second byte of the instruction is inclusive-OR'd with the content of the accumulator. The result is placed in the accumulator. **The CY and AC flags are cleared.**

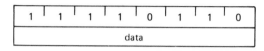

1	1	1	1	0	1	1	0

data

Cycles: 2
States: 7
Addressing: immediate
Flags: Z,S,P,CY,AC

CMP r (Compare Register)

(A) − (r)

The content of register r is subtracted from the accumulator. The accumulator remains unchanged. The condition flags are set as a result of the subtraction. **The Z flag is set to 1 if (A) = (r). The CY flag is set to 1 if (A) < (r).**

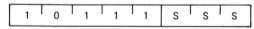

1	0	1	1	1	S	S	S

Cycles: 1
States: 4
Addressing: register
Flags: Z,S,P,CY,AC

CMP M (Compare memory)

(A) − ((H) (L))

The content of the memory location whose address is contained in the H and L registers is subtracted from the accumulator. The accumulator remains unchanged. The condition flags are set as a result of the subtraction. The Z flag is set to 1 if (A) = ((H) (L)). The CY flag is set to 1 if (A) < ((H) (L)).

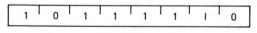

1	0	1	1	1	1	1	0

Cycles: 2
States: 7
Addressing: reg. indirect
Flags: Z,S,P,CY,AC

CPI data   (Compare immediate)

(A) − (byte 2)

The content of the second byte of the instruction is subtracted from the accumulator. The condition flags are set by the result of the subtraction. The Z flag is set to 1 if (A) = (byte 2). The CY flag is set to 1 if (A) < (byte 2).

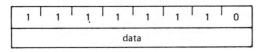

Cycles: 2
States: 7
Addressing: immediate
Flags: Z,S,P,CY,AC

RLC   (Rotate left)

$(A_{n+1}) \leftarrow (A_n) ; (A_0) \leftarrow (A_7)$

$(CY) \leftarrow (A_7)$

The content of the accumulator is rotated left one position. The low order bit and the CY flag are both set to the value shifted out of the high order bit position. **Only the CY flag is affected.**

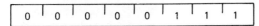

Cycles: 1
States: 4
Flags: CY

RRC   (Rotate right)

$(A_n) \leftarrow (A_{n-1}) ;$ $(A_7) \leftarrow (A_0)$

$(CY) \leftarrow (A_0)$

The content of the accumulator is rotated right one position. The high order bit and the CY flag are both set to the value shifted out of the low order bit position. **Only the CY flag is affected.**

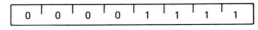

Cycles: 1
States: 4
Flags: CY

RAL   (Rotate left through carry)

$(A_{n+1}) \leftarrow (A_n) ; (CY) \leftarrow (A_7)$

$(A_0) \leftarrow (CY)$

The content of the accumulator is rotated left one position through the CY flag. The low order bit is set equal to the CY flag and the CY flag is set to the value shifted out of the high order bit. **Only the CY flag is affected.**

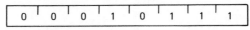

Cycles: 1
States: 4
Flags: CY

RAR   (Rotate right through carry)

$(A_n) \leftarrow (A_{n+1}) ;$ $(CY) \leftarrow (A_0)$

$(A_7) \leftarrow (CY)$

The content of the accumulator is rotated right one position through the CY flag. The high order bit is set to the CY flag and the CY flag is set to the value shifted out of the low order bit. **Only the CY flag is affected.**

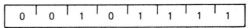

Cycles: 1
States: 4
Flags: CY

CMA   (Complement accumulator)

$(A) \leftarrow (\overline{A})$

The contents of the accumulator are complemented (zero bits become 1, one bits become 0). **No flags are affected.**

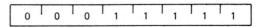

Cycles: 1
States: 4
Flags: none

CMC   (Complement carry)

$(CY) \leftarrow (\overline{CY})$

The CY flag is complemented. **No other flags are affected.**

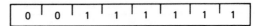

Cycles: 1
States: 4
Flags: CY

STC   (Set carry)

    (CY) ◄— 1

    The CY flag is set to 1. **No other flags are affected.**

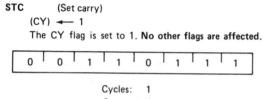

           Cycles: 1
           States: 4
           Flags: CY

Branch Group:

This group of instructions alter normal sequential program flow.

Condition flags are not affected by any instruction in this group.

The two types of branch instructions are unconditional and conditional. Unconditional transfers simply perform the specified operation on register PC (the program counter). Conditional transfers examine the status of one of the four processor flags to determine if a specified branch is to be executed. The conditions that may be specified are as follows:

CONDITION		CCC
NZ	— not zero (Z = 0)	000
Z	— zero (Z = 1)	001
NC	— no carry (CY = 0)	010
C	— carry (CY = 1)	011
PO	— parity odd (P = 0)	100
PE	— parity even (P = 1)	101
P	— plus (S = 0)	110
M	— minus (S = 1)	111

JMP addr   (Jump)

    (PC) ◄— (byte 3) (byte 2)

    Control is transferred to the instruction whose address is specified in byte 3 and byte 2 of the current instruction.

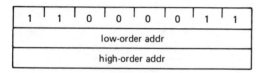

           Cycles: 3
           States: 10
    Addressing: immediate
           Flags: none

Jcondition addr   (Conditional jump)

    If (CCC),

       (PC) ◄— (byte 3) (byte 2)

    If the specified condition is true, control is transferred to the instruction whose address is specified in byte 3 and byte 2 of the current instruction; otherwise, control continues sequentially.

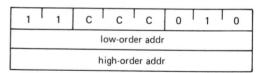

           Cycles: 3
           States: 10
    Addressing: immediate
           Flags: none

CALL addr   (Call)

    ((SP) − 1) ◄— (PCH)

    ((SP) − 2) ◄— (PCL)

    (SP) ◄— (SP) − 2

    (PC) ◄— (byte 3) (byte 2)

The high-order eight bits of the next instruction address are moved to the memory location whose address is one less than the content of register SP. The low-order eight bits of the next instruction address are moved to the memory location whose address is two less than the content of   SP. The content of register SP is decremented by 2. Control is transferred to the instruction whose address is specified in byte 3 and byte 2 of the current instruction.

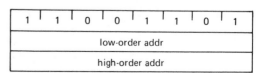

           Cycles: 5
           States: 17
    Addressing: immediate/reg. indirect
           Flags: none

Ccondition addr   (Condition call)

    If (CCC),

       ((SP) − 1) ◄— (PCH)

       ((SP) − 2) ◄— (PCL)

       (SP) ◄— (SP) − 2

       (PC) ◄— (byte 3) (byte 2)

If the specified condition is true, the actions specified in the CALL instruction (see above) are performed; otherwise, control continues sequentially.

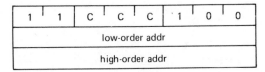

Cycles: 3/5
States: 11/17
Addressing: immediate/reg. indirect
Flags: none

RET (Return)

(PCL) ← ((SP));
(PCH) ← ((SP) + 1);
(SP) ← (SP) + 2;

The content of the memory location whose address is specified in register SP is moved to the low-order eight bits of register PC. The content of the memory location whose address is one more than the content of register SP is moved to the high-order eight bits of register PC. The content of register SP is incremented by 2.

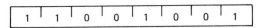

Cycles: 3
States: 10
Addressing: reg. indirect
Flags: none

Rcondition (Conditional return)

If (CCC),
(PCL) ← ((SP))
(PCH) ← ((SP) + 1)
(SP) ← (SP) + 2

If the specified condition is true, the actions specified in the RET instruction (see above) are performed; otherwise, control continues sequentially.

Cycles: 1/3
States: 5/11
Addressing: reg. indirect
Flags: none

RST n (Restart)

((SP) − 1) ← (PCH)
((SP) − 2) ← (PCL)
(SP) ← (SP) − 2
(PC) ← 8 * (NNN)

The high-order eight bits of the next instruction address are moved to the memory location whose address is one less than the content of register SP. The low-order eight bits of the next instruction address are moved to the memory location whose address is two less than the content of register SP. The content of register SP is decremented by two. Control is transferred to the instruction whose address is eight times the content of NNN.

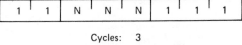

Cycles: 3
States: 11
Addressing: reg. indirect
Flags: none

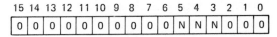

Program Counter After Restart

PCHL (Jump H and L indirect — move H and L to PC)

(PCH) ← (H)
(PCL) ← (L)

The content of register H is moved to the high-order eight bits of register PC. The content of register L is moved to the low-order eight bits of register PC.

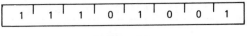

Cycles: 1
States: 5
Addressing: register
Flags: none

Stack, I/O, and Machine Control Group:

This group of instructions performs I/O, manipulates the Stack, and alters internal control flags.

Unless otherwise specified, **condition flags are not affected by any instructions in this group.**

PUSH rp   (Push)

$((SP) - 1) \leftarrow (rh)$

$((SP) - 2) \leftarrow (rl)$

$(SP) \leftarrow (SP) - 2$

The content of the high-order register of register pair rp is moved to the memory location whose address is one less than the content of register SP. The content of the low-order register of register pair rp is moved to the memory location whose address is two less than the content of register SP. The content of register SP is decremented by 2. **Note: Register pair rp = SP may not be specified.**

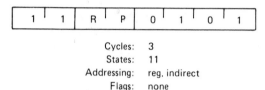

1	1	R	P	0	1	0	1

Cycles: 3
States: 11
Addressing: reg. indirect
Flags: none

PUSH PSW   (Push processor status word)

$((SP) - 1) \leftarrow (A)$

$((SP) - 2)_0 \leftarrow (CY), ((SP) - 2)_1 \leftarrow 1$

$((SP) - 2)_2 \leftarrow (P), ((SP) - 2)_3 \leftarrow 0$

$((SP) - 2)_4 \leftarrow (AC), ((SP) - 2)_5 \leftarrow 0$

$((SP) - 2)_6 \leftarrow (Z), ((SP) - 2)_7 \leftarrow (S)$

$(SP) \leftarrow (SP) - 2$

The content of register A is moved to the memory location whose address is one less than register SP. The contents of the condition flags are assembled into a processor status word and the word is moved to the memory location whose address is two less than the content of register SP. The content of register SP is decremented by two.

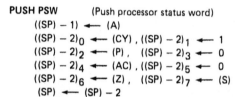

1	1	1	1	0	1	0	1

Cycles: 3
States: 11
Addressing: reg. indirect
Flags: none

FLAG WORD

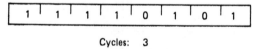

D_7	D_6	D_5	D_4	D_3	D_2	D_1	D_0
S	Z	0	AC	0	P	1	CY

POP rp   (Pop)

$(rl) \leftarrow ((SP))$

$(rh) \leftarrow ((SP) + 1)$

$(SP) \leftarrow (SP) + 2$

The content of the memory location, whose address is specified by the content of register SP, is moved to the low-order register of register pair rp. The content of the memory location, whose address is one more than the content of register SP, is moved to the high-order register of register pair rp. The content of register SP is incremented by 2. **Note: Register pair rp = SP may not be specified.**

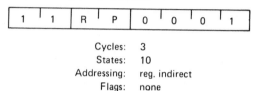

1	1	R	P	0	0	0	1

Cycles: 3
States: 10
Addressing: reg. indirect
Flags: none

POP PSW   (Pop processor status word)

$(CY) \leftarrow ((SP))_0$

$(P) \leftarrow ((SP))_2$

$(AC) \leftarrow ((SP))_4$

$(Z) \leftarrow ((SP))_6$

$(S) \leftarrow ((SP))_7$

$(A) \leftarrow ((SP) + 1)$

$(SP) \leftarrow (SP) + 2$

The content of the memory location whose address is specified by the content of register SP is used to restore the condition flags. The content of the memory location whose address is one more than the content of register SP is moved to register A. The content of register SP is incremented by 2.

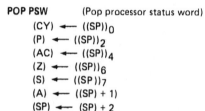

1	1	1	1	0	0	0	1

Cycles: 3
States: 10
Addressing: reg. indirect
Flags: Z,S,P,CY,AC

XTHL   (Exchange stack top with H and L)

$(L) \leftrightarrow ((SP))$

$(H) \leftrightarrow ((SP) + 1)$

The content of the L register is exchanged with the content of the memory location whose address is specified by the content of register SP. The content of the H register is exchanged with the content of the memory location whose address is one more than the content of register SP.

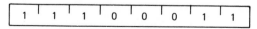

1	1	1	0	0	0	1	1

Cycles: 5
States: 18
Addressing: reg. indirect
Flags: none

SPHL   (Move HL to SP)

(SP) ⟵ (H) (L)

The contents of registers H and L (16 bits) are moved to register SP.

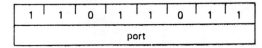

Cycles: 1
States: 5
Addressing: register
Flags: none

IN port   (Input)

(A) ⟵ (data)

The data placed on the eight bit bi-directional data bus by the specified port is moved to register A.

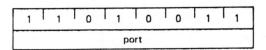

Cycles: 3
States: 10
Addressing: direct
Flags: none

OUT port   (Output)

(data) ⟵ (A)

The content of register A is placed on the eight bit bi-directional data bus for transmission to the specified port.

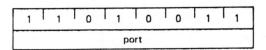

Cycles: 3
States: 10
Addressing: direct
Flags: none

EI   (Enable interrupts)

The interrupt system is enabled **following the execution of the next instruction.**

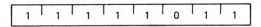

Cycles: 1
States: 4
Flags: none

DI   (Disable interrupts)

The interrupt system is disabled **immediately following the execution of the DI instruction.**

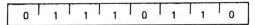

Cycles: 1
States: 4
Flags: none

HLT   (Halt)

The processor is stopped. The registers and flags are unaffected.

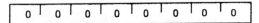

Cycles: 1
States: 7
Flags: none

NOP   (No op)

No operation is performed. **The registers and flags are unaffected.**

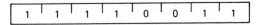

Cycles: 1
States: 4
Flags: none

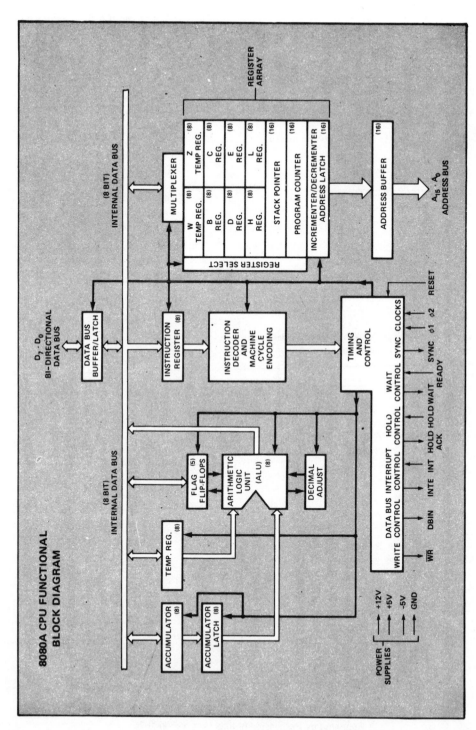

8080A CPU FUNCTIONAL BLOCK DIAGRAM

Courtesy Intel Corporation

Fig. A-1.

NOTES:

1. The first memory cycle (M1) is always an instruction fetch; the first (or only) byte, containing the op code, is fetched during this cycle.

2. If the READY input from memory is not high during T2 of each memory cycle, the processor will enter a wait state (TW) until READY is sampled as high.

3. States T4 and T5 are present, as required, for operations which are completely internal to the CPU. The contents of the internal bus during T4 and T5 are available at the data bus; this is designed for testing purposes only. An "X" denotes that the state is present, but is only used for such internal operations as instruction decoding.

4. Only register pairs rp = B (registers B and C) or rp = D (registers D and E) may be specified.

5. These states are skipped.

6. Memory read sub-cycles; an instruction or data word will be read.

7. Memory write sub-cycle.

8. The READY signal is not required during the second and third sub-cycles (M2 and M3). The HOLD signal is accepted during M2 and M3. The SYNC signal is not generated during M2 and M3. During the execution of DAD, M2 and M3 are required for an internal register-pair add; memory is not referenced.

9. The results of these arithmetic, logical or rotate instructions are not moved into the accumulator (A) until state T2 of the next instruction cycle. That is, A is loaded while the next instruction is being fetched; this overlapping of operations allows for faster processing.

10. If the value of the least significant 4-bits of the accumulator is greater than 9 *or* if the auxiliary carry bit is set, 6 is added to the accumulator. If the value of the most significant 4-bits of the accumulator is now greater than 9, *or* if the carry bit is set, 6 is added to the most significant 4-bits of the accumulator.

11. This represents the first sub-cycle (the instruction fetch) of the next instruction cycle.

12. If the condition was met, the contents of the register pair WZ are output on the address lines (A_{0-15}) instead of the contents of the program counter (PC).

13. If the condition was not met, sub-cycles M4 and M5 are skipped; the processor instead proceeds immediately to the instruction fetch (M1) of the next instruction cycle.

14. If the condition was not met, sub-cycles M2 and M3 are skipped; the processor instead proceeds immediately to the instruction fetch (M1) of the next instruction cycle.

15. Stack read sub-cycle.

16. Stack write sub-cycle.

17. CONDITION   CCC

CONDITION	CCC
NZ — not zero (Z = 0)	000
Z — zero (Z = 1)	001
NC — no carry (CY = 0)	010
C — carry (CY = 1)	010
PO — parity odd (P = 0)	100
PE — parity even (P = 1)	101
P — plus (S = 0)	110
M — minus (S = 1)	111

18. I/O sub-cycle: the I/O port's 8-bit select code is duplicated on address lines 0-7 (A_{0-7}) and 8-15 (A_{8-15}).

19. Output sub-cycle.

20. The processor will remain idle in the halt state until an interrupt, a reset or a hold is accepted. When a hold request is accepted, the CPU enters the hold mode; after the hold mode is terminated, the processor returns to the halt state. After a reset is accepted, the processor begins execution at memory location zero. After an interrupt is accepted, the processor executes the instruction forced onto the data bus (usually a restart instruction).

SSS or DDD	Value	rp	Value
A	111	B	00
B	000	D	01
C	001	H	10
D	010	SP	11
E	011		
H	100		
L	101		

Appendix B

8080 Instruction Timing

MNEMONIC	OP CODE		M1[1]					M2		
	D7 D6 D5 D4	D3 D2 D1 D0	T1	T2[2]	T3	T4	T5	T1	T2[2]	T3
MOV r1, r2	0 1 D D	D S S S	PC OUT STATUS	PC = PC +1	INST→TMP/IR	(SSS)→TMP	(TMP)→DDD			
MOV r, M	0 1 D D	D 1 1 0				X[3]		HL OUT STATUS[6]		DATA→DDD
MOV M, r	0 1 1 1	0 S S S				(SSS)→TMP		HL OUT STATUS[7]		(TMP)→DATA BUS
SPHL	1 1 1 1	1 0 0 1				(HL) ————→SP				
MVI r, data	0 0 D D	D 1 1 0				X		PC OUT STATUS[6]		B2→DDDD
MVI M, data	0 0 1 1	0 1 1 0				X				B2→TMP
LXI rp, data	0 0 R P	0 0 0 1				X			PC = PC + 1	B2→r1
LDA addr	0 0 1 1	1 0 1 0				X			PC = PC + 1	B2→Z
STA addr	0 0 1 1	0 0 1 0				X			PC = PC + 1	B2→Z
LHLD addr	0 0 1 0	1 0 1 0				X			PC = PC + 1	B2→Z
SHLD addr	0 0 1 0	0 0 1 0				X		PC OUT STATUS[6]	PC = PC + 1	B2→Z
LDAX rp[4]	0 0 R P	1 0 1 0				X		rp OUT STATUS[6]		DATA→A
STAX rp[4]	0 0 R P	0 0 1 0				X		rp OUT STATUS[7]		(A)→DATA BUS
XCHG	1 1 1 0	1 0 1 1				(HL)←→(DE)				
ADD r	1 0 0 0	0 S S S				(SSS)→TMP (A)→ACT		[9]	(ACT)+(TMP)→A	
ADD M	1 0 0 0	0 1 1 0				(A)→ACT		HL OUT STATUS[6]		DATA→TMP
ADI data	1 1 0 0	0 1 1 0				(A)→ACT		PC OUT STATUS[6]	PC = PC + 1	B2→TMP
ADC r	1 0 0 0	1 S S S				(SSS)→TMP (A)→ACT		[9]	(ACT)+(TMP)+CY→A	
ADC M	1 0 0 0	1 1 1 0				(A)→ACT		HL OUT STATUS[6]		DATA→TMP
ACI data	1 1 0 0	1 1 1 0				(A)→ACT		PC OUT STATUS[6]	PC = PC + 1	B2→TMP
SUB r	1 0 0 1	0 S S S				(SSS)→TMP (A)→ACT		[9]	(ACT)-(TMP)→A	
SUB M	1 0 0 1	0 1 1 0				(A)→ACT		HL OUT STATUS[6]		DATA→TMP
SUI data	1 1 0 1	0 1 1 0				(A)→ACT		PC OUT STATUS[6]	PC = PC + 1	B2→TMP
SBB r	1 0 0 1	1 S S S				(SSS)→TMP (A)→ACT		[9]	(ACT)-(TMP)-CY→A	
SBB M	1 0 0 1	1 1 1 0				(A)→ACT		HL OUT STATUS[6]		DATA→TMP
SBI data	1 1 0 1	1 1 1 0				(A)→ACT		PC OUT STATUS[6]	PC = PC + 1	B2→TMP
INR r	0 0 D D	D 1 0 0				(DDD)→TMP (TMP) + 1→ALU	ALU→DDD			
INR M	0 0 1 1	0 1 0 0				X		HL OUT STATUS[6]		DATA→TMP (TMP)+1→ALU
DCR r	0 0 D D	D 1 0 1				(DDD)→TMP (TMP)+1→ALU	ALU→DDD			
DCR M	0 0 1 1	0 1 0 1				X		HL OUT STATUS[6]		DATA→TMP (TMP)-1→ALU
INX rp	0 0 R P	0 0 1 1				(RP) + 1 ———→RP				
DCX rp	0 0 R P	1 0 1 1				(RP) – 1 ———→RP				
DAD rp[8]	0 0 R P	1 0 0 1				X		(ri)→ACT	(L)→TMP, (ACT)+(TMP)→ALU	ALU→L, CY
DAA	0 0 1 0	0 1 1 1				DAA→A, FLAGS[10]				
ANA r	1 0 1 0	0 S S S				(SSS)→TMP (A)→ACT		[9]	(ACT)+(TMP)→A	
ANA M	1 0 1 0	0 1 1 0	PC OUT STATUS	PC = PC +1	INST→TMP/IR	(A)→ACT		HL OUT STATUS[6]		DATA→TMP

Fig. B-1.

M3			M4			M5				
T1	T2[2]	T3	T1	T2[2]	T3	T1	T2[2]	T3	T4	T5
HL OUT STATUS[7]	(TMP) —► DATA BUS									
PC OUT STATUS[6]	PC = PC + 1 B3 —►rh									
	PC = PC + 1 B3 —►W		WZ OUT STATUS[6]	DATA ——► A						
	PC = PC + 1 B3 —►W		WZ OUT STATUS[7]	(A) ——► DATA BUS						
	PC = PC + 1 B3 —►W		WZ OUT STATUS[6]	DATA ——► L WZ = WZ + 1		WZ OUT STATUS[6]	DATA —►H			
PC OUT STATUS[6]	PC = PC + 1 B3 —►W		WZ OUT STATUS[7]	(L) ———► DATA BUS WZ = WZ + 1		WZ OUT STATUS[7]	(H) ——►DATA BUS			
[9]	(ACT)+(TMP)→A									
[9]	(ACT)+(TMP)→A									
[9]	(ACT)+(TMP)+CY→A									
[9]	(ACT)+(TMP)+CY→A									
[9]	(ACT)−(TMP)→A									
[9]	(ACT)−(TMP)→A									
[9]	(ACT)−(TMP)−CY→A									
[9]	(ACT)−(TMP)−CY→A									
HL OUT STATUS[7]	ALU —► DATA BUS									
HL OUT STATUS[7]	ALU —► DATA BUS									
(rh)→ACT	(H)→TMP (ACT)+(TMP)+CY→ALU	ALU→H, CY								
[9]	(ACT)+(TMP)→A									

MNEMONIC	OP CODE		M1[1]					M2		
	$D_7 D_6 D_5 D_4$	$D_3 D_2 D_1 D_0$	T1	T2[2]	T3	T4	T5	T1	T2[2]	T3
ANI data	1 1 1 0	0 1 1 0	PC OUT STATUS	PC = PC + 1	INST→TMP/IR	(A)→ACT		PC OUT STATUS[6]	PC = PC + 1	B2 ►TMP
XRA r	1 0 1 0	1 S S S	↑	↑	↑	(A)→ACT (SSS)→TMP		[9]	(ACT)+(TPM)→A	
XRA M	1 0 1 0	1 1 1 1				(A)→ACT		HL OUT STATUS[6]	DATA ►TMP	
XRI data	1 1 1 0	1 1 1 1				(A)→ACT		PC OUT STATUS[6]	PC = PC + 1	B2 ►TMP
ORA r	1 0 1 1	0 S S S				(A)→ACT (SSS)→TMP		[9]	(ACT)+(TMP)→A	
ORA M	1 0 1 1	0 1 1 0				(A)→ACT		HL OUT STATUS[6]	DATA ►TMP	
ORI data	1 1 1 1	0 1 1 0				(A)→ACT		PC OUT STATUS[6]	PC = PC + 1	B2 ►TMP
CMP r	1 0 1 1	1 S S S				(A)→ACT (SSS)→TMP		[9]	(ACT)-(TMP), FLAGS	
CMP M	1 0 1 1	1 1 1 1				(A)→ACT		HL OUT STATUS[6]	DATA ►TMP	
CPI data	1 1 1 1	1 1 1 0				(A)→ACT		PC OUT STATUS[6]	PC = PC + 1	B2 ►TMP
RLC	0 0 0 0	0 1 1 1				(A)→ALU ROTATE		[9]	ALU→A, CY	
RRC	0 0 0 0	1 1 1 1				(A)→ALU ROTATE		[9]	ALU→A, CY	
RAL	0 0 0 1	0 1 1 1				(A), CY→ALU ROTATE		[9]	ALU→A, CY	
RAR	0 0 0 1	1 1 1 1				(A), CY→ALU ROTATE		[9]	ALU→A, CY	
CMA	0 0 1 0	1 1 1 1				(Ā)→A				
CMC	0 0 1 1	1 1 1 1				C̄Y→CY				
STC	0 0 1 1	0 1 1 1				1→CY				
JMP addr	1 1 0 0	0 0 1 1				X		PC OUT STATUS[6]	PC = PC + 1	B2 ►Z
J cond addr[17]	1 1 C C	C 0 1 0				JUDGE CONDITION		PC OUT STATUS[6]	PC = PC + 1	B2 ►Z
CALL addr	1 1 0 0	1 1 0 1				SP = SP - 1		PC OUT STATUS[6]	PC = PC + 1	B2 ►Z
C cond addr[17]	1 1 C C	C 1 0 0	↓			JUDGE CONDITION IF TRUE, SP = SP - 1		PC OUT STATUS[6]	PC = PC + 1	B2 ►Z
RET	1 1 0 0	1 0 0 1			↓	X		SP OUT STATUS[15]	SP = SP + 1	DATA ►Z
R cond addr[17]	1 1 C C	C 0 0 0			INST→TMP/IR	JUDGE CONDITION[14]		SP OUT STATUS[15]	SP = SP + 1	DATA ►Z
RST n	1 1 N N	N 1 1 1			φ→W INST→TMP/IR	SP = SP - 1		SP OUT STATUS[16]	SP = SP - 1 (PCH)	►DATA BUS
PCHL	1 1 1 0	1 0 0 1			INST→TMP/IR	(HL) ────► PC				
PUSH rp	1 1 R P	0 1 0 1			↓	SP = SP - 1		SP OUT STATUS[16]	SP = SP - 1 (rh)	►DATA BUS
PUSH PSW	1 1 1 1	0 1 0 1				SP = SP - 1		SP OUT STATUS[16]	SP = SP - 1 (A)	►DATA BUS
POP rp	1 1 R P	0 0 0 1				X		SP OUT STATUS[15]	SP = SP + 1 DATA	►r1
POP PSW	1 1 1 1	0 0 0 1				X		SP OUT STATUS[15]	SP = SP + 1 DATA	►FLAGS
XTHL	1 1 1 0	0 0 1 1				X		SP OUT STATUS[15]	SP = SP + 1 DATA	►Z
IN port	1 1 0 1	1 0 1 1				X		PC OUT STATUS[6]	PC = PC + 1	B2 ►Z, W
OUT port	1 1 0 1	0 0 1 1				X		PC OUT STATUS[6]	PC = PC + 1	B2 ►Z, W
EI	1 1 1 1	1 0 1 1				SET INTE F/F				
DI	1 1 1 1	0 0 1 1				RESET INTE F/F				
HLT	0 1 1 1	0 1 1 0	↓	↓		X		PC OUT STATUS	HALT MODE[20]	
NOP	0 0 0 0	0 0 0 0	PC OUT STATUS	PC = PC + 1	INST→TMP/IR	X				

224

M3			M4			M5				
T1	T2[2]	T3	T1	T2[2]	T3	T1	T2[2]	T3	T4	T5
[9]	(ACT)+(TMP)→A									
[9]	(ACT)+(TMP)→A									
[9]	(ACT)+(TMP)→A									
[9]	(ACT)+(TMP)→A									
[9]	(ACT)+(TMP)→A									
[9]	(ACT)–(TMP); FLAGS									
[9]	(ACT)–(TMP); FLAGS									
PC OUT STATUS[6]	PC = PC + 1 B3 →W						(WZ) + 1 → PC	WZ OUT STATUS[11]		
PC OUT STATUS[6]	PC = PC + 1 B3 →W						(WZ) + 1 → PC	WZ OUT STATUS[11,12]		
PC OUT STATUS[6]	PC = PC + 1 B3 →W		SP OUT STATUS[16]	(PCH)——— SP = SP – 1	→DATA BUS	SP OUT STATUS[16]		(PCL)→ DATA BUS	(WZ) + 1 → PC	WZ OUT STATUS[11]
PC OUT STATUS[6]	PC = PC + 1 B3 →W[13]		SP OUT STATUS[16]	(PCH)——— SP = SP – 1	→DATA BUS	SP OUT STATUS[16]		(PCL)→ DATA BUS	(WZ) + 1 → PC	WZ OUT STATUS[11,12]
SP OUT STATUS[15]	SP = SP + 1 DATA →W						(WZ) + 1 → PC	WZ OUT STATUS[11]		
SP OUT STATUS[15]	SP = SP + 1 DATA →W						(WZ) + 1 → PC	WZ OUT STATUS[11,12]		
SP OUT STATUS[16]	(TMP = 00NNN000)—→Z (PCL)→DATA BUS						(WZ) + 1 → PC	WZ OUT STATUS[11]		
SP OUT STATUS[16]	(rl) —→DATA BUS									
SP OUT STATUS[16]	FLAGS →DATA BUS									
SP OUT STATUS[15]	SP = SP + 1 DATA —→rh									
SP OUT STATUS[15]	SP = SP + 1 DATA →A									
SP OUT STATUS[15]	DATA →W		SP OUT STATUS[16]	(H)———	→DATA BUS	SP OUT STATUS[16]	(L) ——	→ DATA BUS	(WZ) →HL	
WZ OUT STATUS[18]	DATA →A									
WZ OUT STATUS[18]	(A) —→DATA BUS									

Index